Historic San Francisco

DATE DUE

ILL/PGM			
75065257			
4/29/17			

Demco, Inc. 38-293

Historic
SAN FRANCISCO

A Concise History and Guide

Rand Richards

Heritage House Publishers
San Francisco

Cover design by Larry Van Dyke and Rand Richards
Front cover photo: The third Cliff House (1896–1907), courtesy Marilyn Blaisdell collection.

Heritage House Publishers
P.O. Box 194242
San Francisco, CA 94119
Phone & Fax: (415) 776-3156
E-mail: hhprincon@aol.com

Library of Congress Cataloging-in-Publication Data
Richards, Rand
    Historic San Francisco : a concise history and guide / Rand Richards.
    – 2nd ed.
       p. cm.
    Includes bibliographical references and index.
    ISBN 978-1–879367–05–0
    1. San Francisco (Calif.)—History. 2. Historic sites–California–
San Francisco–Guidebooks. 3. Historic buildings–California–
San Francisco–Guidebooks. 4. Architecture–California–
San Francisco–Guidebooks. 5. Museums–California–
San Francisco–Guidebooks. 6. San Francisco (Calif.)–
Antiquities–Guidebooks. 7. San Francisco (Calif.)–Buildings,
structures, etc.–Guidebooks. 8. San Francisco (Calif.)–Guidebooks.
    I. Title.
F869.S357R53 2007
979.4'61—dc22
                  2007004934

To

Robert C. Ledermann

My father —— and friend

Contents

Illustrations

Preface

I wrote this book for the same reason many authors of non-fiction write: to satisfy my curiosity about something. That something, in this case, was what historic buildings, markers, and artifacts remain from San Francisco's earlier days.

Oddly enough, it was a visit to New Orleans that spurred me to write this book. Three years ago my sister and I, after a visit to our grandmother in Atlanta, stopped in New Orleans for a short vacation before returning to San Francisco. New Orleans, like San Francisco, has a colorful history. The French Quarter in particular has a number of historic structures, and exudes a strong sense of the past. I was vaguely aware of the city's Spanish and French heritage, its role in the War of 1812, and its capture by Union troops during the Civil War. We both wanted to learn more, and more importantly, be able to tie that history to the buildings we were seeing while wandering the streets of the French Quarter. But a search of local bookstores turned up no specific historical guidebook to the city.

On the plane back to San Francisco I wondered if there were any guidebooks to San Francisco such as I had been seeking in New Orleans. Unable to find any after returning home, I decided to write one. The first thing that occurred to me was what, if anything, had survived the 1906 earthquake and fire. In the course of my research I found that despite that catastrophe there are still many things to be found illustrative of the history of this singular city. I hope that the readers of this book will share the sense of discovery I felt as I came upon the vestiges of the San Francisco that was.

Acknowledgments

I must begin by thanking Peter Browning, publisher of Great West Books. He compiled the index, edited the final draft of the manuscript, formatted it on Ventura Publisher®, and was an invaluable source of advice on publishing matters large and small during the production phase of this book.

Another whose contributions deserve notice is Malcolm E. Barker of Londonborn Publications who patiently answered questions about publishing in general and made beneficial suggestions that improved the book's interior layout.

I am also grateful to local authors and historians Gray Brechin and Alex Brammer, both of whom read portions of the manuscript and made useful comments.

My sister, Lise McGrath, also has my gratitude. She helped plant the seed that resulted in this book. And, on the subject of family, I must not neglect my father, Bob Ledermann, who read the manuscript and offered suggestions and encouragement.

Many others, at various stages, were generous with their time and were patient in answering questions. Among them are Marcia Eymann and Mickey Karpas of the Oakland Museum, Pat Akre and Gail Berger of the San Francisco History Room of the San Francisco Public Library, J. Edward Green of the Presidio Army Museum, Don Andreini of the Foundation for San Francisco's Architectural Heritage, Bill Koenig of the San Francisco Fire Department Museum, Bob Chandler and Charles V. La Fontaine of the Wells Fargo History Museum, Gene P. Rexrode and Bob Warren of the Golden Gate Bridge, Highway and Transportation District, Robert L. Osborne and Robert Bridwell of the Department of Transportation for the San Francisco-Oakland Bay Bridge, Eugene Price of the Phoebe Apperson Hearst Museum of Anthropology, Edward P. Von Der Porten of the Treasure Island Museum, and the late Charles S. Hawkins of Fort Point National Historic Site.

Others who were helpful were Elaine Molinari and City Guides, Bob Sharrard of City Lights Publishing, Marshall Moxom of the San Mateo Historical Society Museum, Marilyn Blaisdell, James Lee Carter, and Waldo Church.

I must also thank Dr. Fernando Boneu and the Parador Nacional de Turismo of Lérida, Spain for their kind permission to use the portrait of Gaspar de Portolá which appears on page 14. This alleged likeness—no known portraits from life are known to exist—was first published in Dr. Boneu's biography of the explorer, *Gaspar de Portolá, Explorer and Founder of California.*

I did some of my research at the following institutions and wish to credit their staffs for their assistance: the Bancroft Library at the University of California at Berkeley, the San Francisco Public Library, and the California State Library at Sacramento.

Larry Van Dyke drew the maps and was patient and accommodating with my suggestions for changes.

Finally, thanks are due to all those tour guides, park rangers, docents, and volunteers, from whom I, and many others, have learned much.

Introduction

This book was written for those who would like to know where to find, and to know more about, the historic buildings, sites, museums, and artifacts that help make San Francisco's colorful past come alive.

The core of the book is Chapters 1 through 10. A brief narrative history begins each chapter and is designed to provide background for the subsequent Sites and Attractions section. Next comes a short biography of a key figure of the period. Following that are the Sites and Attractions—the places you can visit that are historically significant and/or have items of interest.

The narrative portion of each chapter highlights key events, but its main focus is on the sites that follow and thus is not designed to be comprehensive. Those wishing to read in greater depth about San Francisco's bygone days should refer to the Select Bibliography in the back of the book.

In the Sites and Attractions section, most of the places mentioned are found in San Francisco. But a few places outside The City, and in three instances outside the Bay Area, are noted either because something significant happened there that had a direct affect on San Francisco—such as at Coloma, where gold was discovered—or there simply is nothing comparable to be found within the city limits—such as the Ohlone Village at Coyote Hills Regional Park in Fremont where an Indian shellmound is still to be found.

Although this book is both a history and a guide, it is intended primarily as a guidebook. The recommended way to use the book is to first read chapters 1 through 10. Then when you visit the sites, turn to the Sites and Attractions Recap, which provides a county-by-county listing of the sites along with a summary of things of interest from all periods at each location. This is especially useful for museums—such as the Oakland Museum History Gallery and the Wells Fargo History Museum—that have items dating from most periods of San Francisco history. In visiting the Oakland Museum, for example, the Recap tells you that there are artifacts from the times of the Indians, from the Spanish/Mexican era, from the gold rush, and so on. But this section is only a summary; if you want further details please refer back to the numbered chapters.

Before visiting the various museums, etc., it is advisable to check their websites or call in advance to make sure that the days and hours information is current.

Parking and Transit Information

With parking in San Francisco and environs becoming tougher to find and more expensive, you should seriously consider taking taxis or public transit whenever it's feasible. Calling the public transit agencies listed below will connect you with an operator who can tell you which buses, streetcars, and BART trains to take to get you from where you are to where you want to go, or visit their websites.

Transit Agency	Phone #	Website
Municipal Railway	(415) 673-6864	www.sfmta.com
A C Transit	(510) 839-2882	www.actransit.org
Golden Gate Transit	(415) 457-3110	www.goldengate.org
Samtrans	(800) 660-4287	www.samtrans.com
BART	(650) 992-2278	www.bart.gov

Municipal Railway is San Francisco; AC Transit is the East Bay; Golden Gate Transit is Marin County; Samtrans is San Mateo County; and BART is the Bay Area except for Marin County.

If you must drive, check the information paragraphs in the Sites and Attractions Recap Section, which highlights where to find the best parking at each location. As a general rule, the cheapest parking in downtown San Francisco can be found at the city-owned garages. There are three: Stockton-Sutter, Fifth and Mission, and Portsmouth Square, which is located at Kearny and Clay streets. When parking on the street in residential neighborhoods, be aware that there is a two-hour time limit in most locations except for those cars that have the requisite stickers on their bumpers.

1

Beginnings (to 1542)

San Francisco's history properly begins in prehistoric times, when geologic changes created the peninsula that now culminates in the city of San Francisco—the guardian at the gate of one of the world's great natural harbors.

San Francisco and the Bay Area's first inhabitants were Indians. The main tribes in the area were the Coast Miwoks and the Ohlone (or Costanoans). They led a peaceful, simple existence for several thousand years until the arrival of European explorers and settlers brought a swift end to their culture and to their very existence.

San Francisco and the Bay are Formed

San Francisco owes much of its special character to its isolation at the tip of a hill-studded peninsula. The city's many hills, and the bay and ocean that border it on three sides, have had a great influence on the way San Francisco developed. Indeed, it is safe to say that much of The City's identity was, and is, shaped by its geology and geography.

The story begins millions of years ago at a time when what is now the state of California was ocean floor. Over time, volcanic convulsions below the earth's crust sent material upward to create new land masses. In northern California this led to the formation of the Sierra Nevada and, farther to the west, the Coast Range, south of San Francisco. This new land was so high above the ocean that what is now San Francisco Bay was dry land—a huge valley. What was to become the city of San Francisco was a coastal knob, a sentinel overlooking the valley and mountains to the east and the ocean to the west.

As the eons passed and the earth continued its upheavals, storms driving in from the Pacific battered the western slopes of the Sierra, causing rivers and streams to form and then flow down to the ocean. Simultaneously, the still upthrusting mountain ranges blocked all of the main rivulets flowing west from the Sierra except for one, and channeled that flow through the only gap—the area northeast of San Francisco now called Carquinez Strait. The rushing waters continued down through the plain, carving the deep valley of Raccoon Strait between Angel Island and Tiburon, and the deepest one of all, the Golden Gate. The runoff then joined the ocean, whose level at that time was several hundred feet lower than it is today; the coastline was about where the Farallon Islands are, seventeen miles away.

In more recent geologic time—that is, within the last two hundred thousand years—several ice ages have alternated with warming trends leading to periodic melting of the snowpack and a rise in the level of the ocean. The valley that became San Francisco Bay first filled with salt water from the rising Pacific Ocean about one hundred thousand years ago. Later the water retreated back out through the Golden Gate until finally, starting about 10,000 B.C., the ocean rose again, filling the bay to today's level and surrounding what would become San Francisco on three sides.

The First Human Inhabitants

The Bay Area's first human inhabitants were Indians, who arrived between five and ten thousand years ago. They were probably descendants of Asian-Siberian peoples who had crossed to Alaska from Siberia and then migrated south. Despite their relative homogeneity as a race, however, once in North America the Indians splintered into a wide variety of tribes and groups. In the years before the coming of the Spanish, as many as fifty-three major cultural groups speaking up to ninety different languages lived in what became the state of California.

In the greater Bay Area there existed four distinct tribes: the Coast Miwoks, the Wintun, the Yokuts, and the Costanoans—or Ohlone as they are more commonly referred to today. (Costanoan was derived from costaños, which is Spanish for 'coast people'). Of these, the Coast Miwoks and Ohlone predominated, with the former occupying Marin and the North Bay and the latter inhabiting the East Bay, the South Bay and San Francisco. San Francisco at the time was primarily sand dunes. Still, a few small groups of Indians lived there mainly clustered around Lake Merced by the ocean and Mission Creek near the bay. In 1776, at the time of San Francisco's founding, Bay Area Coast Miwoks numbered approximately 3,000 and the Ohlone about 10,000.

These Indians were short, with broad faces and flat noses. Many of them painted their bodies and wore plumed headgear and decorated loincloths. They were a Stone Age people, isolated from outside influences, hunter-gatherers who employed only the most simple technology. It was so simple, in fact, they not only had no knowledge of metals but they also did not use the wheel or beasts of burden. The closest they came to agriculture was controlled burning, which promoted the growth of new grasses and plants and whose tender shoots also served to attract game they could trap or hunt. Still, they seemed not to have suffered from these deficiencies. They apparently lacked the motivation to develop further because of the rich abundance of edible plants and fish and game that surrounded them.

Courtesy, The Bancroft Library
Bay Area Indians wearing ceremonial headdresses.

Acorns, because they were so nutritious, high in calories, and plentiful, were a staple of their diet. They could not eat them raw due to the bitter tannic acid, which had to be leached out before they could be consumed. (The early Spanish explorers found this out the hard way when they first ate the acorns raw—to their great intestinal discomfort.) To eliminate the tannin the Indians would first remove the shells, then pound the nutmeats into pulp. The pulp was placed in a basket, strained in a stream, and boiled. The resulting mush was either eaten as porridge or made into cakes.

While acorns served as the Indians bread, they rounded out their diet with a variety of fish, game, and fowl. Besides plentiful rabbits and squirrels, there were deer, elk, grizzly bears, eagles, and many other birds. Slings, traps, clubs, and snares were used to kill game. For gathering fish and shellfish and for hunting seals and sea otters, they constructed boats of tule, a plentiful bulrush found in marshes at the water's edge.

Tule was also used in some cases to construct their huts and dwellings, but it served an even bigger need for the Indians because they used it to make their masterworks: baskets. What plastic containers are to modern-day homemakers, baskets were to the local Indians. They excelled at making baskets, and used them for every conceivable purpose. They used baskets for gathering and storing acorns, fruit, and firewood. They used them for serving mush and for drying fish. They also used them for cooking. Baskets could be woven so tightly they would hold water. That was how they cooked their acorn mush. A bowl-shaped basket was filled with water, and then hot rocks were dropped in to boil the water and thus cook the mush.

Besides using baskets as household containers, the Indians also used them for ceremonial and mortuary purposes. Indeed, baskets were so useful and served so many of their needs that the Miwoks, the Ohlone, and their neighbors never developed the art of pottery making.

In terms of social organization, village life followed a set pattern. Most Bay Area tribes (or more accurately tribelets or groups) consisted of a few hundred people clustered in one or two villages. While there was an overall chief, his or her powers were more those of persuasion than of fiat. Division of labor was generally defined by sex, with men doing the hunting and fishing and women the cooking and basket-making. Shamans and village chiefs were also usually male, although occasionally a woman assumed these duties.

Each tribelet generally moved around within a defined territory in which it had exclusive hunting and fishing rights. Although territorial rights were respected, generosity prevailed, and in cases where one wished to cross a boundary, permission was usually requested and granted. Because of this relatively cordial environment and the abundant wildlife—there was plenty for everyone—warfare was virtually non-existent. Disputes occasionally arose, but these were normally settled quickly and without much bloodshed. No special weapons of war were developed; only hunting weapons made of bone or perhaps deer horn were used in such skirmishes. Whether due to the salubrious environment or the relative social harmony, the Indians of northern California seemed by nature a rather placid, non-aggressive people. They lacked the ferocity of such Plains Indians as the Comanche and the Sioux.

A degree of ferocity might have helped postpone the inevitable. When the Spanish arrived, the Indians relative idyll—which had continued almost unchanged for several thousand years—quickly ended. European diseases such as measles and syphilis, to which they had no immunity, took a major toll. But the confrontations with a technologically superior race, along with the invasion of their habitat and the fatal alteration of their lifestyle by hordes of goldseekers a few decades later, sealed their fate. Despite scattered resistance as white immigration increased, the end was swift. The Indian population of California, which had numbered about three hundred thousand in 1776, plummeted to roughly twenty thousand a little over one hundred years later. Bay Area Indians were particularly hard hit, since that is where the majority of the white settlement was. In 1911 the last "wild" California Indian was captured on a ranch in a remote area in the northeast part of the state.

Ishi (c.1860–1916)

"The Last Wild Indian"

In August 1911 a nearly naked, half-starved Indian was found cowering in a slaughterhouse on a ranch near Oroville, California. He was about fifty years old and was the last of his tribe, the Yahi, and the last Native American in the continental United States to emerge from the wilds and make contact with civilization.

Reporters quickly dubbed him "the last wild Indian," and immediately after his capture they had a field day describing his every reaction to the strange new world he had encountered. They chronicled his wolfing down every food placed before him: beans, doughnuts, and, until he was shown how to peel it, a banana—skin and all.

He spent the first few days of his new existence in the Oroville jail, but his capture was front page news and he quickly came to the attention of anthropologists at the University of California. He was soon placed in their care at the university's San Francisco campus near Golden Gate Park. There his handlers eagerly recorded his every response to civilization. They found that he adapted rapidly to his new surroundings, taking to western clothes right away—although he hated wearing shoes. He liked his new clothes so well, in fact, that he was reluctant to take them off to have his picture taken in his old dress of animal skins. And when his caretakers entreated him to make a camping trip to the wilds he previously inhabited, he consented reluctantly, telling them in sign language that there were no beds or chairs there and very little to eat. The trip back to his old habitat gave the anthropologists an up-close and invaluable look at Ishi's skill in fashioning tools and weapons and in using them to catch fish and game.

Although Ishi adapted well and with equanimity to most of the new experiences that confronted him, he never got used to one thing: the crowds of people that inhabit a big city. Tall buildings, trains, automobiles, and other marvels of an industrialized society he took in stride, but being among large groups of whites made him fearful to the point of near

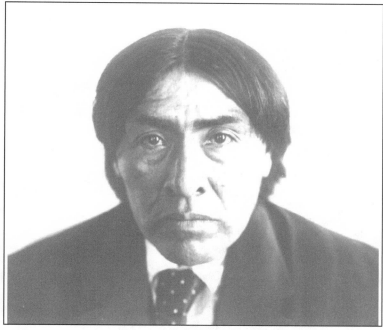

P. A. Hearst Museum of Anthropology, U.C. Berkeley
Ishi, the last of the Yahi.

paralysis. Yet when offered the chance to return to his home territory and previous way of life, he refused. The comforts of civilization outweighed the drawbacks.

Ishi maintained a cheerful demeanor throughout the five years he spent in civilized society. He smiled readily, was never angry, and showed childlike curiosity about even the smallest things. A penny whistle someone gave him delighted him for hours. Still, he was bashful around women, hated to be seen by anyone when he had his clothes off, and preserved his privacy by never revealing his name. So he was called "Ishi," which was the Yahi word for man.

Ishi died in San Francisco on March 25, 1916 of tuberculosis. He was a man between two worlds: he only learned a few words of English and never became an integral part of white society, yet he never desired to return to his old way of life. He remains a fascinating remnant of the past, a distant ancestor brought forward across the centuries to the modern age.

Sites and Attractions

San Francisco's Geologic Formation.

San Francisco Bay Model Visitor's Center.
Location: 2100 Bridgeway, Sausalito. **Phone:** (415) 332-3871. **Hours:** Tuesday – Saturday, 9 a.m. to 4 p.m., with additional summer hours of Saturday, Sunday, and some holidays, 10 a.m. to 5 p.m. Closed federal holidays. Ranger-led tours are available for groups of ten or more. **Admission:** Free. **Website:** www.spn.usace.army.mil/bmvc.

The best place to see what San Francisco and the bay looked like in the distant past before the ocean rose and flooded the valley to create the bay, is at this huge model in Sausalito run by the U.S. Army Corps of Engineers. The purpose of the Bay Model, which is one of the largest working scale models in the world, is to examine the effects of water flows in and out of the bay. But for those wishing to glimpse a bit of geologic history it serves quite well, for the model makes graphic the deep channels the ancient river carved as it wound down from the Sierra through Raccoon Strait and out to the ocean through the Golden Gate, which at 350 feet, is the deepest part of the bay. The model also makes clear just how shallow the rest of the bay is: over 70 percent is less than eighteen feet deep.

The model operates by means of having salt water pumped in and out of the Golden Gate to replicate the ebb and flow of the tides. A full cycle takes fifteen minutes to complete, or one hundred times faster than nature. As interesting as it is to watch the water circulate through the bay, it is perhaps even more visually striking to see the model when it is dry since you can see even better just how deep the Golden Gate is relative to the rest of the bay.

The Indians

Ohlone Village – Coyote Hills Regional Park.
Location: 8000 Patterson Ranch Road (off Paseo Padre Parkway), Fremont. **Phone:** (510) 795-9385. Located within this pleasant county park is an Ohlone shellmound and a reconstructed village. Both are fenced off and are accessible only through docent-led tours. **Hours:** Tours of the shellmound are given Saturdays or Sundays once or twice a month. Call in advance to make reservations and to check dates and times. There is a visitor center in the park that is open Tuesday – Sunday, 9:30 a.m. to 5 p.m. **Admission:** $5.00 per vehicle. Admission is good for the shellmound tour and the visitor center. **Website:** www.ebparks.org.

The Indians of the Bay Area, due to the relatively primitive state of their civilization, the mild climate and the lack of enemies, left behind no forts or permanent structures. They did however leave something else—their trash. Shellfish were such a big part of the diet that archeologists have identified many Indian sites by the huge mounds of discarded shells they left behind. At one time as many as four hundred of these shellmounds were located around the bay shoreline. Today, largely due to development, only a few remain. Despite this lack of material there are several sites and museums that document the area's first inhabitants and their way of life.

The Ohlone Village walk and tour is the best place in the Bay Area to see, on site, just how the local Indians (in this case the Ohlone) lived. The tour is also a particularly fine way for children to learn how the Indians adapted to their surroundings. The guides clearly explain how the Indians lived and back up their talks with hands-on demonstrations in which young spectators are encouraged to participate. Park rangers or volunteer docents lead you on the trail to the shellmound and reconstructed village, and stop along the way at, for instance, a tule marsh, to slice a tule reed down the middle and then demonstrate, with audience help, how by twisting it into strands the natives used it to make rope and weave baskets. (Tule reeds have a spongy, buoyant interior, which explains why the Indians also used them to construct their boats.)

After the ranger unlocks the gate to the enclosure you will cross the shellmound on the way to the village. Archeological digs and carbon dating here have indicated that this site, which was once only forty feet from the bay, witnessed its first human occupation about 400 B.C. The shellmound served not only as a disposal site for discarded oyster and clam shells and fish and bird bones, but also as an Ohlone burial site. About 30 percent of the shellmound has been excavated by archeologists who have found evidence of over five hundred burials.

The reconstructed village, which lies at the edge of the shell-mound, consists of two huts made of cattail and tule reeds, a sweat house, a pit house, and a ceremonial circle. It is reassuring to know that experts are not infallible. The guide on one tour confided that the Ohlone would laugh if they could come back and see the first hut the park employees had constructed, because they had faced the smoke hole at the top into the wind, which would have caused the smoke from any fire within to blow back inside.

Before leaving the park you should also take in the visitor center, located a short distance up the paved road from the gravel parking lot near the entrance (where the shellmound tour begins). This attractive museum houses an eight-foot-long diorama of an Indian village, some Ohlone tools discovered during excavations, and other artifacts. Also on display is a full-size reconstruction of a tule boat.

Kule Loklo Miwok Village.
Location: Point Reyes National Seashore in Marin County. The park's entrance is just north of the town of Olema, at the juncture of Highway 1 and Sir Francis Drake Boulevard. The village is located four-tenths of a mile north of the Bear Valley Visitor Center. **Phone:** (415) 464-5100 (visitor center). Follow the signs and the trail leading through the woods. **Hours:** The Miwok village is open for self-guided tours daily from 8 a.m. to dusk. The visitor center is open weekdays from 9 a.m. to 5 p.m., and weekends and holidays from 8 a.m. to 5 p.m. **Admission:** Free. **Website:** www.nps.gov/pore.

Because of their temporary nature, and the subsequent devastation of the Indians' habitat, no original Native American dwellings survive. The Kule Loklo (it means "Bear Valley" in Miwok) Coast

Miwok Village is a re-creation based on archeological evidence and contemporary accounts, and resembles one such as Sir Francis Drake and his men likely would have seen during their stay on this coast more than four hundred years ago.

The village was constructed using native methods and tools wherever possible. Kule Loklo consists of a sweat lodge, which was used for physical and spiritual cleansing; a ceremonial dance house, which served as a community center; a granary for storing acorns; and other structures.

Rand Richards

Kule Loklo village at Point Reyes.

The Oakland Museum - History Gallery.
Location: 1000 Oak Street (two blocks from Lake Merritt), Oakland. **Phone:** (510) 238-3842. **Hours:** Wednesday – Saturday, 10 a.m. to 5 p.m.; (First Friday to 9 p.m.); Sunday, Noon to 5 p.m. Closed holidays. **Admission:** Adults, $8.00; Seniors, Students, $5.00; Children (under 5), Free. **Website:** www.museumca.org.

Setting the scene as you enter the California History Gallery is a large, realistic mural on the left wall depicting a Coast Miwok village on the Marin shore as it would have appeared prior to the coming of the Europeans.

Indian artifacts on display just beyond the mural include a generous sampling of baskets, some of which are the finest of their kind. Baskets and basket-weaving can be a dry subject, but the Oakland Museum has done a fine job of making it lively and interesting through an appealing and informative visual display.

Other relics remaining from early California Indian life include a fish trap, an acorn granary, bows and arrows, stone mortars, clothing, beads, necklaces, and ceremonial objects. It should be noted that very few Miwok and Ohlone baskets and artifacts survive, so most of the examples on display come from other California Indian groups.

Marin Museum Of The American Indian.
Location: Miwok Park, 2200 Novato Boulevard, Novato. **Phone:** (415) 897-4064. **Hours:** Tuesday – Friday, 10 a.m. to 3 p.m. Saturday and Sunday, Noon to 4 p.m. (call ahead on weekends to be certain volunteer staff are on site). **Admission:** $5.00 donation; Seniors, $3.00. Children, (7–18), $3.00 (under 7), Free. **Website:** www.marinindian.com.

Located on the site of a Coast Miwok village, this compact two-story museum has a nice array of artifacts that depict how the local Indians lived. There are a variety of baskets, bone tools, stone grinding bowls and pestles, and chunks of obsidian. The obsidian, which the Miwoks would have used to make arrowheads, likely was obtained though trade with other Indians since obsidian is not found locally.

The museum's ground floor is great for children because it contains toys and tools such as the Miwoks would have made and used. Children are encouraged to play with them. They can also handle and put on animal skins, including a deer's pelt with the head and horns still attached. Miwoks would have used the latter to disguise themselves while hunting deer.

San Mateo County History Museum.

Location: 2200 Broadway, Redwood City. **Phone:** (650) 299-0104. **Hours:** Tuesday – Sunday, 10 a.m. to 4 p.m. **Admission:** Adults, $4.00; Students, Seniors, Children, $2.00. **Website:** www.sanmateocountyhistory.com.

This museum, located in the former courthouse, which dates from 1908, has a number of exhibits covering historical events that occurred in San Mateo County. A section is devoted to the local Indians, the Ohlone. Highlights here are a full-size reconstruction of a tule hut and a diorama of an Ohlone village.

Artifacts include arrowheads, shells, stone hammers, and bone tools—such as awls and a scapula used as a saw for cutting reeds. There are also several stone mortars and pestles. Some of the artifacts are accessible to children: for example, they are allowed to grind corn and chip flakes from shells.

P. A. Hearst Museum Of Anthropology.

Location: Kroeber Hall, across from the corner of Bancroft Way and College Avenue on the University of California campus, Berkeley. **Phone:** (510) 643-7648. **Hours:** Wednesday – Saturday, 10 a.m. to 4:30 p.m.; Sunday, noon to 4:00 p.m. Closed Monday and Tuesday. **Admission:** Free. **Website:** www.hearstmuseum.berkeley.edu.

Because the Hearst Museum rotates artifacts from its large collection, it is impossible to predict what might be on display at any one time. There usually is something on view related to California Indians and their culture. A recent exhibit included a representative selection of artifacts such as bone tools, scrapers, and knife blades from the Emeryville shellmound, one of the largest and most scientifically excavated Indian shellmounds before it was removed early in this century to make way for a railroad line. A permanent display features Ishi, "the last wild Indian," who died in 1916. On view are bows and arrows he made, and some of his personal effects.

Parador Nacional de Turismo, Lérida, Spain
Gaspar de Portolá, the discoverer of San Francisco Bay.

2

The Discovery of San Francisco Bay (1542–1775)

As Spain expanded her empire she sent explorers up into California, the northernmost—and most remote—part of her New World domain. Several Spanish navigators sailed up the California coast in the second half of the sixteenth century. In 1579 Francis Drake careened his ship Golden Hind *in a "convenient and fit harborough" along what is now the coast of Marin County. None of them saw the entrance to San Francisco Bay as they sailed past.*

Some two centuries later, in 1769, Europeans finally saw San Francisco Bay when the overland expedition of Gaspar de Portolá viewed it from Sweeney Ridge in what is now San Mateo County. Six years after that, Juan Manuel de Ayala sailed through the Golden Gate and mapped the bay for the first time.

Early Spanish Exploration

By the mid-sixteenth century, Spain, the dominant world power, had reached its zenith. Spanish conquistadors had vanquished native peoples and founded colonies throughout much of South and Central America, including Mexico, its most northern possession in New Spain. But the land north of the Rio Grande remained largely unknown territory.

That started to change in 1542 when Juan Rodríguez Cabrillo, sailing north from Mexico, became the first European to explore the California coast. His mission was to explore this completely unknown coastline and find the Strait of Anián, the fabled northwest passage believed to connect the Atlantic and Pacific oceans, thus providing a shortcut to the Orient. Failing to find any such waterway, he sailed as far north as the Russian River before turning back to Mexico. Along the way he sighted Point Reyes, which he named Cabo de Piños for the great clusters of evergreens that could be seen on the hillsides. His ship, the *San Salvador*, did not hug the shoreline closely for fear of being driven onto the rocky shore, and thus Cabrillo became the first of a number of explorers to miss the Golden Gate and the magnificent bay inside.

Cabrillo's journey remained Spain's sole effort at exploring California until after the Spanish conquest of the Philippines started in 1565. A regular trade then began between Mexico and the Philippines, with westbound vessels carrying gold and silver from Acapulco and returning from Manila laden with silks, spices, porcelain, tea, and jewels. While the journey from Acapulco was relatively easy, the eastbound vessels from Manila had to take advantage of prevailing currents that led through the North Pacific and ended in northern California. A port in this area where ships could refit and take on fresh supplies of food and water before sailing home to Acapulco would have been highly desirable. Unfortunately for the Spanish, San Francisco Bay remained undetected, and most of the Manila galleons found shelter in Drakes Bay or in Monterey Bay.

Francis Drake Lands at Point Reyes

In between the comings and goings of the Manila galleons during the late sixteenth century arrived the legendary navigator and freebooter Francis Drake. Drake, who was circumnavigating the globe and plundering Spanish ships along the way, landed on the California coast in the summer of 1579. Although the exact location cannot be pinpointed, he likely careened his ship, the *Golden Hind*, in Drakes Bay. (The bay was not so named until 1792, when another Englishman, sea captain George Vancouver, honored Drake by putting his name on the charts—and perhaps to remind the Spanish of English claims to California.) Drake nailed a "plate of brasse" to a post claiming the land for Queen Elizabeth. He called the new territory Nova Albion, Albion being the Roman name for Britain which, in turn, is derived from the Latin word *albus* or "white." The white cliffs of Drakes Bay no doubt reminded him of similar cliffs at Dover, England. Drake remained for six weeks. When he continued his journey he stopped at the Farallon Islands outside the Golden Gate to stock up on bird's eggs and seal meat before leaving the area for good. Due to prevalent fog, Drake too sailed past the entrance to San Francisco Bay without seeing it.

Rand Richards

The white cliffs at Drakes Bay.

Further Spanish Exploration

The next visitor of any consequence was Sebastián Cermeño, a Portuguese navigator sailing for Spain. After a grueling four-month journey across the Pacific from the Philippines, his ship, the *San Agustin*, leaking and in need of repair, anchored in Drakes Bay in November 1595. While Cermeño and his men were exploring ashore, a winter storm struck, sinking the *San Agustin*. The group set out in a small launch they had brought from the ship and, amazingly, made it all the way back to Acapulco. Preoccupied with their near brush with disaster and unable to undertake any further exploring from their small boat, they, like all others before them, missed the entrance to the Golden Gate. Before leaving, Cermeño rechristened Cabrillo's Cabo de Piños, Punta de los Reyes (King's Point), which has been shortened to the name we know it by today—Point Reyes.

In 1602 Sebastián Vizcaíno, who had been one of Cermeño's officers, sailed back up the coast to Drakes Bay hoping to find and salvage cargo from the *San Agustin*. He found nothing, and returned to Acapulco. Vizcaíno explored the California coastline more thoroughly than his predecessors, and in his report to the viceroy in Mexico City he particularly praised the safe anchorage that Monterey Bay provided. Still, despite his diligence, he too passed right by the entrance to San Francisco Bay.

The Vizcaíno expedition brought to a close the end of the initial explorations of the California coast. Trade between Manila and Acapulco had, by this time, already dwindled to just one ship a year. Spain, whose empire was starting to contract, decided to concentrate on her colonies in South and Central America. Alta California (San Diego northward), the most far flung outpost of her empire, was left to the Indians. San Francisco Bay remained undiscovered for almost another two centuries.

What finally rekindled Spain's interest in Alta California was fear of the Russians. Russian traders and trappers, lured by the rich bounty of sea otter pelts, had by the eighteenth century ventured down the coast from Alaska as far as northern California. Alarmed by this encroachment, Spanish authorities decided to mount an overland expedition to the area to establish a Spanish presence.

Portolá Discovers San Francisco Bay

Gaspar de Portolá, a captain of dragoons serving in Mexico, was named governor of Baja and Alta California and given command of the expedition. Part of his task was to install Franciscan friars in the Baja California missions in place of the Jesuits—whom King Don Carlos III had expelled from Spanish dominions two years earlier—and to establish new Franciscan missions in Alta California.

On March 9, 1769 Portolá left Velicatá, Baja California, about two hundred miles south of San Diego, with approximately sixty men, including soldiers, Franciscan priests, muleteers, and Christian Indians, along with one hundred mules loaded with six months' provisions. Their objective was Monterey Bay, which had been so highly praised by Vizcaíno.

They reached Monterey Bay on September 30 after a long and arduous journey, but they did not recognize it when they saw it. Perhaps they envisioned an enclosed harbor, or maybe Vizcaíno's extravagant praise led them to expect something more impressive. They also were expecting to rendezvous with a supply ship coming from San Diego, but it was nowhere to be seen. So they marched on to the north.

By the end of October they were camped on the ocean shore at present-day Pacifica. Portolá sent a small scouting party on ahead under the command of Sergeant José Ortega. Meantime, Portolá and his men climbed the western ridge of Montara mountain and sighted the Farallones and, farther north, Cermeño's Bahía de San Francisco (Drakes Bay). They were confused. Some were certain they had already passed Monterey Bay, but others were not so sure.

On November 2, a small band of soldiers who had been deer hunting returned to camp with the news they had discovered an immense estuary to the east that extended to the north and south as far as they could see. The following day Ortega and his men returned to camp, reporting they too had seen this vast body of water, and that the strait through which it joined the ocean prevented them from going farther north. Portolá saw the bay for himself on November 4 when he crossed Montara Mountain's Sweeney Ridge and descended the eastern side. So, ironically, after two centuries of exploration of the coastline by ships, it was an overland expedition that first sighted San Francisco Bay.

Despite the fact that they were the first Europeans to gaze upon this newfound body of water they failed to recognize it as such, thinking instead that what they were viewing was a larger inner arm of Cermeño's Bahía de San Francisco. Portolá and his men, no doubt suffering disappointment from the now certain realization that they had overshot their target of Monterey Bay, paid scant attention to their discovery. Portolá did send Sergeant Ortega ahead to loop around the southern end of the bay and up the other side to see if a way could be found to reach Point Reyes. When Ortega returned after a few days to report that his way had been blocked by unfriendly Indians and marshy tributaries and swamps, which drained to Carquinez Strait, Portolá called a council of his officers. They decided to retrace their steps. After a difficult and trying journey, during which they had to slaughter some of their emaciated mules for food, they arrived in San Diego in January 1770. Although they marched along the coast, they once again failed to recognize Monterey Bay.

Ayala Explores the Bay

Lieutenant Juan Manuel de Ayala, in command of the packet boat *San Carlos,* became the first European to sail through the Golden Gate, when on August 5, 1775 he anchored his vessel near present-day Fort Point. His mission was to explore and map the bay and to rendezvous with an overland expedition coming from Mexico under the command of Captain Juan Bautista de Anza.

Ayala spent most of his forty-four days in the bay anchored off Angel Island in the cove that now bears his name. While two of his officers explored the far reaches of the bay in launches, Ayala himself stayed aboard the *San Carlos.* He was nursing what must have been a painful wound, having accidentally been shot in the foot several weeks into the voyage when a loaded pistol discharged as it was being packed away.

Painting by Walter Francis

Ayala sails through the Golden Gate.

Nevertheless, he put his time to good use, keeping a log and writing a comprehensive report of the trip for his superiors. He also tagged many of the bay's landmarks with the names we know them by today: Angel Island (Isla de los Angeles), Sausalito (Saucelito—"little thicket of willows" and Alcatraz (Isla de Alcatraces—"island of pelicans"). The latter name he actually applied to Yerba Buena Island, but an English sea captain mapping the bay in 1826 mistakenly assigned the name to the rock we now know as Alcatraz.

When the bay reconnaissance was complete, and with no sign of the overland de Anza expedition—which got off to a late start and did not arrive until the following year—Ayala hoisted anchor and returned to Baja California. His thorough mapping of the bay had proved conclusively that Drakes Bay and San Francisco Bay were two separate bodies of water, and that the latter's huge size and good shelter made it a harbor of great importance.

The age of exploration was over. San Francisco was about to be founded.

Gaspar de Portolá (c.1718–1786)

"The Discoverer of San Francisco Bay"

Gaspar de Portolá was born in either 1717 or 1718 in Catalonia, Spain, the son of a land-holding nobleman. He joined the King's army as a junior officer at about age seventeen and slowly worked his way up through the ranks, fighting various battles in Italy and Portugal.

In 1764, having reached the rank of captain, he was sent to New Spain (now Mexico), the far distant outpost of Spain's declining empire. It was an assignment he had not volunteered for, but as a career military man and loyal officer he accepted it without complaint.

Whether Portolá ever grew to love his new surroundings is not known, but he spent most of the remaining two decades of his life in the New World. In 1767 he was made military governor of Baja and Alta California, with his assignment being to arrest and expel the Jesuits from their missions. He carried this out smoothly, and pleased not only his superiors, for even the Jesuits praised him for his considerate treatment of them.

Two years later Portolá received the assignment that would make him a charter member of the early pioneers who put California and San Francisco on the map. At the request of the viceroy in Mexico City he led an expedition of subordinate officers, soldiers, and Franciscan friars on an overland journey from San Diego northward up the California coast. Their mission was to locate the harbor of Monterey, which had been sighted and praised by Sebastián Vizcaíno, an earlier Spanish explorer. They failed to recognize Monterey Bay when they reached it, and continued on north where, in early November 1769, Portolá and his men became the first Europeans to behold San Francisco Bay. Portolá was less than inspired by his discovery. Disappointed that he had failed to locate Monterey Bay, he mentioned the sighting of this "great arm of the sea" only as an afterthought in his follow-up report to his superiors.

Although contemporary descriptions of Gaspar de Portolá are few, he seems to have been a humane commander who consulted his officers before making decisions, and who looked

after the welfare of his men. He noted with pride upon returning to San Diego after his trek that not a single life had been
lost. Forced to slaughter their mules to survive the return journey, Portolá's only recorded gripe was about having to eat
half-roasted mule meat without salt. It was a remarkably mild
complaint considering that during a six-month march in an
alien, untamed wilderness he and his men had encountered
Indians and wild animals and had experienced earthquakes
and drenching rains.

Portolá made one more expedition up the California coast,
the following year, when he finally was successful in locating
Monterey Bay. Summoned to Mexico City afterward, his explorations were celebrated and he was promoted to colonel. A few
years later he was appointed governor of nearby Puebla, a position he held for nine years.

In early 1786, Gaspar de Portolá finally returned to Spain.
The never-married career officer served as the king's royal
deputy for his native province of Lérida in Catalonia. He soon
became ill, and died a few months later in Lérida where, coinci-
dentally, he was buried in the Church of Saint Francis of Assisi,
the namesake of the great bay six thousand miles away that
Portolá himself had discovered.

Sites and Attractions

Francis Drake and the Early Explorers

Drakes Bay – Point Reyes National Seashore.
Location: On the Marin County coast near the town of Olema, which is
at the juncture of Highway 1 and Sir Francis Drake Boulevard. **Hours:**
The park itself is open from sunrise to sunset. The Bear Valley Visitor
Center is open weekdays, 9 a.m. to 5 p.m., and weekends and holidays
from 8 a.m. to 5 p.m. **Phone:** (415) 464-5100. The Kenneth C. Patrick
Visitor Center at Drakes Beach is open only weekends and holidays, 10
a.m. to 5 p.m. Phone: (415) 669-1250. Park rangers are on duty at both
stations during business hours. **Admission:** Free. **Website:**
www.nps.gov/pore.

Scenic Drakes Bay, the probable location of Francis Drake's
thirty-six day stopover in June and July of 1579, and the site of
Sebastián Cermeño's wreck of the *San Agustin* sixteen years later,
is located an hour's drive north of San Francisco. Besides a monument on the beach marking where historians believe is the most
likely area for Drake's landfall, there are other items of interest in
the park related to both the Drake and Cermeño landings.

The place to start is the Bear Valley Visitor Center and park
headquarters, a short distance inside the park's entrance. The visitor
center has a roomful of exhibits covering the history as well as the
flora and fauna of the park. On display are several pieces of Ming
Dynasty porcelain from the Cermeño wreck that were recovered
from archeological digs at local Miwok Indian sites.

Before departing the visitor center for Drakes Bay, pick up one
of the park's official map and guide pamphlets. It shows all of
the park's major roads and hiking trails and provides some background material on Drake and Cermeño and their time spent in the
area.

Rand Richards

Drake landing site monument.

Sixteen miles further along Sir Francis Drake Highway is the Kenneth C. Patrick Visitor Center at Drakes Beach. Available at the small bookstore here is a pamphlet reprinted from the Geographical Magazine of London describing the Drake Navigators Guild's "proof positive" that Drake landed there. Their finding is based on distinct pottery fragments retrieved from local Indian digs that they claim could only have come from Drake.

Behind the visitor center, on the open-air deck, is a series of panels describing Drake, the man, and his remarkable voyage around the world.

Drake's landing site is located on the beach about a mile northeast of the visitor center. Along the way you pass, and can see up close, the white cliffs that reminded Drake of England and caused him to name the area Nova Albion. The monument, which is inland a little bit from the main part of the beach and consists of a ten-foot-high wooden pole posted behind an anchor and a plaque embedded in stone, can be difficult to find. The best way there is to hike along the beach until you reach the channel leading to Drakes Estero. Turn left following the bank of the channel for about two hundred yards, then turn left inland through the swamp grass and rounded dunes. The monument is about fifty yards in.

As to the wreck of the *San Agustin*, it still lies somewhere in Drakes Bay, buried under at least thirty feet of sand and mud. Several private salvors have made proposals to excavate it. It seems only a matter of time before it is located and salvaged. Its recovery would represent a significant archeological find, since it would surely shed further light on the early Spanish explorations of California. The remains of the *San Agustin* would also be the first Manila galleon ever salvaged.

Drake's Plate of Brass.
Location: At the Bancroft Library on the campus of the University of California at Berkeley. The plaque is on view in the waiting area of the reading room. Anyone who is at least eighteen years old and a high school graduate can use the library. **Phone:** (510) 642-6481. **Hours:** Monday – Friday, 9 a.m. to 5 p.m.; Saturday, 1 p.m. to 5 p.m. (while classes are in session.) **Admission:** Free. **Website:** http://bancroft.berkeley.edu. The Bancroft Library is **closed** for renovation.

On permanent display here in the lobby of the Bancroft Library is the Plate of Brass that Francis Drake was thought to have left behind before departing northern California in 1579. Or, rather, what is a clever forgery.

The plaque was discovered on a hill near San Quentin prison on the east side of Marin County by a young department store clerk on a picnic during the summer of 1936. For almost forty years the preponderant scholarly opinion was that the plate was genuine. In the mid-1970s, with advances in technology, further metallurgical and other tests were conducted that led scholars to conclude that the plate was a forgery. The type of metal found in the plate differed from known examples of sixteenth-century brass, and it was shown that the plate had been produced by machine-made rolling rather than the hammer shaping that Drake's era would have produced.

The plate also bears a hole in its lower right corner because, according to the account of the voyage, a sixpence coin was placed in a hole in the plate when it was "nailed to a firme post" to proclaim Queen Elizabeth's sovereignty over Nova Albion. In 1974 an Elizabethan sixpence dated 1567 was found buried under the ceremonial dance floor of a Coast Miwok village site near Novato. Intriguing as it is to speculate whether this was the coin (now in the Bancroft Library but not on display) that once lodged in Drake's plate, there is no way to confirm it.

Still surrounding the Plate of Brass is the mystery of who forged it, when, and why. Theories have ranged from Captain George Vancouver who visited the area in 1792, to a student of a local college history professor who only half-jokingly told his students to keep an eye out for Drake's plate.

The Bancroft Library also places recent acquisitions dealing with all phases of California history on temporary display in the glass cases in the lobby. One recent item relating to San Francisco history was a beautiful hand-colored map of the bay done by José Canizares, one of the two officers who explored the shoreline of San Francisco Bay for Manuel de Ayala in 1775.

The Oakland Museum – History Gallery.
Location: 1000 Oak Street (two blocks from Lake Merritt), Oakland. **Phone:** (510) 238-3842. **Hours:** Wednesday – Saturday, 10 a.m. to 5 p.m.; (First Friday to 9 p.m.); Sunday, Noon to 5 p.m. Closed holidays. **Admission:** Adults, $8.00; Seniors, Students, $5.00; Children (under 5), Free. **Website:** www.museumca.org.

The era of exploration is one of the least well covered areas of the History Gallery's collection, no doubt due to the fact there just is not a lot remaining from the period. On display are nautical and navigational instruments: an astrolabe, telescope, and compass. There are also prints of the Indians drawn by early explorers, and reproductions of early maps—including one showing California as an island.

Portolá's Discovery of San Francisco Bay

Portolá Discovery Site.
Location: Sweeney Ridge, San Mateo County between Pacifica and San Bruno. **Phone:** (415) 556-8371. Sweeney Ridge is part of the Golden Gate National Recreation Area. **Hours:** Open daily, 8 a.m. to dusk.**Admission:** Free. There are several trails leading to the discovery site. The easiest and most accessible one starts from the end of Sneath Lane in San Bruno. Others start from parking lot #2 behind Skyline College in San Bruno and from behind the Shelldance nursery off Highway 1 in Pacifica. **Website:** www.nps.gov/goga.

Atop Sweeney Ridge in San Mateo County is a stone monument commemorating the sighting of San Francisco Bay by the Gaspar de Portolá expedition of 1769. Most historians credit November 2 as the date the bay was first seen, since that was the date the hunting party returned with the news of its sighting. The monument lists November 4 as the date, which is also accurate since that is when Portolá himself first saw it.

Portolá and his men were lucky to see the bay. Sweeney Ridge can be enshrouded in fog on days when it is sunny and clear in neighboring locales. Fortunately for Portolá he was there in the fall, which is when the Bay Area enjoys its most extended stretches of warm, fog-free weather. From the ridge, when the air is clear, you can see not only the bay but also some of the other landmarks seen by Portolá and his men—the Farallones to the west, Point Reyes to the northwest, and Mount Hamilton to the southeast.

As noted above, the best trail to the summit is the one starting at Sneath Lane in San Bruno but if you find yourself in Pacifica on the other side of the ridge there are a couple of other Portolá related things to see. On Crespi Drive just off Highway 1 is where the explorer and his band last camped before hiking up onto Sweeney Ridge to sight the bay. A plaque marks the spot. Just yards away, in the Pacifica Community Center's parking lot, is a new, stylized bronze sculpture of Portolá that was donated by the governor of Catalonia, Spain in honor of its native son.

When hiking to the discovery site a jacket or windbreaker is recommended, since even on days of fine weather it can be cool and breezy at the summit.

San Mateo County History Museum.
Location: 2200 Broadway, Redwood City. **Phone:** (650) 299-0104. **Hours:** Tuesday – Sunday, 10 a.m. to 4 p.m. **Admission:** Adults, $4.00; Students, Seniors, Children, $2.00. **Website:** www.sanmateocountyhistory.com.

The museum has a few items relating to the Portolá expedition, including a map of San Mateo County showing Portolá's route to the discovery of San Francisco Bay. Each spot where he is known to have camped is marked. Other items include a reproduction of what is believed to be a likeness of Portolá, and a fine oil painting depicting Portolá's discovery of San Francisco Bay.

Ayala at Angel Island

> **Ayala Cove – Angel Island.**
> **Location:** Angel Island, the largest island in San Francisco Bay, is located off the Tiburon peninsula. There is a visitor center at Ayala Cove that can provide maps and more information. **Phone:** (415) 435-3522. Public access to the island is by ferry only. Primary points of departure are San Francisco and Tiburon. The Blue & Gold Fleet, **Phone:** (415) 705-5555, located at Pier 41, San Francisco, and the McDonough ferry, **Phone:** (415) 435-2131, which departs from 21 Main Street, Tiburon, both serve the island daily during the summer. Call the above numbers for departure times and the winter schedule. **Admission:** Angel Island itself is free. The ferry tolls on the Blue & Gold Fleet are: Adults, $14.50; Children (6–12), $8.50; under 6, Free. The McDonough ferry: Adults, $10.25; Children (5–11), $8.00; Bicycles, $1.00. **Websites:** www.angelisland.org and www.parks.ca.gov.

It was in this cove that Manuel de Ayala anchored his ship *San Carlos* "within a pistol shot" of the shore while his subordinates explored and mapped the bay. The graceful arc of the shoreline in this charming and protected cove appears to have changed little since Ayala's time. What has changed is the island's vegetation. Two hundred years ago Angel Island was heavily forested with native oak, bay, and madrone trees. The arriving Yankee traders (who called it "Wood Island") and the later gold rush hordes soon stripped the island bare of its timber for use as firewood and as lumber for construction. Angel Island's vegetation today is primarily eucalyptus, which was planted by the U.S. Army after 1850. Current plans call for the eucalyptus to be removed, and for the island to be reforested with native trees.

Ayala Cove was, until 1900, known as Raccoon Cove. The name was then changed to Hospital Cove due to a U.S. Army hospital built there as part of a now vanished quarantine station. In 1969 it was renamed Ayala Cove to honor the Spanish explorer.

3

The Founding of San Francisco (1776–1847)

The first settlers arrived in 1776 and established the Presidio, overlooking the Golden Gate, and, farther inland, Mission Dolores. The first mass held at the latter location, on June 29, 1776, marks the official founding of San Francisco.

But Spain's empire was near collapse. In 1821 Mexico declared its independence from the mother country, and San Francisco became part of Mexico. A new elite—the Californios—soon came to power in California, and built large ranchos on appropriated former mission lands.

Mexican rule was even briefer than that of Spain. In 1846, when war broke out between the United States and Mexico, the village of Yerba Buena (as San Francisco was then known) was seized by U.S. troops without a shot being fired. Less than a year later Yerba Buena was renamed San Francisco.

The Presidio and Mission Dolores

In late 1775 the de Anza expedition, a group of about two hundred colonists accompanied by a military escort, left Tubac, Sonora (near present-day Tucson, Arizona). Their objective was to establish a mission and presidio at the tip of the San Francisco peninsula as the nucleus of a new colony in Alta California.

After leaving most of the party at already established Monterey, Captain Juan Bautista de Anza and a small advance guard, including his lieutenant, José Moraga, and Pedro Font, a Franciscan priest, went on ahead. On March 28 they reached the bluff at the very tip of the peninsula (Fort Point occupies the site now) where de Anza planted a cross signifying the location of the future presidio. The site was chosen because of its strategic location overlooking the entrance to the bay. Father Font, enraptured by the view and pondering the future city, wrote in his diary that day ". . . I think that if it could be well settled like Europe there would not be anything more beautiful in all the world. . . ."

While the site for the presidio was perfect for its strategic value, the windswept, rocky ledge was less than ideal for a mission settlement. So the next day, after exploring further, the small band came upon a sheltered valley three miles inland to the southeast. Here the soil and climate were better and there was abundant fresh water provided by a stream-fed lagoon. Because it was the Friday before Palm Sunday—the Friday of Sorrows—they called their encampment Laguna de los Dolores.

Having established sites for both presidio and mission, the advance guard then headed south. De Anza returned to Mexico, while Lt. Moraga went to Monterey where he and Father Junipero Serra, head of the Franciscan order in California, assembled the waiting colonists and escorted them to the mission site.

The settlers celebrated with a mass held under a shelter made of branches on June 29, 1776. This ceremony, held just five days before the Declaration of Independence was ratified three thousand miles away in Philadelphia, marks the official founding of San Francisco. Two months later a supply ship sailed into the bay with skilled carpenters, tools, and other equipment. Logs were cut and the carpenters constructed a warehouse, a barracks for the soldiers, and a new chapel made of mud-plastered boards.

On October 9 the formal dedication of Mission San Francisco de Asis (named in honor of Saint Francis of Assisi, founder of the Franciscan order) was held. After the ceremony the celebrants enjoyed a barbecue and feast. The Indians, perhaps anticipating what the future would bring, appeared less than enthusiastic, as Father Francisco Palou noted in his diary that day: "The day has been a joyful one for all. Only the savages did not enjoy themselves on this happy day."

At the same time the fledgling mission was under way, the Presidio (presidio derives from the Latin word *praesidium,* which is what the Romans called their fortified camps) was being built near the entrance to the bay. Although de Anza had marked the bluff overlooking the Golden Gate as the spot for the presidio, after his departure, Lt. Moraga chose a spot a mile to the southeast that was less exposed to the wind and closer to fresh water. A square compound of about 250 yards on a side was laid out and encircled by walls made of the only building materials at hand—California live oak, and mud. This rough enclosure was dedicated on September 17, 1776. Two years later it was almost entirely washed away by a violent rainstorm. A more permanent fortification was then built, and the enclosure eventually boasted a chapel, the commandante's headquarters, and barracks for the troops, all built around a central courtyard.

The Presidio, located where it was—inland and not on the bluff overlooking the entrance to the bay—was a less than ideal place from which to defend against any invasion. The Spanish did not immediately follow up by fortifying the bluff where de Anza had planted the cross. Apparently they felt no threat from any foreign power, and thus nothing was done for some years after the Presidio was founded.

That changed in 1792 when a British Royal Navy ship under the command of Captain George Vancouver sailed into San Francisco Bay. He was cordially received by the Spanish garrison—perhaps too cordially, for the Presidio's commandante was later reproved for allowing Vancouver to observe the lack of defenses.

Work was soon begun on the construction of a fort on the bluff overlooking the southern entrance to the Golden Gate. This fort, the Castillo de San Joaquin, was completed in 1794. It was an inadequate structure, built on sand and crumbling rock and garrisoned by only seven soldiers. The adobe walls shook whenever one of its cannons was fired. Munitions were in such short supply that when, in 1806, a Russian ship entered the bay and fired a friendly salute, the Spanish soldiers had to row out to the vessel to borrow enough powder to fire a return salute.

Despite shortages and the primitive lifestyle of the residents of these frontier outposts, the first few decades of existence for both the Presidio and Mission Dolores were moderately prosperous. The mission established a growing, if not self-sufficient, community. The priests used Indian labor to plant and harvest crops, and a new, larger, solidly built church (the present-day building—Mission Dolores—which dates from 1791) was constructed.

San Francisco Becomes Mexican Territory

The period of relative calm soon came to an end. Spain's empire contracted, and its American colonies started agitating for independence. By 1810, Mexico was in open revolt against the mother country. Preoccupied with combating the rebellion, Spain could no longer afford to aid or supply the missions and presidios in faraway Alta California. So they were essentially abandoned, and were obliged to rely on their own resources.

Cutoff and isolated, Spain's three fortifications in San Francisco, the Castillo de San Joaquin, the Presidio, and Mission Dolores, went into a progressive decline. Racked by wind, rain, and periodic earthquakes, all three structures began to crumble—Mission Dolores less so, since it was more solidly constructed. The human toll was even worse. The garrison's soldiers, no longer receiving wages from Spain, came to rely on the mission for their food and other necessities. But Mission Dolores had problems of its own. The Indian neophytes, kept under guard while being converted to

Mission Dolores, in the 1870s.

Christianity, suffered greatly. The change in diet, the adjustment to a foreign discipline, and the exposure to new diseases such as measles, to which they had no immunity, took a dreadful toll.

Spain's rule over Alta California came to an end in 1821, when Mexico, after a decade of revolution, declared its independence. San Francisco became Mexican territory, although word did not reach it until 1822.

Spanish influence vastly changed the way of life—that of the Indians—that had existed in San Francisco and the surrounding area for thousands of years. The Spanish introduction of agriculture, the use of metal instead of stone, the changeover to different social, political, and religious systems, constituted a total transformation of the way things had been. Less than a century later, the Indians and the remnants of their culture would be almost gone.

Secularization and the Rise of the Californios

The coming of Mexican rule brought more changes to San Francisco and the rest of Alta California. The most important one occurred in 1834, when the Mexican congress passed the Secularization Act, which ended the Franciscans' control of the missions. This act freed the remaining Indian neophytes and, more importantly, stripped the missions of their vast land holdings.

Pressures had been building for years from Alta California settlers and would-be settlers, such as former soldiers who coveted mission land. The Mexican government realized that if Alta California was to develop its potential, growth in population would be essential to this sparsely settled region.

The missions, which had always been intended as temporary institutions—with the idea that the Christianized Indians would one day take on the duties of citizenship and gain title to the mission lands—found the timetable accelerated. But the Indian neophytes were simply not prepared to assume such responsibility. Mission overseers, appointed by the rulers in Mexico City, turned out, in many cases, to be either incompetent or corrupt, and the Indians found themselves cheated of their due. Some of them returned to the wilderness, while others hired on as laborers or servants at nearby ranchos.

Prior to secularization a few land grants had been made to individual settlers, but after 1834 the floodgates opened and the various successive governors of Alta California started doling out huge land grants to local settlers, retired soldiers, and to almost anyone, in fact, who was willing to take out Mexican citizenship. Some of these parcels were as large as 48,000 acres—the kind of acreage that would support cattle ranching on a large scale.

Large cattle baronies—or ranchos—arose on these lands, consolidating power in the hands of a small group of families, who quickly became the dominant social and political force in Mexican California. They were known as the Californios. Typically they were grouped into large, close-knit, patriarchal families. The Californios, their ranchos supported by Indian labor, lived a relatively carefree life that was punctuated by frequent fiestas and sporting events. Mariano Vallejo was one of the best known and most respected of the Californios. He amassed parcels of land totaling 175,000 acres, including much of what is today Napa and Sonoma counties.

San Francisco Public Library

A Californio fandango.

San Francisco itself was part of a dozen ranchos, including Rancho San Miguel, Rancho Laguna de la Merced, and the Rancho Rincon de las Salinas y Potrero Viejo, among others.

At Mission Dolores, secularization was the final blow to the already crumbling structure. It closed in 1834, and for the next quarter century it served variously as a tavern and dance hall, while the grounds were sometimes used for bull versus bear contests. It was not until 1859 that Mission Dolores reopened as a Catholic church. It remains an active parish to this day.

The Presidio and the Castillo de San Joaquin also fell into ruin. The Castillo was vacated in 1835, and its garrison moved to Benicia, across the bay. What little remained of the fort was razed in 1853 to make way for the construction of Fort Point. The original Presidio was occupied until 1835, when it too was abandoned. Its remaining walls were carted away a few years later to help build a customs house at the growing community on Yerba Buena cove.

The Birth of Yerba Buena

When Mexico severed ties with Spain in 1821, the latter's previously monopolistic trade practices came to an end, and California's ports were officially opened to trade with other nations. Trade was slow at first, but by the 1830s Yankee trading vessels, which had come around Cape Horn, were anchoring regularly at Yerba Buena—a protected cove on the northeast corner of the peninsula—to buy hides and tallow for leather tanneries and factories in New England.

By 1835, trade had reached the point where at least one settler decided to erect a permanent dwelling on the hillside facing the cove. This first resident was William A. Richardson, a British seaman who stayed behind when his ship returned to England in 1822. He took Mexican citizenship, and soon married the Presidio commandante's daughter. Richardson established himself as a harbor master and pilot, and later took on additional duties as a broker for the growing hide and tallow trade, acting as a middleman between the Californios and the American ships anchoring in the cove.

Richardson's first dwelling, nothing more than a ship's sail
stretched over four posts, was put up in October 1835, and stood just
one hundred yards west of the shoreline, which at that time was a
little east of where Montgomery Street is today. He quickly supplemented this with a wooden shack. In 1836 he replaced this structure
with one made of solid adobe bricks. In that same year a Yankee settler, Jacob Leese, built a house just a few yards south of Richardson.
By 1839 several more dwellings had been built on the cove, and a
dirt path called the Calle de la Fundacion was carved out as the first
"street"—roughly where Grant Avenue is today. Richardson named
the fledgling community *Yerba Buena* ("good herb"), after a local
mint-flavored plant that grew wild in the area, and which the Indians and Spanish used to make tea.

With the little town starting to grow, it was decided to lay out a
town plan so that the granting of additional lots could proceed in a
more orderly fashion. The Mexican authorities asked a Swiss new-
comer named Jean-Jacques Vioget, the only one in town with surveying instruments, to create a rough plan and draw a map. Vioget,
who had lived in Chile, followed the traditional Spanish pueblo
model of a square commons—a plaza—as a focal point in a grid
pattern of streets. He laid out a large rectangle encompassing the
plaza—later named Portsmouth Square—and all of the existing lots.
Two men on horseback bearing lengths of chain measured in varas
(one vara equaled thirty-three inches) carried out the physical
survey. Thus was the plan of the infant city born. No names were
applied to any of the streets that appeared on Vioget's map, but
today the north-south streets can be identified as Kearny and Grant,
and the east-west streets as Sacramento, Clay, Washington, Jackson,
and Pacific.

Vioget probably never imagined that little Yerba Buena would
one day grow into a big city, or that his simple grid would be
extended, causing parallel streets to rise up and over steep hills and
distant ridges. Thus an almost casual decision, made a century and
a half ago, created the basic plan for much of the physical layout of
the city as it exists today.

The Coming of the Americans

The 1840s saw the beginning of the inexorable force that led California to change from Mexican to U.S. rule. With the increasing frequency of trade emanating from Yerba Buena, word of California's fertile soil, mild climate, and lack of an effective Mexican military presence soon reached the east. In 1841 the first overland party, led by John Bidwell, crossed the plains and the Sierra into California. He was soon followed by others, and by the mid-1840s a recognizable trail had been worn from Missouri to California.

Unlike the pre-1840 American-born residents who had married into Mexican families and adapted to local culture, the new arrivals were not interested in assimilating. They were looking for lands to occupy and settle. They were the vanguard of the idea of Manifest Destiny that would soon extend American territory beyond the Mississippi River to the Pacific Shore.

San Francisco Becomes American Soil

It was foreordained that with the inexorable pressure of steady and continued migration from the East, California would eventually become part of the United States. But the precipitating cause that led this to occur earlier than it would have otherwise was the Mexican War. The major source of friction between the U.S. and Mexico in the 1840s was who would gain control of Texas. But it was no secret that the U.S. coveted California as well. President Andrew Jackson had even offered to purchase San Francisco Bay and northern California in 1835 for $3.5 million, but Mexico declined to sell.

With tension between the two countries mounting, a clash on the Texas border in 1846 led to war. The war was short, not very bloody, and ended in total victory for the United States in early 1848, with Mexico ceding both Texas and California to her more powerful neighbor.

San Francisco played only a small part in the drama. John C. Frémont, in California on his second exploring expedition to the West, along with a few of his men, rowed from Sausalito past the entrance to the bay—which he named *Chrysopylae*, the Golden

Gate, "on the same principle that the harbor of *Byzantium* (Constantinople afterwards) was called *Chrysoceras* (golden horn)"—to the undefended Castillo de San Joaquin. There he, Kit Carson, and the rest of his group spiked the ancient bronze cannons. In his memoirs, Frémont made this sound like a heroic task but, in truth, the cannons were lying in the dirt, inoperable, their wooden carriages rotted away.

The most significant event occurred in Yerba Buena cove. On July 9, 1846, Captain John B. Montgomery and a small detachment of sailors and marines rowed ashore from the warship U.S.S. *Portsmouth,* anchored in the bay, and raised the American flag over the plaza, which was soon to be named for the ship. There was no resistance, and the small Mexican pueblo of Yerba Buena effectively became U.S. soil.

How San Francisco Got Its Name

If a rose by any other name would not smell as sweet, then San Francisco, had it remained Yerba Buena, would not be quite the same city. Luckily for San Francisco, two promoters of a rival town forced Yerba Buena to take action to claim the name it was destined to have.

In 1847, friends of Mariano Vallejo, Thomas O. Larkin, and Robert Semple, convinced that a town on the eastern shore of the bay, closer to John Sutter's increasingly important colony at Sacramento, would be a better location for a major city, petitioned Vallejo for a land grant on Carquinez Strait. The grant duly given, the two promoters named their soon-to-be city Francisca. It seemed the perfect choice, since it capitalized on the association with San Francisco Bay while at the same time honoring their patron's wife, one of whose given names was Francisca.

Residents of Yerba Buena, on hearing this, decided that their town deserved to be linked with the name of the magnificent bay, and they persuaded Alcalde (a combination mayor and judge) Washington A. Bartlett to change the name of Yerba Buena to San Francisco. On January 23, 1847 Bartlett issued a proclamation stating that henceforth Yerba Buena was to be known as San Francisco in all future dealings. Larkin and Semple relented and changed the name of their town to Benicia, one of Señora Vallejo's other names.

The names Yerba Buena and San Francisco actually had been used interchangeably by the Mexicans virtually since the pueblo's founding. Bartlett's proclamation formalized what had heretofore been the community's secondary designation.

The O'Farrell Plan

Later in 1847, alcalde Bartlett asked Jasper O'Farrell, an Irish engineer and surveyor who had been in town four years, to extend the city's boundaries, because continued growth had filled most of the existing lots on the relatively scarce flat ground adjacent to the water's edge. Pressure was growing from residents who looked at the shallow water just beyond the beach and realized that additional lots could be formed (and money could be made) by filling in the cove. So O'Farrell, expanding on the earlier Vioget plan, continued the grid pattern by extending lines into the bay. These lines soon became wharves, and then streets.

O'Farrell had originally wanted to open up the Vioget plat, and suggested widening the existing streets from sixty to eighty feet and also terracing nearby Telegraph Hill. Both these proposals were rejected by business and property owners, who wished to avoid the expense of realigning existing buildings. Continuing the grid also offered a couple of advantages: it could easily be extended and, more importantly, subdivided—a prime consideration for those lusting after real estate profits.

O'Farrell's main departure from the Vioget plan was to lay out Market Street, a 120-foot-wide boulevard, running at a diagonal to the initial grid. In designing such a grand avenue O'Farrell likely envisioned it as the social and commercial center of what he surely saw would someday be a great city. He pointed it at Twin Peaks, a prominent landmark to the west. This also was the direction of Mission Dolores, one of San Francisco's main focal points. But what led O'Farrell to the idea of Market Street in the first place was happenstance. In expanding the southeast corner of the fifty-vara-lot main grid toward the waterfront—in what is now the area south of Market around First Street—he discovered that it overlapped

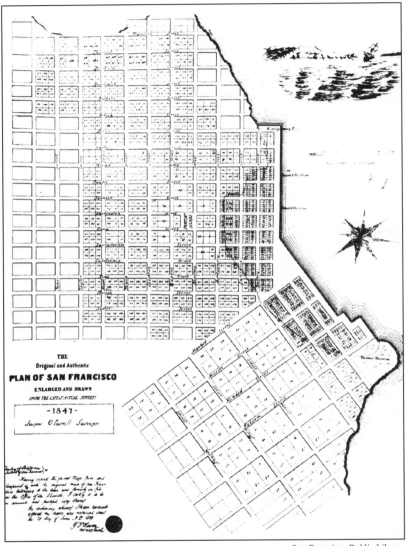

Jasper O'Farrell's 1847 plan for San Francisco,
showing the original shoreline.

with some previously granted one-hundred-vara lots. Forced to resurvey both areas, he probably decided he could avoid a squabble by placing a boundary street, cut at a diagonal to the main grid, between the two. Thus Market Street was born. Combined with the benefit of providing the town with a grand boulevard, it surely must have seemed an ideal solution.

South of Market, O'Farrell aligned the streets parallel and perpendicular to his new promenade, and continued the one-hundred-vara lot survey on that side. This is why city blocks south of Market from First Street to the bay are twice the area of those north of Market and east of Sansome Street, where the lots are fifty varas on a side.

When seen on a map or from the air, the downtown portion of the city today looks like two completely different town grids stitched together with Market Street as the seam, a veritable Frankenstein monster of city planning. And it is a monster that comes alive for every motorist trying to cross Market Street, since few of the streets ending at Market directly connect with any on the other side.

In any event, the O'Farrell plan, which grew by stages to its eventual perimeter—north of Market to Francisco and Leavenworth and south of Market to Townsend and Fourth streets—permanently fixed the grid pattern on the city. In the decades to come, as the city grew beyond the O'Farrell boundaries, the grid spread, creating a network of streets marching up, over, and—later on—sometimes through, some of the steepest hills found within any city's limits.

The Calm Before the Storm

As 1847 drew to a close, the young community nestled on the cove was growing, and San Franciscans (all five hundred of them) were looking forward to more growth. But even the most visionary resident could not have foreseen the kind of explosive change that was about to hit San Francisco with the force of a hurricane. One hundred and thirty miles away in the Sierra foothills, at Coloma, a sawmill was under construction. There, a discovery was about to be made that would electrify the world and draw fortune hunters from all over the globe to the small village on Yerba Buena cove.

Society of California Pioneers

Jasper O'Farrell.

Jasper O'Farrell (1817–1875)

"San Francisco's City Planner"

Jasper O'Farrell was born near Dublin, Ireland in 1817. Unlike many of his countrymen, who came from poor families, O'Farrell was raised in relative comfort. Trained as a civil engineer, he arrived in San Francisco (then still the Mexican pueblo of Yerba Buena) in 1843 aboard a U.S. coastal survey ship, after having spent almost two years mapping the west coast of South America as part of a British surveying expedition.

He learned Spanish, adapted readily to the Californio way of life, and was known as Don Gaspar O'Farrell until the U.S. established its authority in 1846. With his language fluency and his professional training he soon became an indispensable man, serving the Mexican authorities, Californio rancheros, and the arriving Yankees as a surveyor and engineer.

In 1847, at the request of the American alcalde, Washington Bartlett, he revamped and made some minor corrections to the initial Vioget survey of Yerba Buena of 1839 and, following the established grid, extended the city limits far beyond the original town centered on Portsmouth Square.

O'Farrell's main legacy to San Francisco is Market Street, the grand boulevard that bisects downtown and served as the centerpiece of his plan. At 120 feet wide it was twice the width of most other city streets at the time. This extravagant use of valuable land for a public thoroughfare nearly got O'Farrell lynched. According to friends and family members, when O'Farrell's map was first published, in 1847, a mob formed in protest and talked of lynching the surveyor. Hearing of the threat, O'Farrell rode to North Beach, took a boat for Sausalito, and stayed away from San Francisco until the furor died down.

O'Farrell, who was usually awarded land in payment for his surveying services in San Francisco and elsewhere, soon managed to acquire some large holdings. Combined with some success in gold mining at the start of the gold rush in 1848, he soon retired to a 60,000-acre ranch near Sebastopol in Sonoma County.

In later years he dabbled in politics, getting elected to the state senate in 1858. After losing a race for lieutenant governor in 1861 he gave up statecraft and lived out his remaining years on his ranch. He visited San Francisco frequently, and on one such visit, in November 1875, he died suddenly of an apparent heart attack at age fifty-eight. He left a wife and eight children. Some of his descendants still live in northern California today.

Sites and Attractions

The Spanish Era

Mission Dolores.
Location: Sixteenth and Dolores Streets, San Francisco. **Phone:** (415) 621-8203. **Hours:** Open daily during summer, 9:00 a.m. to 4:30 p.m.; during winter, 9 a.m. to 4 p.m. Restricted visiting hours on religious and major holidays. Closed Thanksgiving and Christmas. **Admission:** Adults, $5.00; Students, Seniors (65+), $3.00. **Website:** www. missiondolores.org.

Mission Dolores is the oldest building in San Francisco—a proud survivor from the days of Spanish rule. Although the mission was officially christened Misión San Francisco de Asis (after Saint Francis of Assisi), the more colloquial Mission Dolores stuck, and is the name it is known by today.

The first chapel and mission of 1776 were located on Camp Street, a small alley a block east of the present site. In 1788 work began on a permanent church building. It was completed in 1791 and stands today, looking much like it did originally. The only other remnant of the mission's early days is that part of the cemetery immediately adjoining the chapel. Other buildings that once housed priests and Indian neophytes have long since disappeared.

Constructed of more than thirty-six thousand large adobe bricks, with walls over four feet thick, the church has a solid, almost stocky appearance. Despite that, it is well proportioned, even graceful. The mission's original bells, in the three niches on the façade, were brought from Mexico in the 1820s.

The chapel survived the 1906 earthquake—and the one of 1989 —virtually unscathed, but the larger parish church next door, which had been constructed in 1876, collapsed during the 1906 quake. It was replaced by the present basilica, which dates from 1913 but whose façade was substantially remodeled in the 1920s.

Inside the church the simple wooden pews are offset by a hand-carved altar and figurines made in Mexico about 1800. The painted ceiling and beams replicate Indian-designed patterns, the colors of which were originally made from vegetable dyes. The roof still has the original timbers, which at one time were fastened together with wooden manzanita pegs and rawhide thongs. In 1918, as an earth-quake-proofing measure, the beams were strengthened with steel reinforcing ties. Also at that time clapboard siding on the church's exterior walls was taken down, revealing the whitewashed adobe walls once again. Buried beneath the chapel floor are William Leidesdorff, a pre-gold rush San Francisco businessman, and Lt. José Moraga, leader of the settlement party of 1776.

There is a small museum in back of the nave (reached via the door marked "To Museum") where relics from the mission's early days are on display. Among the items are the church's first baptismal register, started in 1776, sacred artifacts donated by Father Junipero Serra, and various secular objects reflecting everyday life at the mission. There is also a cutaway section of a wall showing the rough adobe bricks behind the white plaster finish.

Beyond the museum is the oldest cemetery within the city limits. The mission's burial ground was originally as much as five times larger. Burials occurred soon after the mission was established, but none of the very early grave markers, which were made of wood, has survived.

One of the earliest remaining headstones is that of Luís Argüello, the first Mexican governor of Alta California (1822–1825), who died in 1830. Several other Spanish-Mexican notables who have San Francisco streets named after them, such as Francisco Guerrero and José Noe, are buried here.

The cemetery reflects the international character of San Francisco. Beside the tombstones of the Hispanic founders are ones marking the graves of early French, German, Italian, Irish, Scottish, and Australian residents. A statue of an Indian maiden commemorates the as many as five thousand native Americans who were buried on the mission grounds. Some of these nameless dead are likely still buried under nearby streets and buildings.

The Presidio.

Location: The Presidio, which is a National and California State Historic Landmark, occupies over one thousand acres in the northwest corner of San Francisco. The main entrance is at the western end of Lombard Street. Other city entrances are through the north end of Arguello or via Lincoln Boulevard, the main drive along the western edge. The Presidio can also easily be reached from Marin County by taking the first right turn after exiting the Golden Gate Bridge toll booths. The military officially vacated the Presidio in 1994. Since October 1 of that year the entire post has been part of the Golden Gate National Recreation Area, and is operated by the National Park Service and the Presidio Trust. **Website:** www.nps.gov/prsf.

Artifacts that illustrate the Presidio's early history can be seen at several locations:

The Old Hospital – Former Presidio Museum.

Location: Lincoln and Funston streets in the Presidio, San Francisco. No phone. Interior not open to the public.

Rand Richards

The City's oldest relic—a cannon from the Castillo de San Joaquin.

This building, with the open veranda on the second floor, served as the Presidio's hospital from 1864 to 1899, and then was used for other medical functions up until as late as 1973. It is truly a museum piece in its own right, but the building does not date from 1857 as the bronze plaque on the front façade would have you believe.

The structure originally faced west toward the parade ground but was turned around in 1878 to face east at the same time as the officers quarters to the north were. The three-story octagonal tower was added in 1897 as a surgery and laboratory.

Under the front porch is one of the six remaining cannon from the Castillo de San Joaquin, the Spanish fort of 1794 that stood where Fort Point is now. Dated 1623, this cannon is the oldest verifiable relic related to The City's history. The wooden gun carriage is a replica.

The Officers Club and Parade Ground.
Location: At the intersection of Moraga and Arguello streets, about a quarter of a mile southwest of the Old Hospital. The Officers Club currently serves as the Presidio's temporary visitor center. At a later date the visitors center will move to Building 102 by the parade ground. **Phone:** (415) 561-4323. **Hours:** Daily, 9 a.m. to 5 p.m., except holidays. **Website:** www.nps.gov/prsf.

A sign on the front lawn of the Officers Club identifies this as the oldest building in San Francisco. But this is inaccurate and

Courtesy, Park Archives, GGNRA

The Presidio Officers Club.

misleading. It is the *site* of San Francisco's first permanent construction, but nothing from the earliest presidio remains. Within the present walls there are, however, some adobe bricks from the Spanish commandante's headquarters that date from about 1810 to 1820.

A small sampling of these bricks is visible inside the Officers Club. Frankly, there is not much to look at, but in the main dining room on the west wall by the stage is a plastic window set in the wall. Pushing the adjacent button lights a dim bulb that reveals a few cobweb-festooned dun-colored adobe bricks.

Flanking the front door of the Officers Club are two more of the Castillo's cannon. Two others are located on either side of the flagpole on the parade ground a short distance away. These bronze cannon—and their brethren, one each located at the Army Museum, as noted above, and at Fort Point—were all cast in Peru in the seventeenth century. They bear not only the coat of arms of the Royal House of Spain, which is distinguished by the cross-hatched castles of Aragon and lions of Castile, but also the crests of the Peruvian viceroy who happened to be regent at the time the cannon were cast. The former insignia are located atop the base of the cannon and the latter are embossed on the forward part of the barrel. It is not known how these pieces came to Mexico from Peru, but they were brought by frigate up the California coast from San Blas in Baja California specifically to arm the Castillo de San Joaquin. These rare cannon are the only surviving artifacts from the old Spanish fortification. They were some of the ones spiked by Frémont and his men in 1846. Evidence of that spiking can still be seen on the piece west of the entrance to the Officers Club. If you look closely you can see a broken-off piece of a rat-tail file jammed in the firing vent—the small hole where the fuse would go.

Before leaving the area, look at the stone marker with an embedded bronze tablet, on the eastern rim of the parade ground near the flagpole. This tablet allegedly marks the northwest corner of the presidio of 1776. Two hundred and fifty yards to the east, at the edge of the parking lot, is another stone marker, anchoring what was believed to be the northeast corner. While it is certain that the original presidio stood in this area, recent archeological excavations indicate that the walls may have extended farther to the north than previously believed. The walls were fourteen feet high and five feet thick, made of adobe and mud-covered twigs and branches.

It hardly needs saying that the vistas and landscapes surrounding the original eighteenth century compound have changed greatly. All the trees and vegetation visible are of a later time; the surrounding eucalyptus and Monterey pine were planted by the army in the 1880s. When the Spanish first arrived, the Presidio, like much of San Francisco, was largely bare of vegetation. There were only sand dunes, with an occasional scrub oak.

Fort Point.
Location: In the Presidio at the end of Marine Drive, underneath the south end of the Golden Gate Bridge. **Phone:** (415) 556-1693. **Hours:** Open Friday - Sunday, 10 a.m. to 5 p.m. Closed Thanksgiving, Christmas, and New Year's Day. Park ranger-led tours are given at regular intervals. **Admission:** Free. **Website:** www.nps.gov/prsf.

Once inside the fort, immediately to your left you will see the finest of the six remaining bronze cannon from the Spanish Castillo. It was cast in Peru in 1684. Beyond it, through the second door to the left, in the powder magazine is a scale model of the Castillo de San Joaquin as it looked about 1795. As the model and the map on the adjoining wall indicate, it was a rather simple, even primitive, fort.

The Mexican – Californio Era

The Petaluma Adobe.
Location: 3325 Adobe Road, Petaluma. **Phone:** (707) 762-4871. **Hours:** Open daily, 10 a.m. to 5 p.m. Closed major holidays. **Admission:** Adults, $2.00; under 17, Free. **Websites:** www.parks.ca.gov or www. petalumaadobe.com.

The Petaluma Adobe was the headquarters of General Mariano Vallejo's Rancho Petaluma, a 66,000-acre (over 100 square miles) land grant he had received from the Mexican authorities in the 1830s as a reward for his military service. (Vallejo had been commandante of the San Francisco Presidio prior to its being abandoned in 1835.)

Set on a low hill with a commanding view of the surrounding valley, the Adobe was constructed over a ten-year period starting in 1836. It was nearly completed in 1846, when it was raided by Captain Frémont and his band during the Bear Flag revolt. They

Marilyn Blaisdell Collection

The Petaluma Adobe, as it looked in the 1930s.

stripped it of its horses, cattle, and various supplies. The rancho and the building went into a progressive decline that continued until the 1950s, when a restoration effort was begun. By that time one half of the original four-sided building had disintegrated.

The remaining portion of the Adobe has been lovingly restored. Most of the rooms have been re-created to show what went on in them and what life on the rancho was like. Although the furnishings are either replicas or period pieces, since none of the originals survived a century of neglect, the atmosphere evoked is authentic. With the roosters crowing and the sheep bleating on the surrounding grounds, if it were not for the traffic whizzing by on Adobe Road you could easily imagine that you had stepped back in time to the 1840s.

Highlights of the Adobe's interior include the ranch foreman's room with its bed, writing table, and a saddle resting on its stand, and the tallow and hide workroom with its candle-dipping machine arrested in mid-motion as if its operator had just stepped out for a moment and would be right back. Also not to be missed is the Vallejo family apartment on the second floor. The dining room in particular gives a vivid picture of the graciousness of upper-class Californio domestic life.

To even better convey the feeling and flavor of ranch life, a local association sponsors a "living history days" at the Adobe two weekends a year, in May and October, in which costumed volunteers demonstrate the crafts and activities that took place on the rancho.

Portsmouth Square and Yerba Buena Cove.

Location: Portsmouth Square, now the heart of Chinatown, is bounded by Clay, Kearny, and Washington streets, and, at its western edge, by Walter U. Lum Place. The cove, which began just east of Montgomery Street, was filled in as the early city expanded, and now lies beneath San Francisco's financial district.

Virtually nothing remains of the hillside community of Yerba Buena-San Francisco that existed before the gold rush. The passage of a century and half has changed the area beyond recognition. Portsmouth Square itself is still there in its original dimensions with the exception of its Kearny Street side, which was shaved slightly when the downtown streets were subsequently widened. The plaza's landscaping and layout has undergone a number of transformations—including the addition of the underground parking garage in 1960—making it a much different place from the simple commons it was in the 1840s.

On nearby Grant Avenue, a half block to the west, a plaque at 823–827 marks the site of first resident William A. Richardson's dwelling. A half block south of Richardson's dwelling, where the intersection of Clay Street and Grant Avenue is today, stood the house of Jacob P. Leese, the second resident of Yerba Buena. Here, in 1836, the transplanted American held the area's first Fourth of July celebration—this despite the fact it was Mexican territory.

A block away, just off Portsmouth Square at 743 Washington Street, the Bank of Canton building marks the site of another early landmark. A small plaque embedded in cement near the door identifies this as the location of Sam Brannan's *California Star,* the first newspaper in San Francisco. It was here, in January 1847, that

Brannan published—begrudgingly, because he preferred Yerba Buena—the declaration officially changing the name of the town to San Francisco.

Walk down Washington Street into Portsmouth Square and cut diagonally across the plaza as if you were heading to the southeast corner. Not far past the granite monument to Robert Louis Stevenson you will find a bronze plaque marking the spot where the U.S. flag was first raised over Yerba Buena, on July 9, 1846.

A final place to take note of in the neighborhood is one block east of the plaza. At the southeast corner of Clay and Montgomery streets, a plaque commemorates the landing of the U.S.S. *Portsmouth*. Captain Montgomery and his men actually came ashore half a block farther east, about where Leidesdorff Alley meets Clay Street. This is where the water line was in 1846. Everything east of this point to the Embarcadero is filled-in land.

The National Maritime Museum.
Location: At the foot of Polk Street adjacent to Aquatic Park, San Francisco. **Phone:** (415) 561-7100. **Hours:** Open daily, 10 a.m. to 5 p.m. **Admission:** Free. **Closed** until 2009 for renovation. **Website:** www.nps.gov/safr.

This appealing museum has a variety of exhibits related to the area's maritime history. Of interest from the pre-gold rush era is a large, hand-crafted scale model of the U.S.S. *Portsmouth,* the ship that carried the sailors and marines who raised the Stars and Stripes over San Francisco. The *Portsmouth* was built in 1843 at the naval shipyard at Portsmouth, New Hampshire. She saw action in California during the Mexican War, and later served off the African coast, capturing ships engaged in the slave trade. During the Civil War the *Portsmouth* did duty as part of Admiral Farragut's fleet. She ended her career on the East Coast as a training ship.

The Oakland Museum – History Gallery.

Location: 1000 Oak Street (two blocks from Lake Merritt), Oakland.
Phone: (510) 238-3842. **Hours:** Wednesday – Saturday, 10 a.m. to 5 p.m.;
(First Friday to 9 p.m.); Sunday, Noon to 5 p.m. Closed holidays. **Admission:** Adults, $8.00; Seniors, Students, $5.00; Children (under 5), Free.
Website: www.museumca.org.

The History Gallery has evocative exhibits on both the Spanish and Mexican eras. Included in the former are various religious objects such as a censer, a missal, a ciborium (a combination plate and chalice), a crucifix, several bibles, priest's vestments, and some altar clothes. On the secular side there is hand-crafted furniture, tools and implements of various kinds, and a huge, wooden olive press.

From the Californio period there is a representation of a household dining-living room. A rough-hewn table rests on top of an animal-hide floor covering. In the background are a wooden chest and a leather saddle. On one wall is a fine oil portrait of Mariano Vallejo.

A final display illustrating this period includes items that Yankee traders brought with them around Cape Horn to exchange with the Californios for hides and tallow—items such as beads, chinaware, a hair comb, and a small guitar.

San Mateo County History Museum.

Location: 2200 Broadway, Redwood City. **Phone:** (650) 299-0104. **Hours:** Tuesday – Sunday, 10 a.m. to 4 p.m. **Admission:** Adults, $4.00; Students, Seniors, Children, $2.00. **Website:** www.sanmateocountyhistory.com.

On display from the days of the Californios is a leather trunk, and a fine saddle made in Chile but used on a San Mateo peninsula rancho in the mid-nineteenth century. Note the hand-wrought silver horn with its intricate design. The bridle is made of silver and silk.

Also on exhibit is an adobe brick in its wooden frame and some hides, and candles made of tallow. The Californios would exchange the latter for finished goods brought by traders—such as fine cloth and silk fans.

4

The Gold Rush (1848–1849)

In 1848 gold was discovered in California, an event of great consequence and one that literally created the city of San Francisco. Gold seekers and fortune hunters came from all over the globe, and the population of San Francisco quickly developed into a polyglot mix of peoples, languages, and cultures.

The early days of the city were ones of turmoil and dramatic change as the infusion of gold sent prices for food, lodging, and real estate skyrocketing. Gambling, prostitution, and other entertainments flourished.

The gold rush was one of the pivotal events in American history. The quest for gold transformed not only San Francisco but the nation as well, giving dramatic credence to the belief that, in America, anyone could strike it rich.

The Discovery

By the 1840s the number of newcomers to California had reached the point where residents were starting to explore beyond the initial coastal settlements. One such pioneer was John Augustus Sutter, a Swiss émigré, who had arrived in California in 1839, on the run from creditors and a bad marriage. With the permission of the Mexican governor he built an adobe fort near the American River in what is now downtown Sacramento, and set up a semi-feudal ranch and estate supported by Indian and immigrant labor.

By 1847, with more immigrants arriving and San Francisco growing, the need for building materials, particularly sawed lumber, was increasing. The trees in the Sacramento area proved unsatisfactory, and it was soon discovered that the straightest trees that made the best lumber were to be found in the Sierra foothills. Sutter, accordingly, sent James Marshall, a carpenter and millwright in his employ, out scouting to find a suitable location for a lumber mill. Marshall located an ideal spot on the South Fork of the American River near an Indian village called Cullomah ("beautiful vale"). There were abundant tall, straight pine trees on the site, and swift-running water to power the mill. Construction started in September, and by January 1, 1848 the mill's foundation was complete, and the tailrace, which carried the diverted water back to the river, was under construction.

On the morning of January 24, 1848, with the other workers busy at their appointed tasks, Marshall, who was inspecting the tailrace, which he felt was not deep enough, saw a small, golden nugget about half the size of a pea lying on the sandy bottom in about one foot of water. Many years later he recalled the moment: "I reached my hand down and picked it up; it made my heart thump, for I was certain it was gold."

Doubt immediately set in, however, for this small nugget was more the color of brass than the reddish-tinged gold he had seen elsewhere. But it compared favorably to a five-dollar gold piece, he found it malleable when pounded, and saw that it did not tarnish when boiled in lye. Now much more convinced, and with the discovery of other golden nuggets and particles, he set off with a small pouch of samples to inform Sutter.

Back at New Helvetia, Sutter's self-styled barony, he and Sutter consulted several books, performed other tests, and concluded that the nuggets were pure gold. Excited, but realizing that the mill would never be completed if word of the discovery spread, they swore each other to secrecy. But Marshall was hardly out the door before Sutter had let the word slip to some of his employees. And back at Coloma (as "Cullomah" later was modified to), Marshall found his millworkers spending their free time searching the nearby riverbanks for more gold.

Small amounts of gold had been found in California before. In 1842, two Californios uncovered some gold nuggets in a canyon north of Los Angeles, a find that led to a minor flurry of activity. And the Indians before that had, on occasion, brought specks of gold with them to the missions. But these small quantities had not been enough to get anyone terribly excited. This strike, however, was different. It was a rich one, with nuggets soon showing up in almost every pan. Marshall's initial find was the match that lit the bonfire.

It took several more months before the rush started in earnest. News of the discovery had been reported in San Francisco newspapers as early as March, but was greeted with skepticism. It was only in May, when a natural-born promoter named Sam Brannan trumpeted the find, that gold fever struck. Brannan, who had been visiting the Coloma area in response to the news, returned to San Francisco with a generous collection of gold samples. Owner of a hardware store, Brannan, in order to whip up enthusiasm for his goods, appeared in Portsmouth Square brandishing a bottle filled with nuggets, shouting: "Gold! Gold! Gold from the American River!" San Francisco emptied. The rush to El Dorado was on.

The News Spreads

By early summer the news had reached southern California and northern Mexico. By late summer word had reached Hawaii on a ship sent to pick up mining supplies. Inasmuch as Honolulu was a Pacific crossroads, it was not long before vessels were bound for San Francisco from China, Australia, and South America. As 1848 came to an end, an estimated eight to ten thousand miners were already at the diggings.

But it was just the beginning. On December 5, President Polk, in a message to Congress, confirmed the rumors that Easterners had been hearing for several months: "The accounts of the abundance of gold in that territory are of such an extraordinary character as would scarcely command belief were they not corroborated by . . . authentic reports . . . ." Polk's words were backed by an ample display of California nuggets forwarded to Washington from the gold fields.

The news electrified the East Coast and soon crossed the Atlantic, where English, French, and other Europeans found themselves preparing to join the rush. Gold fever was so strong that some felt their greatest worry was not the length of the journey facing them or the hardships they might encounter, but how they would make it home loaded down with all that gold.

By early 1849, land and sea expeditions, organized and otherwise, were departing from East Coast and European cities. Some of the forty-niners made the perilous sea journey around Cape Horn, the storm-plagued southern tip of South America. Others tried a shorter route—by sea to Panama or Nicaragua—and then overland through miasmic swamps and jungles to the Pacific shore, hoping to book passage on ships heading north up the coast. Still others made the arduous trek overland through the blistering deserts and snowy mountain passes. Whatever the route, it took an average of six months to make it to California from the East. Upwards of one hundred thousand Argonauts set out for the gold fields in 1849. In that fateful year, nearly eight hundred vessels left New York harbor alone for San Francisco.

Rand Richards collection

At the diggings.

The California gold rush was the greatest peacetime migration in modern history—all of it touched off by the discovery of a piece of gold the size of a pebble.

At the Diggings

Once arrived at San Francisco, most seaborne travelers could not get to the diggings fast enough. (Those who came overland usually went straight to the mines.) Ships' crews deserted and struck out for the gold fields along with their passengers, leaving Yerba Buena cove thick with abandoned vessels.

From what became the town of Downieville, in the north, to Mariposa, in the south, gold was being found throughout the Sierra foothills. And, as prospectors spread across other parts of the state, gold was discovered elsewhere too. In fact, gold was eventually discovered in fifty-four of California's fifty-eight counties. Ironically, San Francisco, whose name has always been closely linked with the gold rush, is one of the four counties where no gold has ever been found. But the heart of the "Mother Lode" (an expression that arose from the miners' mistaken belief that one great vein of ore—the source of all the riches—was waiting to be found) remained that stretch from Downieville to Mariposa. In between these two sprang up towns whose gold rush heritage lives on in their names—Gold Run, Rough and Ready, Fairplay, Placerville.

Once at the diggings, miners set up camp and staked claims along any available section of riverbed. Using shallow bowls or their own frying pans, the forty-niners braved icy streams to wash dirt and gravel, hoping to find, when the water and lighter particles had been sluiced away, the "flash in the pan," the heavier gold at the bottom. When the easy to find gold became scarce, pan washing gave way to cradles and "long toms," which were wooden boxes lined with riffles to catch the gold, and designed to wash more dirt and gravel than pans.

In 1848, particularly during the first few months when the news had not yet spread and prospectors were few, finding gold was easy and nuggets were plentiful. Some claims were so rich they yielded up to five *pounds* of gold a day. (Gold's official price on the East Coast at this time was $18 an ounce, but in California, when vast quantities started surfacing, the price went as low as $8 to $9 an ounce.) Obviously, not all gold seekers were so lucky, but it is estimated that in the first year the typical miner was making ten to fifteen dollars a day. This was at a time when the average wage earner east of the Mississippi was earning little more than a dollar a day.

Gold Rush Days in San Francisco

The gold rush had an immediate and dramatic effect on San Francisco. After the initial virtual abandonment of the city in the spring of 1848 by gold-bug-bitten residents heading for the foothills, San Francisco soon was beset by hordes of newcomers. Winter rains brought miners down from the hills to wait for better conditions and to pick up supplies, while at the same time sailing vessels filled with new arrivals started anchoring in Yerba Buena cove with ever greater frequency. San Francisco's population rose from about one thousand in early 1848 to two thousand in February 1849, and to twenty thousand or more at the end of that landmark year.

With this mushrooming of population, San Francisco found itself virtually under siege by the forty-niners, many of whom were laden with bags of gold dust and nuggets, roaming the town looking for food, shelter, and entertainment.

Most of the miners were either bachelors or had left their families back in the States. Since family life was virtually nonexistent, dining in restaurants became popular. San Francisco today is noted for its restaurants; the wide ethnic variety to be found has its roots in the gold rush era when people from all over the world descended on the city and brought their native dishes with them. But with edible commodities of all types scarce, and with gold abundant, prices were steep. A breakfast of coffee, ham, and eggs could cost six dollars. A loaf of bread which might cost four cents in New York would cost fifty cents or more in San Francisco.

Shelter was also a scarce commodity. With few buildings that were more than leaky tents or haphazard board shacks, desirable sleeping quarters commanded premium prices. A private room could cost as much as one thousand dollars a month. Even raw bunks without mattresses went for fifteen dollars a night, and some enterprising landlords sold sleeping places on benches, tables, and even on board planks stretched across sawhorses. Paying such exorbitant prices did not guarantee a restful night's sleep. Fleas, lice, rats, and other vermin were frequent bedtime companions.

Inflated prices were not just confined to food and lodging. Real estate in particular rocketed to astronomical heights. One piece of property purchased for $23,000 in late 1848 sold for $300,000 a year later. And a choice parcel on Portsmouth Square that went for $6,000 in the spring of 1849, changed hands in the fall for $45,000. Also fronting the square was the El Dorado, a gambling emporium which, in its initial incarnation, was nothing more than a canvas tent fifteen feet by twenty–five feet. It leased for $40,000 a year.

Courtesy, The Bancroft Library
Miners being separated from their gold dust at a game of faro.

Gambling was the premier recreation of early San Francisco. There were no restrictions as to who could operate a parlor, so dozens, and later hundreds, of gambling halls were in full swing. Three sides of Portsmouth Square were at one time virtually nothing but storefronts housing games of chance.

There were two other popular diversions of the day. Drinking, which was pursued almost as an avocation by some, was just as popular as gambling, as the numerous saloons could attest. Even with whiskey costing thirty dollars a quart, demand was great, and large quantities of liquor were consumed. Prostitution, the other popular vice, no doubt would have received equal favor but for the fact that women were scarce in early San Francisco. The first state census, in 1850, revealed that only 8 percent of the population was female.

San Francisco Public Library

Portsmouth Square in 1849.

The Legacy of the Gold Rush

The gold rush profoundly altered the once sleepy backwater that was California. The transformation was sudden and dramatic, and was marked by changes even more sweeping than those that had preceded it. The area's first inhabitants, the Indians, had lived a pastoral, spiritual existence in relative harmony with the land. The Spanish had come to extend their empire and glorify God. For the Californios of the Mexican era (for the landed gentry anyway) the focus had been on living the good life.

But the discovery of gold in 1848 quickly obliterated these previous ways of life. And the change that swept San Francisco affected the rest of the nation as well. America has always seen itself as the land of opportunity, a place where anyone could pick up and move on, and create a new, better life elsewhere. But the distinguishing characteristic of the gold rush was that, for the first time, it held out the promise to ordinary Americans that they could become wealthy virtually overnight. No more working long hours for low pay in a dull, subsistence level job. With lumps of gold just lying on the ground waiting to be pocketed by whoever found them, many a carpenter, farmhand, and dollar-a-day wage earner stayed awake nights dreaming vivid dreams of having mansions, liveried footmen, and twenty-dollar gold pieces without limit to spend. The new belief was that any man, of whatever background, could wake up one morning and find himself equal to the Astors or Vanderbilts. While very few would actually become rich through gold mining, the motivating factor was the belief that it could happen. San Francisco was the focal point, the new frontier, not just physically but psychologically as well.

Sam Brannan (1819–1889)

"The First San Franciscan"

Sam Brannan arrived in Yerba Buena cove on board the ship *Brooklyn* on July 31, 1846. A Mormon elder, and leader of a group of over two hundred men, women, and children, Brannan and his charges were seeking to establish a new colony in virgin territory, far from U.S. soil. Unfortunately for them, the Mormons arrived just weeks after Captain Montgomery and his men had raised the American flag in Portsmouth Square, claiming California for the United States. Brannan, seeing the Stars and Stripes as he landed, reportedly exclaimed in disgust: "There's that damned flag (or rag) again."

Brannan, a natural entrepreneur and promoter, did not take long to adjust to the new reality. Apparently financed by tithes he collected from his fellow Mormons (and which he refused to turn over to emissaries sent from Salt Lake City by Brigham Young), he established San Francisco's first newspaper, the California Star, located just off Portsmouth Square. He also bought property; at one time he owned one-fifth of the city's real estate. He also set up a trading post at Sutter's Fort.

When gold was discovered in 1848, it was promoter Brannan who started the stampede to the Sierra foothills; he returned to San Francisco with some of the first nuggets found, and trumpeted the find to everyone within earshot at Portsmouth Square. With strong demand for shovels and other hardware from his Sacramento store, and with real estate prices increasing sharply, Brannan soon became one of California's wealthiest men. When crime raged in 1851, he spearheaded the formation of the First Committee of Vigilance.

Brannan's magic touch and good fortune did not last. He started drinking heavily, his reach exceeded his grasp, and he made increasingly poor investments. In 1859 he purchased land in the Napa Valley, which he developed as a hot springs resort. Brannan was going to name it Saratoga, after the famous spa in New York State, but at the dedication Brannan was drunk. He stood up and announced, "I'll make this place the Calistoga of Sarafornia." The name Calistoga stuck, but the resort proved to be a financial drain that helped dissipate his fortune.

As the years passed, Brannan took to the bottle even more. His wife divorced him, and in the settlement he gave her his valuable San Francisco holdings, while hanging on to his money-losing resort. One day he surprised trespassers on the grounds; he was shot eight times, but recovered.

Brannan eventually went broke and moved to southern California. He died a pauper near San Diego in 1889 at the age of seventy. Despite his importance in early San Francisco, Sam Brannan's only legacies are a few cabins still left standing in Calistoga from his original resort and a street named for him in San Francisco.

Courtesy, California State Library

Samuel Brannan.

Sites and Attractions

The Gold Rush

Marshall's First Nugget (The "Wimmer" Nugget).
Location: At the Bancroft Library on the campus of the University of California at Berkeley. The Wimmer nugget is on display in the reading room of the library, which is located through the doors to your right as you enter. **Phone:** (510) 642-6481. **Hours:** Monday – Friday, 9 a.m. to 5 p.m., Saturday, 1 p.m. to 5 p.m., (while classes are in session). **Admission:** Free. The Bancroft Library is **closed** for renovation. **Website:** http://bancroft.berkeley.edu.

On view here is what is purported to be the first nugget that James Marshall picked up in the tailrace at Sutter's Mill at Coloma. The nugget acquired its name from Peter Wimmer, one of the workers at the mill, whose wife boiled it in lye after its discovery as part of the test to see if it was really gold.

While there is an accompanying statement from an authority certifying that this is the original nugget, one has to wonder if this truly could be it. Given the excitement the discovery generated, and the fact that it was taken to Sutter's Fort for further tests (along with other nuggets), and then only later permanently left with Mrs. Wimmer, leaves one feeling skeptical.

Marshall himself stated that the nugget he found was half the size of a pea, whereas the Wimmer nugget in its pounded-out form seems to be of a bigger mass. Marshall's biographer suggests that this nugget was found by another member of the sawmill's crew. Whatever the case, it does seem likely that, if not the first, this particular nugget was found in January 1848 and was one of the earliest discovered.

The Old Mint.

Location: Fifth and Mission Streets, San Francisco. The Old Mint is closed but plans to reopen as a museum of San Francisco history at some unspecified date after refurbishing. **Website:** www.sfhistory.org.

San Francisco had a pressing need for coinage in the wake of the gold rush. To accommodate the demand a mint was constructed on Commercial Street in the heart of the financial district in the 1850s. Within a decade however that facility outgrew its cramped location. A new site was selected south of Market Street and between 1869 and 1874 this Greek Revival structure was erected.

Over the next few decades this was the busiest mint in the country, churning out the silver dollars and gold coins needed as a medium of exchange for the growing economy. It also served to store gold bullion, and in fact once held one-third of the nation's gold reserves.

The "Granite Lady," as the Old Mint was known, served as a museum from the 1970s to 1995 and housed a great collection of artifacts from several periods of San Francisco history.

Some of the artifacts from that collection that may return to the new museum are gold mining equipment such as a sluice box, a rocker, and ore carts and buckets. There also will no doubt be a sampling of gold coins from the era. Also probably returning will be a length of timber from Sutter's original mill at Coloma.

Another item of interest was an actual miners cabin. Although it dated from the 1930s when hard times brought a brief resurgence to gold mining, it might as well have dated from 1849, since it captured the mood and spirit of a gold panner's shack. It was a vivid, if slightly romanticized, reconstruction.

The Oakland Museum – History Gallery

Location: 1000 Oak Street (two blocks from Lake Merritt), Oakland. **Phone:** (510) 238-3842. **Hours:** Wednesday – Saturday, 10 a.m. to 5 p.m.; (First Friday to 9 p.m.); Sunday, Noon to 5 p.m. Closed holidays. **Admission:** Adults, $8.00; Seniors, Students, $5.00; Children (under 5), Free. **Website:** www.museumca.org.

On display from the heyday of the gold rush are some original artifacts, including a gold-washing pan, shovels, pickaxes, and a long tom. Nearby rests the desired end result of the miner's labor—a leather pouch spilling gold nuggets.

The forty-niners did not spend all their time digging for gold. Also on view are an opium pipe, period liquor bottles, playing cards, and, in a display case, a Colt revolver. In the corner to your right a tableau features a few more objects, such as a faro table set with liquor bottles, and an aging wooden chair with a Kentucky rifle slung over the back.

The new invention of photography captured early images of the gold rush. On the walls, surrounding this part of the exhibit, are daguerreotypes of forty-niners.

Around the wall in the next section is a complete assay office, which stood for over a century in Nevada City in the Sierra foothills. Assaying increased in importance after the easy-to-find nuggets had been harvested. As gold became harder to find in its pure state, it became necessary to assay the ore to see if it was profitable to mine. Assay offices soon became permanent fixtures of Mother Lode towns. This fine example was built in the early 1850s and saw continuous use until 1910. Behind the glass fronted façade you can see assaying paraphernalia such as brass scales, chemical bottles, and crucibles, as well as ledgers and reference books the assayer would have consulted in his research.

Across the room is a reconstruction of a miner's kitchen from the town of Rough and Ready. It is an evocative setting, consisting of a period table, chairs, and cupboard surrounded by painted pine-plank walls. The cast-iron wood-burning stove in the center would have radiated the warmth this cozy scene exudes.

Wells Fargo History Museum.
Location: 420 Montgomery Street (between California and Sacramento), San Francisco. **Phone:** (415) 396-2619. **Hours:** Monday – Friday, 9 a.m. to 5 p.m. Closed bank holidays and weekends. **Admission:** Free. **Website:** www.wellsfargohistory.com.

Illustrative of the gold rush era are samples of gold from all the major Mother Lode rivers. What is interesting is how varied they are in shape, texture, and especially color. Darker gold could indicate the presence of copper, while a paler gold might contain silver.

These samples makes you realize that, for the miners, identifying the gold was sometimes as difficult as finding it.

The Bank of California Museum.
Location: In the basement of the main branch of Union Bank of California, 400 California Street (between Sansome and Montgomery), San Francisco. There is no phone or website for the museum. **Hours:** Monday – Friday, 9 a.m. to 4:30 p.m. Closed bank holidays and weekends. **Admission:** Free.

On display here are dozens of gold nuggets of all shapes and sizes. Nuggets such as these are fairly rare, since most of the ones found in the early days of the rush were melted down to make coins, ingots, or gold bars. Some of the nuggets are in their original state, that is, the gold still clings to the quartz rock in which it was found. Other nuggets show their "pure" state, that is after extraneous matter has been removed.

A Walking Tour of Gold Rush San Francisco.
Location: Downtown San Francisco from First and Market streets north to Broadway and Battery, ending at Clay and Sansome streets. (See map on page 73.)

You only have to look at the skyscrapers standing shoulder-to-shoulder in San Francisco's financial district, the area that once was Yerba Buena cove, to know that nothing visible remains from the fateful year of 1849. But if you are downtown to see the Wells Fargo History Museum and the Bank of California Museum, a stroll through the area—and a little imagination—will give you some idea of what San Francisco was like in its infancy.

With the discovery of gold, Yerba Buena Cove quickly became the center of activity, as ship after ship arrived in response to the news. While the cove itself was ideal for an anchorage, protected as it was from the swift bay currents, the land immediately surrounding the cove was not. Within just a block or two of the shoreline the land sloped sharply upward, leading to the precipice of 376-foot-high Nob Hill, only five blocks away from the water.

Nob Hill (at one time spelled Knob Hill—the K was later dropped) was too steep and too solid to be leveled, as other, smaller hills near the cove were, so the only viable option was to expand eastward into the cove itself. This was initially done by building wharves extending into the bay, and then later by filling in the spaces between them with soil and sand from nearby dunes and with anything else that was handy, usually spoiled merchandise or other trash.

At one time all of the east-west streets east of Montgomery between California and Broadway were wharves. Commercial Street, for example, an alley half a block south of Clay Street, was once called Long Wharf, and eventually extended 2,000 feet into the bay—to about where the Embarcadero is today. Connecting planks were laid to facilitate movement between the wharves. As the bay was filled in, these planks became part of Jasper O'Farrell's grid pattern of streets. Battery, Front, and Davis streets were once plank thoroughfares connecting the wharves.

A good way to get a sense of the early city and to see just how much of downtown San Francisco rests on landfill is to walk along the original shoreline. The place to start a walking tour is the southwest corner of Market and First streets, where a plaque embedded in the sidewalk notes that at the time of the gold discovery at Coloma in 1848, the shoreline was twenty-five feet to the northeast, or about in the middle of the intersection.

Cross over Market Street to Battery, where anchored in the sidewalk near the Donahue mechanics monument you will find another plaque marking the shoreline. At the corner of Bush and Battery, just to the north, go west one block on Bush to Sansome. (The original shoreline angled to the northwest under the Shell Building—part way through the block—but obviously it is impossible to follow the outline of the old cove exactly, due to the grid pattern of streets and buildings). Turn right on Sansome to Pine, left on Pine half a block to Leidesdorff, turn right through the alley to California Street, then left to Montgomery.

At the intersection of California and Montgomery streets, the heart of the financial district, go four blocks north to Jackson Street. This stretch of Montgomery Street was the young city's main commercial street at the time, but was still little more than a dirt thoroughfare. The winter of 1849–1850 was an especially rainy one;

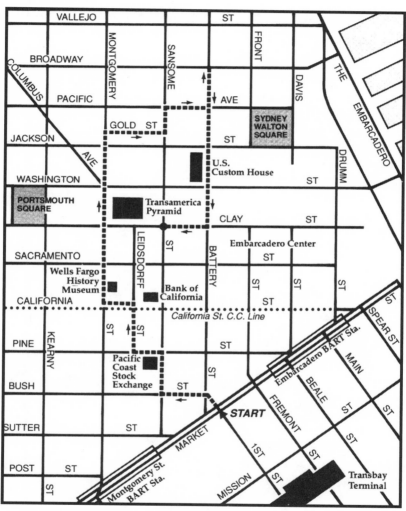

Map by Larry Van Dyke

Gold Rush Walking Tour.

it turned Montgomery Street into a sea of liquid mud so deep that William T. Sherman, later of Civil War fame, who was living nearby, claimed to have seen several mules stumble and drown in it. As you cross Sacramento, Commercial, Clay, and Washington, look east down these streets and try to visualize them as the wharves they once were, with ships at anchor next to them.

At Jackson and Montgomery streets you will have reached the approximate westernmost edge of Yerba Buena cove. This intersection was once a small lagoon that fed into the cove. Continue north on Montgomery and make a right into the little alley, Gold Street.

Go to the end of Gold Street (you will pass another little alley called Balance, named for a gold rush ship buried nearby) and turn left on Sansome Street. On Pacific Avenue, half a block up, take a right to Battery and go left one block to the intersection of Broadway. This marks the northern end of the financial district portion of the original shoreline.

Walk south on Battery Street four full blocks to the intersection of Clay Street. Entombed beneath your feet here and for several blocks around on all sides lie the remains of several gold-rush ships that were abandoned by their crews in their haste to get to the gold fields. Two of the more notable ships were the *Euphemia*,

Courtesy, California State Library.

The *Niantic*—high and dry.

which was used by the city government as a floating prison after it was abandoned, and the *Niantic,* which served as a hotel and was also partitioned into offices and a storehouse. The *Euphemia* lies a block to the south near the intersection of Battery and Sacramento. To finish your tour, walk one block to the west, where a plaque on the northwest corner of Clay and Sansome marks the *Niantic's* final resting place. In 1978, during the construction of the present office building on the site, the *Niantic's* remains were rediscovered. Among the artifacts retrieved were bolts of cloth, metallic pieces of firearms, and almost twelve dozen bottles of French champagne.

The National Maritime Museum.

Location: At the foot of Polk Street adjacent to Aquatic Park, San Francisco. **Phone:** (415) 561-7100. **Hours:** Open daily, 10 a.m. to 5 p.m. **Admission:** Free. **Closed** until 2009 for renovation. **Website:** www.nps.gov/safr.

Part of the ship *Niantic* was saved and ended up here. On display in the main lobby is a bottom portion of the stern including part of the rudder. Both pieces have much of their original copper sheathing still nailed in place.

Just steps away is an evocative diorama of the *Niantic* after she had had her sails removed, a roof put on, and she had been converted into a storeship at Clay and Sansome streets at what was then the shore of the bay.

Other exhibits of interest include a map of the sea routes to the gold fields, and a model of the Clipper Ship *Flying Cloud.* Among the enlarged photos on the surrounding walls is the earliest known photo of San Francisco showing Yerba Buena cove thick with a forest of ships' masts.

Visitor Center, Haslett Warehouse.

Location: 499 Jefferson Street, corner of Hyde. **Phone:** (415) 447-5000. **Hours:** 9:30 a.m. to 5 p.m., with extended summer hours. **Admission:** Free. **Website:** www.nps.gov/safr.

The Visitor Center in the old Haslett Warehouse, across from the Hyde Street Pier, has some smaller artifacts from the *Niantic,* found during the 1978 excavation. Among the items are a hatchet head, a percussion pistol fragment, a duck's head letter holder, and a French champagne bottle. Next to these is a piece of the copper-sheathed stern of the gold-rush ship *Apollo.*

Gold Discovery Site – Coloma.

Location: The Marshall Gold Discovery State Historic Park, as it is officially known, is located northeast of Sacramento in Coloma on Highway 49 between Auburn and Placerville. **Phone:** (530) 622-3470. **Hours:** The visitor center and the park's other buildings are open daily, 10:00 a.m. to 4:30 p.m. The park itself is open from 8 a.m. to sunset. Closed Thanksgiving, Christmas, and New Year's Day. **Admission:** $5.00 per vehicle. **Website:** www.parks.ca.gov.

For a general orientation, stop first at the visitor center where there is a museum with a number of exhibits, including some on Marshall and Sutter, the gold discovery, and what a miner's life was like. On display are various tools of the period, including Marshall's rifle and some artifacts from the original mill.

Across the road, next to the picturesque American River, is a replica of the famous sawmill, completed in 1967. The original—that portion of it that had not been cannibalized by wood-hungry miners in the 1850s—was washed away by a flood in 1862. Some of the foundation timbers resurfaced in 1924, leading to renewed interest in the gold discovery site. The timbers are on view in a display case next to the sawmill.

Just downstream a few yards you can visit the spot at the riverbank where Marshall made his historic discovery. Nearby is a reconstruction of Marshall's cabin, and his monument and grave-site marker. A pamphlet at the visitor center has a map showing how to get there.

Rand Richards

Sutter's Mill today.

5

Growing Pains (1850–1859)

The decade following 1849 was a tumultuous one for San Francisco. Six major fires swept the city in the first two years after the gold rush; at least some of them the result of arson. Other kinds of crimes were rampant as well, and civic leaders twice took law enforcement into their own hands, forming vigilante groups to punish wrongdoers.

Gold production declined, which led to San Francisco's first business depression, in 1855. The City weathered the storm, however, and the economic base broadened as agriculture, construction, and banking grew in importance. Newly-made fortunes created an elite group that clustered on Rincon Hill, San Francisco's first upper-class residential neighborhood.

As the decade came to a close, political and social strife still prevailed. In 1859, San Francisco resident and U.S. Senator David Broderick was killed in a duel. Disputes between Californios and the American newcomers over who owned title to rancho lands dragged through the courts. Some were not settled for decades, but in the main the Californios were the losers, thus writing a final chapter to several centuries of Spanish and Mexican control of the region.

The Lawless Early Days

Life in early San Francisco was exciting, unpredictable, and dangerous. Like many a frontier town founded on a mining boom, it not only had few of the settling influences of civilization but it also suffered various natural catastrophes and endured periods of lawlessness.

The city was extremely vulnerable to fire. Most structures were of wood or cloth, were built flush to each other, and were illuminated by whale-oil lamps. Once a fire started it became hard to contain due to the lack of an adequate water supply and the often present winds, which easily spread the flames from building to building. Not surprisingly, the city suffered a number of major fires in its first few years, each one causing extensive damage, with several wiping out much of the downtown area.

Most of these fires were probably started by accident. Nevertheless, a gang of hooligans known as the Sydney Ducks, a band of Australian ex-convicts who had descended on the city following the news of the gold rush, took full advantage of the situation. They and their confederates looted shops and warehouses while everyone else was busy fighting the fire. Their base of operations was a strip of the waterfront between Pacific Avenue and Broadway, known as Sydney Town.

Rand Richards collection
The fire of May 3–4, 1851, destroyed much of downtown San Francisco.

The Vigilance Committees

In May 1851, after the fifth major fire in less than two years had devastated the city, San Francisco's merchants and property owners—those who had lost the most from thievery and the ruinous fires—had had enough. With the local courts and the fledgling police force seemingly unable to control crime, Sam Brannan and some other leading citizens banded together and formed what later was known as the First Committee of Vigilance. Their aim was to rid the town of its criminal element. They largely succeeded. The Committee was active for only a few months, but during that time four Sydney Towners were hanged for crimes ranging from burglary to murder. The message having gotten across, many other undesirables either fled or laid low, and relative calm was restored.

Crime receded in the public consciousness over the next few years, but in May 1856 a Second Committee of Vigilance quickly assembled in response to a new threat to public order. The spark that led to its formation was the assassination of James King of William—he added the William to distinguish himself from a James King in another county in his native Maryland—a crusading newspaper editor shot down by a corrupt politician who had been exposed by King's paper. The Committee members, worried that the assassin, James Casey, might escape or be released from the city jail, decided to take matters into their own hands. They massed a large force of supporters and forced the jailers to hand over Casey and another prisoner—Charles Cora, who had killed a U.S. marshal. The two prisoners were "tried," found guilty, and hanged from rafters suspended from Fort Gunnybags, the Committee's Sacramento Street headquarters. After hanging two more murderers and deporting scores of undesirables, the Second Committee of Vigilance disbanded in August 1856, having intimidated the town's criminal element once again.

San Francisco's New "Fireproof" Buildings

One of the tangible results of the fires, looting, and thievery of the early years was the construction of new buildings designed to protect property from any such future occurrences. Downtown San Francisco in the 1850s saw the construction of a multitude of two- to three-story buildings of brick or stone, with iron shutters over doors and windows. A number of these structures had been built before the last major fire, in 1851, and although the walls held, some storekeepers lost their inventories to the intense radiant heat. Still, the solid construction was a vast improvement over the old haphazard canvas and wood construction of the infant city.

A Diversified Economy

The gold rush and the infusion of capital the gold brought to California caused a ripple effect that led to the birth and rapid growth of many industries designed to service the miners and their needs. Not only did the demand for beef lead to a burgeoning cattle industry, but in response to the demand for fresh fruits and vegetables, agriculture boomed as grapes, wheat, barley, and other crops were planted. Lumber too was in great demand, since it was needed as timbering in the mines, for flumes to carry water, and for many other utilitarian uses—not to mention the need for construction in San Francisco.

Freight, steamship, and stagecoach lines sprang up. Wells Fargo, a name long associated with the history of the West, began operation in San Francisco in 1852 and grew into a large express and banking concern.

Banking, in fact, was one of The City's leading commercial activities in the 1850s. It was given impetus by two factors. The first was that in order to facilitate the rapid growth, a medium of exchange more manageable than gold nuggets and dust was needed. The obvious solution was to mint coins. Since this was prior to the time when the central government had the sole power to coin money, a number of private banks sprang up, each churning out gold coins, most of them containing less gold than the face amount.

The second great need for banking services grew out of the changing situation in the Mother Lode. By the early 1850s most of the richest placer deposits, consisting of the relatively easy to find surface gold, had been located and exhausted. There was still plenty of gold left, but it was deeper underground, and new methods would have to be developed to get at it. Deep tunneling, quartz mining that required stamp mills to crush the gold-bearing rock, and high-pressure hydraulic cannons that washed away whole hillsides were the new techniques. All required capital investment, and the banks, flush with gold on deposit, were more than willing to provide the financing.

The City's Elite

The infusion of so much money and so much prosperity, by no means evenly distributed, led to the rise of the city's first elite. As would be expected, they were primarily merchants, bankers, and industrialists. Surprisingly few were miners. While gold strikes brought moderate prosperity to scores of miners, there was no one big bonanza such as would soon occur at the Comstock Lode.

As with all such groups they tended to congregate near one another in prime locations and to visibly display their wealth. San Francisco's first elite were no exception. In the early 1850s they started to settle in the Rincon Hill area south of Market Street. Rincon Hill was well situated in that it was close to downtown, the rise effectively separated it from the working class down below, and the climate was good since it was protected from the wind. It remained the residential area of choice until Nob Hill superseded it in the 1870s.

Protecting San Francisco from Attack

Construction of Fort Point, San Francisco's largest surviving brick building, also began in the early 1850s. It replaced the Spanish fort on the site, the Castillo de San Joaquin. (The Castillo and the one-hundred-foot-high bluff on which it stood were leveled to make way for Fort Point.)

The idea for a stronghold guarding the Golden Gate can be traced back to the War of 1812. After the British attacked Washington and sacked the White House and the Capitol, the federal government took steps to strengthen coastal defenses. Over the decades, forts and gun emplacements sprang up along the East Coast and, as the West Coast became U.S. territory, the coastal defense plan was extended to the Pacific. Three forts were planned: one for San Diego, one at the mouth of the Columbia River in Washington State, and one at the entrance to San Francisco Bay. The latter was the only one completed; the Fort at Fort Point (later shortened to just Fort Point) was also the last of thirty coastal forts built. It is the only casemated brick and masonry fort on the West Coast.

In 1850 President Millard Fillmore reserved for military use all of the strategic points guarding the bay: the Presidio (which includes the bluff where Fort Point was built), Angel Island, Alcatraz, Mare Island, Benicia, and Point San Jose (now Fort Mason). Construction on Fort Point started in 1853, when Congress approved an initial $500,000 appropriation. The fort was completed in 1861, just as the Civil War was starting. Except for verbal skirmishes between Union supporters and southern sympathizers, the Civil War had no affect on San Francisco, and the garrison at Fort Point never fired a shot in anger.

Rand Richards collection
Fort Point, in 1904, from outside the Golden Gate.

Hard Times

When construction of Fort Point was just getting underway, downtown San Francisco's building program ground to a halt as the city found itself in the grip of its first depression. By the spring of 1854, after five years of rapid growth brought on by the gold rush, business started to contract. The richest placers had been exhausted—1852 was the peak year of gold production in California—and the remaining gold was deeper and more expensive to mine. The city's merchants soon found themselves in a classic squeeze: more goods and supplies were arriving at a time when the amount of money in circulation was starting to decline. With inventories accumulating and sales declining, many shopowners were forced into bankruptcy.

The City's banks were affected too. Many were already overextended in loans to mining ventures that were contracting or proving unprofitable. Coupled with retail businesses going under, a number of financial institutions, including two of the largest, also collapsed. In the midst of all this, one of the city's councilmen, a wharf owner named Henry ("Honest Harry") Meiggs, looted the city treasury of several hundred thousand dollars—nearly all of its gold reserves—and fled to South America.

The Broderick - Terry Duel

But boom times typically follow bust, and by the late 1850s San Francisco, center of an increasingly broad-based economy, had started to recover. The political climate, however, had become quarrelsome and contentious. Two of the principal antagonists were David C. Broderick and David S. Terry. Broderick, a U.S. Senator from California, was San Francisco's leading politician. Terry, a hot-tempered Southerner, had been Chief Justice of the California Supreme Court until he resigned the day before the duel. The two men, once political allies, had a bitter falling out. Terry seized on an alleged slander and challenged Broderick to a duel.

On the morning of September 13, 1859 the two men faced off in a ravine near Lake Merced, straddling the San Francisco-San Mateo County line. Upon the command to fire, Broderick raised his pistol only to have it discharge prematurely, sending the ball into the dirt in front of him. Terry took dead aim, mortally wounding Broderick who was taken by wagon twelve miles across town to the Leonidas Haskell house at Fort Mason, where he died three days later. Broderick was a corrupt politician, but his death made him a martyr, and Terry wisely and hurriedly left San Francisco. The outcry over Broderick's death was so great that it brought an end to public dueling in California.

The End of the Ranchos

The 1850s also saw the start of the swift decline of the Californios and their ranchos. The beginning of the end came with the initial gold discoveries of 1848. Ranch hands and vaqueros were just as susceptible as others to gold fever, and they deserted for the mines along with everyone else. The second major blow came with the hordes of forty-niners, many of whom soon became squatters on rancho land. Squatting was illegal: the Treaty of Guadalupe Hidalgo, which ended the Mexican War, had declared that Mexican property rights would be respected. But with large numbers of gold seekers fanning out everywhere it was virtually impossible for the Californios to defend their vast, lightly tenanted, and unfenced ranchos.

Their only recourse was legal action. A U.S. Land Commission was established in 1851 to deal with the problem, and many Mexican landowners pressed their claims through the commission. The litigation, in most cases, was protracted. Some of the disputes were not settled for decades. In the end, the majority of the rancheros lost title to their lands. Even the winners sometimes ended up losers. Point Reyes, for example, was originally part of two ranchos. The Mexican owners won their case and established their title, but it was so costly to litigate that, when the case ended, they were forced to turn their deeds over to their American attorneys to pay their legal bills.

Shades of Things to Come

As the decade ended San Francisco had grown in ten short years from a canvas and wood encampment nestled on a quaint cove to a solidly built city with a bustling port and over fifty thousand inhabitants. With gold production steadily declining, many residents might have predicted that San Francisco would settle comfortably into a role as a modest outpost on the western edge of the United States. But The City was about to be transformed to almost as great a degree as it had ten years earlier when the gold rush started. The transforming agent would, once again, be metallic, but this time silver rather than gold.

William T. Sherman (1820–1891)

"Gold Rush Banker"

William Tecumseh Sherman was born in Ohio in 1820. His father died when he was nine, and he was adopted by a U.S. Senator who, in due course, got him appointed to West Point, where he graduated sixth in his class. Sherman suffered from asthma his whole life, but it did not preclude a military career and the young lieutenant soon found himself in California, at that time a lonely outpost in the war with Mexico.

He was present at the creation, so to speak, for he arrived at Monterey in January 1847 to become adjutant to the military

Courtesy, The Bancroft Library
William T. Sherman.

governor, Richard B. Mason. He visited the fledgling town of San Francisco that year and described it as a "horrid place." The wind blew incessantly, piling up huge drifts of sand near the few rude buildings nestled around Yerba Buena cove. Given the opportunity to buy fifty-vara lots for sixteen dollars apiece at the first municipal auction of land, in 1847, he turned it down. San Francisco had no future that he could see.

Early in 1848 Sherman was present in Colonel Mason's office in Monterey when Sutter and Marshall's first samples of gold from Coloma arrived. The two officers tested the nuggets and, convinced of their authenticity, rode on horseback to Coloma where they found the Sutter's Mill crew busy at work panning for gold. Sherman later helped draft the official announcement of the find, which was sent to President Polk in Washington. Polk used it in his report to Congress in December 1848—a report that started the stampede to the gold fields the following year.

After making a profit on a half-interest in a store he had purchased in Coloma (Army officers only made seventy dollars a month and were allowed to supplement their incomes with private ventures), Sherman stayed in California until January 1850, when he was sent east with military dispatches.

He resigned his army commission in 1853 and returned to San Francisco with his wife and young family, and started his career as a banker, opening a branch of Lucas, Turner & Company, a St. Louis-based bank owned by his father-in-law's brother. Initially business was robust and profitable, but by early 1855 the economy was souring, rumors about the stability of various financial institutions had become rife, and in February panicky depositors descended on all of San Francisco's banks and demanded their money. In the run on his bank the steely-eyed Sherman showed courage, determination, and coolness under fire—the same qualities that would serve him well as a Civil War general. While Page, Bacon & Company, San Francisco's largest bank, and several others failed during the run, Sherman's bank weathered the crisis (thanks to his prudence it was better capitalized than most) and stayed in business.

The following year Sherman briefly became involved in the activities surrounding the Second Committee of Vigilance. He disliked the threat of mob rule posed by the Committee, and when asked to lead a U.S.-backed militia effort to stop it, he agreed. But he became caught in political double-dealing, and backed out. It left him with a mistrust of politics that lasted the rest of his life.

In 1857, with his asthma getting worse and with the city's commercial hub having moved away from the bank's Jackson-Montgomery location toward Market Street, it was decided to close the branch. Sherman left San Francisco for New York to manage a Lucas, Turner branch there.

With the outbreak of the Civil War, in 1861, Sherman returned to military service where he won enduring fame for his march through Georgia in 1864. The once junior military officer and relatively obscure banker returned in triumph to San Francisco in 1876, where he was feted as a war hero and lionized as a native son.

Sites and Attractions

City Strife

San Francisco Fire Department Museum.
Location: 655 Presidio Avenue (between Bush and Pine), San Francisco.
Phone: (415) 563-4630. **Hours:** Thursday – Sunday, 1 p.m. to 4 p.m.
Closed the rest of the week and all holidays. **Admission:** Free. **Website:**
www.sffiremuseum.org.

San Francisco has been destroyed so many times by fire it seems only fitting that The City should have a museum devoted solely to its fire department. Located next to an active firehouse and staffed by volunteers, the museum is packed with artifacts from all periods of San Francisco's fire-fighting history, including a particularly strong collection of objects from the very early days.

The premier item is The City's first fire engine, an 1810 hand pumper that was brought around Cape Horn from New York to San Francisco. It was on the waterfront, waiting to be shipped to the Mother Lode to pump water from flooded mine shafts, when San Francisco's first major fire broke out on December 24, 1849. It was used in that conflagration, and stayed in The City and saw service until 1866, when it was retired in favor of new steam-driven equipment. Trimmed with a leather fringe and painted in its original blue and yellow colors, it has been lovingly restored to mint condition.

Other artifacts on display include riveted buffalo-hide water buckets (it was a city fire prevention law in the 1850s that every dwelling had to have at least six of these, filled with water, on the premises), fused window glass from an 1851 fire, and a couple of oil lamps of the period. It is easy to see, when looking at the latter, how readily fires could be started by one of these fragile and easily upset lamps.

Scattered about the floor of the museum are fire hydrants from the nineteenth and twentieth centuries. The oldest one, painted silver, dates from 1863. What is noteworthy is how little change there has been in the basic design over the years. Many inventions have gone the way of the dodo bird, or have changed beyond recognition during the past century, but the lowly fireplug is not one of them.

Jackson Square and Sherman's Bank.
Location: Downtown San Francisco. The area of prime interest is Montgomery Street between Washington and Jackson, and Jackson Street from Montgomery to Sansome.

The 1906 earthquake and fire, which wiped out virtually all of the downtown, spared a small area, principally the two blocks between Washington and Pacific and bounded by Montgomery and Sansome. This charming area today is known as Jackson Square, and contains San Francisco's oldest surviving commercial buildings. These structures are typical of the two- and three-story brick buildings put up after the disastrous fires of 1849 to 1851. In the 1850s many of these brick façades were covered with stucco scored to look like stone to make them more impressive. Despite the removal of the stucco, a walk down these streets provides a glimpse of what the city was like in its earliest days.

The Belli Building at 722 Montgomery Street typifies the period. Only the brick façade of this circa 1853 structure remains. The building originally housed a tobacco warehouse, but it was soon converted to a theater. Singer and actress Lotta Crabtree is known to have performed here. In subsequent decades the building served as medical offices, a garment factory, and a paper warehouse. From the late 1950s until 1989 when it suffered some structural damage in the Loma Prieta earthquake it housed the law offices of the flamboyant attorney the late Melvin Belli.

Next door, at 728 Montgomery, also with just its façade remaining, is the Genella Building. It was erected in 1851 or early 1852. Author Bret Harte once lived in the residence above the ground floor warehouse, and wrote his most famous story, "The Luck of Roaring Camp," while there. This building weathered 1906, but during the

1989 quake a chunk of bricks from the upper story peeled off and crashed onto the sidewalk. Right next door at 730 is the Golden Era Building, built about 1852. The Golden Era was a weekly newspaper that published stories by Mark Twain and Bret Harte early in their careers.

A few steps north, on the northeast corner of Montgomery and Jackson streets, is what was the Bank of Lucas, Turner & Company, colloquially known as Sherman's Bank. William Tecumseh ("War is hell") Sherman, prior to his later fame as a Civil War general, managed the San Francisco branch of a St. Louis bank at this location.

Sherman, at the behest of his employers, purchased the lot in 1853 for $32,000, and then spent $50,000 during the following year building this structure. It opened for business in July 1854. He had high hopes for its success, having selected the site with the belief that the heart of the city's business district would stay at the foot of Broadway. Trade shifted toward Market Street, however, and in 1857 Sherman closed the bank and moved to New York.

Rand Richards

Sherman's Bank today.

Sherman's bank today looks somewhat different from its 1850's appearance, the major change being that the building no longer has a third story. It was removed after the 1906 quake as a safety measure. Another change is that half of the windows on the Jackson Street side have been bricked up. The stucco or whatever other facing once covered this side has also been removed. The decorative granite on the Montgomery Street side is the original, but it is not from California; it might have come from China.

Stroll east down Jackson Street toward Sansome and you will see other representative buildings on both sides of the street. The plainer red brick buildings on the north side mostly date from the 1850s, while the more ornate ones on the south side are primarily from the 1860s. A notable exception to the latter is 415 Jackson, which dates from 1853. From 1855 until 1894 it served as the Ghirardelli chocolate factory headquarters. Next to Sherman's Bank, at 472 Jackson, is a fine example of the rather plain brick-fronted commercial buildings that went up in many northern California towns during the 1850s. This one dates from between 1850 and 1852, and once housed the French consulate.

The stylish, classical three-story building at 451 Jackson was originally a liquor warehouse. Known as Hotaling's, it was erected in 1866.

Also downtown, a few blocks to the southeast, on Sacramento Street across from Embarcadero Two, is the site of the Second Vigilance Committee's headquarters, "Fort Gunnybags." This is where the assassin James Casey and his unlucky cell mate, Charles Cora, were hanged in 1856. A bronze plaque bearing the committee's trademark—an all-seeing eye—marks the spot. Casey and Cora are buried in Mission Dolores cemetery.

Wells Fargo History Museum.
Location: 420 Montgomery Street (between California and Sacramento), San Francisco. **Phone:** (415) 396-2619. **Hours:** Monday – Friday, 9 a.m. to 5 p.m. Closed bank holidays and weekends. **Admission:** Free. **Website:** www.wellsfargohistory.com.

Several exhibits related to San Francisco's early days are spread over the museum's two floors. The ground floor has a large array of gold on display.

Upstairs is a life–size wooden mockup of a stagecoach. Sit inside, and while the coach rocks back and forth on its creaking leather springs a recording gives a narration of an actual stagecoach journey taken by a young man in 1859 from St. Louis to San Francisco. It provides a graphic re-creation of just how uncomfortable such a trip must have been.

Around the corner is an extensive collection of mail that was delivered to early San Franciscans. No zip codes or even street addresses were needed in those days. A letter addressed to "Messrs. Fretz & Ralston, Bankers, S.F." was delivered just fine. The postmarks on some of these letters are from mining towns that no longer exist. In a glass case across from these is a medallion worn by one of the members of the 1856 Committee of Vigilance.

Located in the very back, across from the elevator, is a detailed, five-panel color panorama of San Francisco in 1863. It is a virtual snapshot of the city at that time. The view is from Russian Hill—about where 999 Green Street is today—and provides an almost 360-degree sweep of the growing metropolis. The streets and more than one hundred buildings—several of which still stand today—are numbered and identified.

The Bank of California Museum.

Location: In the basement of the main branch of the Bank of California, 400 California Street (between Sansome and Montgomery), San Francisco. There is no phone or website for the museum. **Hours:** Monday – Friday, 9 a.m. to 4:30 p.m. Closed bank holidays and weekends. **Admission:** Free.

Against the west wall, in a glass case, are the beautifully detailed and formidable looking Belgian-made dueling pistols once believed to have been used in the Broderick-Terry duel. The pistols used were known as the "Aylette pistols," because they were lent to Terry by a neighbor, a Dr. Daniel Aylette. Terry practiced with them for two months prior to the duel, and allegedly found that one—the one used by Broderick—had an exceptionally sensitive trigger. This discovery, and the fact that Terry had aimed his weapon with the intent to kill, after Broderick's gun discharged prematurely, led to cries for Terry's scalp, but no murder charges were filed.

Recent research indicates that the "Aylette pistols" are in the possession of a private collector. It is possible, however, that the pistols on display belonged to Broderick and were present on the day of the duel, and were not used, since Terry had won the toss as to the choice of weapons.

Exhibited in the glass cases in the center of the room are some gold coins that circulated in San Francisco during the first few years after the gold rush. It may seem odd, but prior to 1864, when the federal government decreed that henceforth only the coins it minted would be legal tender, states and territories were prohibited from coining money, but private citizens were not. This led to the birth of private banks. On display are samples of both government and private-issue coins. Most of the latter are quite rare, because when it was discovered that they contained less gold than the face amount—and virtually all of them did—they were melted down.

The Broderick – Terry Duel Site.

Location: 1100 Lake Merced Boulevard, San Francisco (in the southwest corner of the city near the San Mateo County line). **Directions:** From Lake Merced Boulevard look for the brown historical signs and turn in at the sign, "Lake Merced Hill, Private Club," with the above address beneath it. Park by the tennis courts and walk to the end of the lot where the state historical marker is. **Admission:** Free.

To reach the site of the duel, walk through the opening in the fence at the historical marker and continue down the paved path. Go past the small granite plinth that says "Duel Site." Approximately two hundred yards farther on, under a canopy of trees, are two small stone markers showing where Broderick and Terry each stood on the morning of September 13, 1859.

The pair had originally faced off the previous morning, September 12, but because of publicity about the event the San Francisco Chief of Police was on the scene and arrested the two men, since dueling was prohibited by state law. The antagonists were released by a judge later that day, and quietly agreed to meet the following morning at the same place. Shortly before seven o'clock Terry fired a bullet into his opponent's chest, mortally wounding him. Senator Broderick was thirty-nine years old.

It is hard to know what the surroundings were like in 1859, but the eucalyptus and Monterey Pine covering the site today are obviously recent. The area probably was bare of vegetation, since this part of the city is not far from the ocean, and was, at that time, mostly rolling sand dunes.

Protecting San Francisco From Attack

> **Fort Point.**
> **Location:** In the Presidio at the end of Marine Drive, beneath the south end of the Golden Gate Bridge. **Phone:** (415) 556-1693. **Hours:** Open Friday - Sunday, 10 a.m. to 5 p.m. Closed Thanksgiving, Christmas, and New Year's Day. Park ranger-led tours are given at regular intervals. **Admission:** Free. **Website:** www.nps.gov/fopo.

This massive brick and granite fort, which somewhat resembles Fort Sumter in South Carolina, is one of the best examples in the United States of a nineteenth-century coastal fortification. It looks much the same today as it did when it was completed in 1861, the only major change being that its guns have been removed—around the turn of the century—from their positions overlooking the gate and the bay.

The fort was just becoming operational as the Civil War began, and naturally its first task was to guard against any possible Confederate attack. With the war being fought two to three thousand miles away, such an attack would, on the face of it, seem to be absurd. Surprisingly, however, a Confederate raider did sail up the northern California coast. But the war had ended shortly before it arrived at the Golden Gate, and thus Fort Point was cheated of its chance to defend San Francisco.

Except for the garrison's occasional foray outside the Bay Area to quell Indian uprisings, the fort played no active role during its military life. As a defensive barricade it was obsolete shortly after it was completed. By 1862, more accurate and more deadly rifled cannon, whose pointed projectiles could easily penetrate brick walls, had been developed. Fort Point, despite its up to twelve-foot-thick walls, would quickly have been reduced to rubble by such artillery. By the late 1880s its guns were outmoded too, its muzzle-loading cannon having been superseded by larger, more powerful seacoast rifles, which could hurl a projectile up to twenty-five miles.

Inside the fort there are exhibits on the first three of the four levels. Almost all the rooms and casemates—where the guns are placed—are open to visitors. Cheerful park rangers, and volunteers dressed in Civil-War-era uniforms, give tours and are available to answer questions.

Across the courtyard on the casemate side of the ground floor are a caisson and various guns and mortars of the period. On the barracks side, ground floor, is the sutler's store (now the gift shop), and the powder magazine. The former barracks has exhibits on a typical soldier's life, along with representative artifacts, photographs, and a display of armaments featuring cannon balls and projectiles.

The second floor is where the fort's hospital, kitchen, and officers' quarters were. All three have been partially re-created using period utensils and pieces of furniture and some replicas. Fort Point is invariably windy, even in these relatively protected rooms, and you cannot help feeling how cold and drafty they must have been, since the only heat they had came from small coal-burning fireplaces.

If the officers' quarters were less than deluxe, one can only imagine what life was like for the enlisted soldiers, who billeted on the third floor. A reconstruction here shows six hard, wooden, double bunks made `comfortable' by mattresses stuffed with straw. Men slept two to a bed, twenty-four to a room. How anyone got any sleep—with snoring and periodic nighttime shiftings of position—in these cramped quarters is hard to picture.

It is difficult to see how Fort Point could have been anything other than a hardship post for those stationed there. And if cramped conditions, constant wind, and numbing chill were not deadly enough, then a trip to the mess hall might prove to be. As part of their training, company cooks were admonished: "Remember that beans, badly boiled, kill more than bullets . . . ."

Due to the constant breeze here at the Golden Gate be sure to take a sweater or windbreaker when visiting Fort Point.

Fort Mason.
Location: On Bay Street between Van Ness Avenue and Laguna Street. Auto access is via Franklin Street. Fort Mason is part of the Golden Gate National Recreation Area (GGNRA). The headquarters for the park is the old hospital building on MacArthur Avenue at Fort Mason. **Phone:** (415) 561-4700. **Hours:** The park headquarters is open Monday – Friday, 9:30 a.m. to 4:30 p.m. Fort Mason itself, like the rest of the GGNRA parkland, is open from 8 a.m. to sunset. **Admission:** Free. **Website:** www.nps.gov/goga.

Along with Jackson Square, Fort Mason is one of the few places left in San Francisco that evokes The City as it was during the first decade of its existence. It was named for Richard B. Mason, an early U.S. military governor of California (1847–1849). Like the Presidio, it was one of the key military installations designed to defend San Francisco. A number of dwellings still survive from the 1850s and 1860s.

The buildings of most interest are located on the east side of Franklin Street, just north of the entrance to the Officers Club parking lot. The center portion of the clapboard-sided Officers Club dates from 1855; the structure was enlarged and remodeled in 1877. Just beyond it are three residences, numbered 2, 3, and 4. They were built in the mid-1850s by squatters. While the word `squatters' gives the impression of poor people putting up shacks, in this case some of The City's leading citizens, including a prominent banker and John C. Frémont, built or bought houses here in this choice location with superb views of the bay.

The army, which claimed title to all of Fort Mason under President Fillmore's directive of 1850, simply did not have the manpower in the 1850s to evict these interlopers. But in 1863, with the Civil War underway and with the threat of a possible attack by a Confederate warship that was known to be in the Pacific, the army mustered its forces, evicted the squatters, and turned the houses into officers' quarters. The displaced residents, including Frémont and his family, sued the government and requested compensation for their losses. The case went all the way to the U.S. Supreme Court, which in 1867 ruled for the army.

To see these former squatters' homes walk north on Franklin Street. Since they are private residences, please do not trespass. The houses are visible from the sidewalk. Number 2, with its graceful circular carriage driveway, veranda, and sweeping view of Aquatic Park and the bay, once served as the residence of Fort Mason's commanding general. Number 3—the Leonidas Haskell house—has a bit of history associated with it in that U.S. Senator David Broderick died here after his duel with David Terry near Lake Merced. Number 4 is perhaps the nicest of all, with its commanding view out over the bay. On the bluff just west of number 4 was the location of the Frémont home, which he and his family occupied from 1859 to 1861. Frémont then leased out the one-story Gothic cottage until it was torn down in 1863 to make way for gun emplacements.

As you turn back toward Franklin Street on the west side across from numbers 2, 3, and 4 is a row of Victorian-era enlisted men's houses. Most of these date from 1864 and 1865. Before you wander past these, you might take a short detour down Funston Street, which intersects with Franklin near the north end of the oval turn-around. Half a block down on the right, in what is now a youth hostel, was a Civil-War-era enlisted men's barracks. Directly behind it is a restored gun battery—with one representative cannon.

Camp Reynolds – Angel Island.

Location: Angel Island, the largest island in San Francisco Bay, is located off the Tiburon peninsula. Camp Reynolds is on the west side of the island in the West Garrison area. There is a visitor center at Ayala Cove that can provide maps and more information. **Phone:** (415) 435-3522. Public access to the island is by ferry only. Primary points of departure are San Francisco and Tiburon. The Blue & Gold Fleet, **Phone:** (415) 705-5555, located at Pier 41, San Francisco, and the McDonough ferry, **Phone:** (415) 435-2131, which departs from 21 Main Street, Tiburon, both serve the island daily during the summer. Call the above numbers or check the website for departure times and the winter schedule. **Admission:** Angel Island itself is free. The ferry tolls on the Blue & Gold are: Adults, $14.50; Children (6–12), $8.50; Children under 6, Free. The McDonough ferry: Adults, $10.25; Children (5–11), $8.00; Bicycles, $1.00. **Websites:** www.angelisland.org and www.parks.ca.gov.

A final fortification that served as a defense point for protecting San Francisco and the bay in the early years, of which something tangible still remains, can be found on the west side of the island. Camp Reynolds at Angel Island boasts the finest collection of wooden Civil War buildings left in the United States.

It was not until late 1863 that the Army got around to constructing the outpost, named for John F. Reynolds, a Union Civil War general killed at Gettysburg by a Confederate sniper.

The two restored officers' quarters at the top of the parade ground (officially the buildings numbered 10 and 11) are the highlights. Building number 10 is open for tours seven days a week during the peak tourist season; otherwise, on weekends only. The buildings date from 1865. They were actually constructed on Yerba Buena Island, and were ferried to Angel Island in 1882. The Bakery, immediately adjacent, was built on the site in 1863. The remaining structures, on the southern end of the parade ground leading toward the water, were constructed beginning in 1863 and housed the camp's officers. Enlisted men's barracks originally stood directly across from the officers' quarters, on the opposite side of the parade ground, but have long since been torn down.

The City's Elite

> **South Park.**
> **Location:** In the center of the area bounded by Bryant, Brannan, Second, and Third streets in San Francisco. The easiest access by auto or on foot is from either Second or Third streets.

Looking at South Park today, it is hard to believe that it was once the most fashionable address in San Francisco. But in the 1850s its oval common was ringed with elegant London Regency-style townhouses. South Park was part of the neighboring Rincon Hill area, an elevated knob of land that, in the 1850s and 1860s saw the construction of grand Victorian homes, many with stables and carriage houses in the rear. It was home to many of the young city's leading citizens.

In a couple of decades, however, the area became increasingly industrial, began to decline as a residential district, and later was changed beyond recognition. In 1869, Second Street was extended south, cutting through the hill, and in 1873 the invention of the cable car opened the steeper Nob Hill to development, allowing The City's newer millionaires to build there. The 1906 disaster destroyed the remaining Rincon Hill mansions, and in the 1930s most of what remained of the hill itself was leveled to make way for the Bay Bridge anchorage.

The only vestige of this once upper-class enclave is the oval common of South Park. Today the area is a mixture of residential and commercial buildings surrounded by old warehouses. An attractive restaurant and other small businesses have opened around the oval in recent years.

Courtesy, Cowell Foundation, Oakland Museum
South Park, about 1855. Rincon Hill in the background.

6

The Bonanza Age
(1859–1880)

The discovery in 1859 of the Comstock Lode, a rich vein of silver ore twenty miles northeast of Carson City, Nevada, transformed San Francisco almost as much as did the gold rush.

While the rush to Washoe (named for the Washo Indians) and Virginia City was in its early stages, four Sacramento merchants—who came to be known as the Big Four—built the Central Pacific Railroad, the western half of the first transcontinental railroad, which would link San Francisco to the East Coast. Its completion, in 1869, led to increased competition and a painful economic downturn. The Chinese, many of whom had come to California to work on the railroad, were blamed by a vocal minority for The City's economic misfortunes, and were so greatly harassed that they withdrew into their enclave—Chinatown—for protection.

In the 1870s it was silver rather than the railroad that captured the public's imagination. Four other men—the Bonanza Kings, as they were sometimes called—became wealthy and powerful when they tapped into the "Big Bonanza," an abundant vein of silver.

But the dominant figure of his day was banker William C. Ralston, a prime beneficiary of the Comstock wealth, and a man who invested his money in the development of San Francisco. His untimely death in 1875 signaled the end of an era. Soon thereafter the high-grade Nevada silver ore was exhausted. By 1880 the Comstock was history.

Discovery of the Comstock Lode

In 1859, a prospector named James Finney (called "Old Virginny" after his native state) stumbled on what soon proved to be the richest discovery of silver ore in history. He and several other prospectors, including Henry Comstock, who gave his name to the lode, staked claims to a dusty, hardscrabble piece of ground in western Nevada. They originally were attracted by the discovery of modest amounts of gold. But in their shoveling and sluicing they became at first irritated and then puzzled by large quantities of thick, blue clay that kept clogging their rockers. After a period of cursing this stuff that was making their task more difficult, someone had the presence of mind to send samples to be assayed. When the results came back it was found that this "blue mud" was extremely rich in silver. The rush to Washoe was on. The consequences for San Francisco would be nearly as great as that of the gold rush ten years earlier.

By the end of 1863 the Comstock had produced $22 million, modest by the gold production standards of a decade earlier but enough to warrant the serious attention of miners everywhere in the West. It was only the beginning. During the next fifteen years the Comstock Lode generated more than $300 million in wealth. Alas, its original discoverers were not to profit from it. Finney, Comstock, and the other first claimants sold out early for only a few thousand dollars. Most died broke. The main beneficiary of the "Big Bonanza" was not even Virginia City, the town that rose from the ground above this Aladdin's treasure. The real winners were San Francisco and a handful of shrewd speculators.

William Ralston and the Bank of California

William C. Ralston, who was to become San Francisco's leading citizen of the 1860s and 1870s, was in the 1850s a relatively obscure banker in the city in partnership with several others. But in 1864 he formed a new partnership with Darius O. Mills, and together they organized the Bank of California. They immediately opened a Virginia City branch.

It was a propitious time to start a Virginia City operation. The initial boom had ended, and mining that year had mostly been halted due to flooding in the mines at the five-hundred-foot level. With mounting debt, and production at a standstill, mine owners were facing bankruptcy. Ralston, sensing an opportunity, had the Bank of California's Virginia City branch, under the direction of a crafty and at times devious manager named William Sharon, start lending money to keep the mines going. In return, the bank took shares of stock as collateral, and, through foreclosures and supplying additional loans, quickly gained a controlling interest in many of the Comstock mines.

To increase their leverage even further, Ralston and his partners bought the nearest forests to supply lumber for timbering in the mines. They completely denuded the shores of Lake Tahoe, developed sawmills and the local water works, and built the Virginia & Truckee Railroad, the only rail line to Virginia City. This monopoly on supplies and transportation, combined with controlling interests in many of the mines, gave "Ralston's Ring," as it came to be called, a lock on the Comstock's wealth.

After the initial flooding problems in the mines were resolved, even richer ore bodies were discovered, and by 1867, when the next mining boom started, the Bank of California's shares rose astronomically, making William Ralston rich.

Ralston's Building Program

It was not long before Ralston, a man who gloried in grandiose projects, set to work investing the bank's money and his own. He envisioned a San Francisco with an unlimited, glorious future. His objective was to make the growing metropolis independent of Eastern manufacturers. He spread his cash around, starting a woolen mill, a carriage company, a furniture-making operation, and even a silkworm factory among a number of enterprises. He also built the California Theater (it was located on Bush Street near Kearny) which was The City's leading stage for many years. And he owned two showplace residences, one in San Francisco and the other, a palatial estate, in Belmont on the peninsula.

But his biggest and most consuming project was the construction of the Palace Hotel on Market Street. This huge edifice and city landmark, when completed in 1875, contained 800 rooms, making it, for a time, the largest hotel in the United States. Only a few years earlier, the site had been nothing more than windswept sand dunes.

The Palace Hotel, shortly after it opened.

The Comstock, and its Effect on San Francisco

William Ralston dominated the city during his prime, but in the overall picture he was merely an agent for the Comstock silver wealth that flooded San Francisco. The ore might have been mined in Nevada, but San Francisco was the major recipient of the mines' bounty. Not only had Ralston and The City's other financiers supplied the capital that led to the development of the mines, but San Francisco also provided 90 percent of the necessary supplies and materials. Virtually everything the Washoe mines and miners consumed, from assaying equipment, drills, and shovels to foodstuffs and clothing, was either manufactured in the San Francisco area or, like fine imported champagne, was landed at city wharves and then transported to Virginia City.

All this economic activity led to widespread prosperity, which in turn generated a building boom. Several thousand new buildings went up in San Francisco during the 1860s and 1870s. Among them were a new U.S. mint at Fifth and Mission streets, completed in 1874 and a new sub-treasury building, which opened in 1877 on Commercial Street near Montgomery, the site of the first mint (1854–1874).

A boom based on mineral wealth, however, can be a mixed blessing. With San Francisco's fortunes closely tied to Comstock silver, the ups and downs of the mines played havoc with the city's economy. This was particularly evident on the floor of the Mining Exchange, where share prices sometimes gyrated wildly. More than one stock during the era went from two dollars a share to well over a thousand dollars on news of a major find. Share prices could and did fall just as rapidly on news that a bonanza had gone to "borrasca"—meaning that a vein of ore had terminated in barren rock. Speculative fever ran high, and San Francisco wage earners, who dreamed of living the life of a William Ralston, too often found themselves either caught paying high prices for shares soon to be driven down by a manipulator with inside information, or else paying assessments on worthless stock.

The Bonanza Kings

Although William Ralston was San Francisco's dominant figure during his tenure at the Bank of California, by the early 1870s a quartet of Irishmen, who came to be known as the "Bonanza Kings," had started to generate headlines of their own.

John Mackay, James Fair, James Flood, and William O'Brien, like so many other young men, had emigrated to California in the wake of the gold rush. Mackay and Fair enjoyed modest success at mining, but their small stakes merely served to whet their appetites for more.

With the Comstock the center of action, the four formed a partnership. Mackay and Fair provided the mining expertise while Flood and O'Brien, late of the Auction Lunch, a popular saloon where they had been the proprietors, served as stockbrokers on the Mining Exchange. Mackay and Fair identified a depressed but potentially lucrative mining stock controlled by the Ralston/Sharon team, and Flood and O'Brien quietly were able to buy up enough shares to gain control. The mine hit a new ore vein, the share price rose dramatically, and the four were on their way.

Armed with several million dollars, the group began buying up several smaller mines at the northern end of the lode. (The entire wealth of the Comstock was contained in an area less than two miles long and only a few hundred feet wide.) These they combined into one big mine they called the Consolidated Virginia. In early 1873, miners below the one-thousand-foot level struck what became known as the fabled "Big Bonanza," a massive body of concentrated silver ore more than four hundred feet deep. It was worth in excess of $100 million, and it made the formerly poor Irishmen California's richest men.

The Death of William C. Ralston

By the summer of 1875, William Ralston, always a profligate spender and heavy borrower, found himself overextended. The problems leading to his downfall began when the vein of ore in his leading Comstock mine, the Ophir, started petering out. (There has been speculation that William Sharon, Ralston's Virginia City agent, may have hastened Ralston's demise by intentionally, and prematurely, dumping shares on the market.)

With the source of his wealth gone and with many of his previous business ventures proving to be non-paying investments, he found himself strapped for cash. He desperately started selling off his assets, but it was too late. His fortune was inextricably linked with that of the Bank of California, and when a run started on the bank on August 26 it could no longer meet its obligations, and closed its doors. Ralston tendered his resignation at the request of the board of directors, and went for his customary afternoon swim at the Neptune Bath House at the foot of Larkin Street (where Aquatic Park is now). A short time later he was pulled from the water, lifeless, apparently the victim of a stroke. Title to the Palace Hotel, his greatest legacy, which was just weeks away from completion, was taken by William Sharon, who also claimed the keys to his Belmont estate.

August 26, 1875: failure of the Bank of California.

The Big Four and the Transcontinental Railroad

William Ralston and the Bonanza Kings were not the only ones active in big business and high finance in the 1860s and 1870s. Another quartet, soon to be known by their own moniker, the "Big Four," directed the most ambitious undertaking the West had known when they backed the building of the western half of the transcontinental railroad. The idea for a railroad linking the East and West coasts had been bandied about almost since the time California was admitted to the union in 1850. All through the 1850s the matter had been stalled in Congress over the slavery question. Northern states wanted the line to cross free states and end in northern California, while southern states wanted it to cross slave states and terminate in southern California.

The secession of the southern states in 1861 resolved the issue. In 1862, Congress, now free of the opposition of southern Congressmen and anxious to tap the Nevada silver mines to help finance the Civil War, approved the Pacific Railroad Act. Two companies, the Union Pacific and the Central Pacific, were awarded contracts. The Union Pacific would lay track from Omaha west, while the Central Pacific was to link up with the former by building east from Sacramento. The U.S. Government would provide a generous subsidy of loans and land grants.

Four Sacramento merchants—Charles Crocker, Mark Hopkins, Collis P. Huntington, and Leland Stanford—provided the seed capital to build the Central Pacific. Construction began in 1863. Laying track was easy at first, since Sacramento and its environs lie on a plain. But as the rails advanced into the foothills and beyond, further advances became small incremental steps when it became necessary to blast tunnels through Sierra mountainsides. Finally, six laborious years after they started, the two railroads met at Promontory, Utah. On May 10, 1869, the "golden spike" was driven, signifying the linking of the East and West coasts, the symbolic completion of America's Manifest Destiny. Travel from one coast to the other would now take only seven days rather than the previous four to six months.

San Francisco celebrated wildly when the telegraph flashed the news of the driving of the golden spike. "San Francisco annexes the United States" said one banner carried by Montgomery Street revelers. But the euphoria evaporated quickly. The anticipated benefits of a link with the rest of the country not only failed to materialize, but the ending of San Francisco's isolation had just the opposite effect. No longer insulated from price competition with eastern markets, The City's artificially high prices sank when faced with the abundant and cheaper goods that were shipped over the newly completed railroad. To make matters worse, the rail link was a convenient means for thousands of unemployed job seekers to come to California, driving down both wages and prices. As a result, San Francisco soon found itself in the midst of a depression. Despite the infusions of wealth the silver discoveries of the following decade were to bring, the 1870s, at least in terms of societal change, were to prove a turbulent and trying time.

Courtesy, California State Library

Chinese laborers building a railroad trestle in the Sierra Nevada.

The Chinese

Perhaps no group suffered more during this time than the Chinese. It had taken a while for their numbers to grow and their presence to be noticed. Chinese are known to have arrived in San Francisco as early as 1848, when a local newspaper recorded that four "Celestials" had found employment. The excitement created by the gold rush failed to take root as strongly in China as in other countries, however, and so the Chinese were slow to emigrate. At first, when they were few in number (by 1850 only 500 of 58,000 miners were Chinese), and the gold was plentiful, the Chinese were welcomed—or at least tolerated. But as gold became scarcer and the number of Chinese increased, eventually amounting to a quarter of all miners in the Mother Lode, the Chinese found themselves subjected to ill treatment. Despite their efforts to avoid direct competition and conflict with Americans, mainly by working claims that had been abandoned, they were sometimes rousted from even these meager diggings by frustrated and jealous Yankees.

What gave impetus to further discrimination was the Central Pacific's hiring of Chinese workers. Early in the construction, track-laying had gotten off to a slow start. This was partly due to the lack of reliability of the mostly Irish laborers. As an experiment, Chinese were hired. They proved to be hard-working and dependable; the call soon went out for more. They so well proved their mettle when blasting tunnels through the Sierra and in handling other hazardous tasks, that by the time the two railroads met in Utah, 85 percent of the Central Pacific's work force was Chinese.

Their very success, however, along with their now increased numbers, made them easy targets when the depression followed the completion of the railroad. In 1869, with construction at an end, twenty thousand Chinese were suddenly out of work. Some moved on to other railroad jobs in the West, but most drifted back to San Francisco. At the same time, thousands of other Chinese were landing at city docks; throughout the early 1870s tens of thousands more arrived. With unemployment high, and Chinese competing for jobs and willing to work for lower wages, they soon became scapegoats and victims of abuse.

Faced with white hostility, the Chinese were forced into menial occupations.   →

Rand Richards collection

Soiled linen for the laundry

Vegetable peddler

The abuse had started as early as the 1850s, but as the years passed and the Chinese population increased, so did the viciousness. One particularly savage incident occurred in 1868, when a band of young whites accosted a Chinese crab fisherman, robbed and beat him, branded him with a hot iron, and then slit his ears and tongue.

In such an environment it is not difficult to understand the climate of fear that must have prevailed among the Chinese when a young Irish-born firebrand named Denis Kearney organized the Workingman's Party with the rallying cry, "The Chinese Must Go!" A powerful sandlot orator, Kearney in 1877 stirred crowds into mob action that led to the looting and burning of a number of Chinese laundries and other businesses. He soon faded from prominence, but his anti-Chinese rhetoric echoed the feelings of a vocal minority who made their presence felt with legislators.

Anti-Chinese legislation had first been enacted in the mid-1850s, when a miners' tax aimed at Chinese was passed. By the 1870s, discriminatory legislation was being enacted at both the state and local levels. Some of these laws were either unenforceable or were overturned by the courts, such as the petty "Queue Ordinance" passed by the San Francisco Board of Supervisors in 1876, which mandated that all Chinese prisoners confined in the county jail be shorn of their pigtails. Most of the laws, however, like the earlier miners' tax, were aimed at occupational pursuits such as agriculture and fishing where Chinese were competing directly with whites. Despite occasional victories in the courts, the pressures against the Chinese were inexorable. In 1879, at the state constitutional convention, a new amended charter was ratified, which contained numerous other anti-Chinese restrictions—even including a statute prohibiting Chinese from voting.

The effect of this overt and codified racism was to exclude the Chinese from most occupations and to deprive them of full participation in a society they had helped to pioneer. The result was that they withdrew into an enclave—Chinatown—where they were among friends and were relatively safe from the predations of white ruffians. There they operated laundries, Chinese restaurants, and other businesses that offered little or no competition for whites.

William C. Ralston (1826–1875)

"The Man Who Built San Francisco"

William Ralston was born on a farm in Ohio, migrated to New Orleans when he was a teenager, and worked as a clerk and ship's carpenter on Mississippi riverboats. He was twenty-three in 1849 when the gold rush started, but he was in no hurry to join the hordes moving west—probably because he saw that an easier way to make money was to provide services for the forty-niners rather than be one.

He made his way to Panama where, in conjunction with two partners, he started a successful banking operation, and then branched into shipping, transporting gold seekers by steamship up the coast to San Francisco. He first arrived in The City

Courtesy, California State Library

William C. Ralston.

in 1851 as captain of one of his vessels. He did not stay long, however, and during the next few years made the journey several more times.

Ralston settled in San Francisco for good in 1854. He soon went into banking. By 1864 he had built enough of a reputation that he was able to align himself with Darius O. Mills, the city's leading banker. The two of them established the Bank of California, an institution still active today, with its headquarters at California and Sansome streets, on the same site as the earlier Ralston/Mills bank.

Ralston, as aggressive as Mills was cautious, soon had the Bank of California's capital invested in speculative Comstock silver mines. It was a gamble that paid off: when the mines started yielding their abundant wealth in the late 1860s and early 1870s, the Bank of California profited mightily.

Ralston, flush with cash, started businesses and spread money around with abandon. He soon had his and the bank's money (the two became intertwined) tied up in various ventures—woolen mills, hydraulic mining, Alaskan fisheries, sugar refineries, and many other endeavors. And, of course, there was his peninsula estate and his pet project, the Palace Hotel. Ralston was such an energetic civic booster that whenever San Francisco lacked something, rather than seeking the cheapest source of supply, he would produce it locally, whatever the cost.

But his passions bordered on recklessness. And when the crunch came, as it usually did in the boom and bust times characteristic of the early West, Ralston, overextended, could not meet his obligations. Runs on banks thought to be in trouble were a real threat in Ralston's day, and when rumors circulated about his profligacy, the inevitable run started. On August 26, 1875, the Bank of California, besieged by panicky investors, closed its doors early, its reserves of gold and silver exhausted.

William Ralston, San Francisco's leading citizen, under obvious stress, died of an apparent stroke while on his customary afternoon swim the next day after resigning his position at the bank. He was forty-nine years old. A virtual symbol of San Francisco's can-do optimism, he was widely mourned and was given the largest funeral San Francisco had ever seen.

Sites and Attractions

William Ralston and the Bank of California

> **The Bank of California Museum.**
> **Location:** 400 California Street (between Sansome and Montgomery),
> San Francisco. **Phone:** (415) 765-0400. There is no separate phone or
> website for the museum. **Hours:** The bank's and the museum's hours are
> the same: Monday – Friday, 9 a.m. to 4:30 p.m. Closed bank holidays and
> weekends. **Admission:** Free.

William Ralston's Bank of California (now Union Bank of California) still occupies its main location in downtown San Francisco on the northwest corner of California and Sansome streets. The present building was erected in 1908, Ralston's original structure having been torn down just before the 1906 earthquake. The earlier bank building, sheathed in blue sandstone and modeled after the Library of Saint Mark in Venice, was built in 1866.

In the bank's basement is the previously mentioned museum. There are several exhibits here on the Comstock's history. On view are several illustrations: a map showing the location of the major mines on the lode; a lithograph depicting a network of wooden timbers that supported the tunnels extending deep into the earth; and some photos of the Virginia & Truckee Railroad, the line that hauled all of the treasure out of Virginia City to the outside world. Along one wall, framed and behind glass, are the original rich assay pellets of 1859 that started the rush to Washoe. In one of the glass cases in the center of the room can be seen a quite rare (only two are known to exist) small gold ingot dated 1867 and stamped with the name of William Sharon, the bank's Virginia City branch manager.

Interior of the original Palace Hotel.
The Garden Court occupies the space today.

The Palace Hotel.

Location: Market and New Montgomery streets, San Francisco. **Phone:** (415) 512-1111. **Website:** www.sfpalace.com.

Construction of the Palace Hotel, William Ralston's greatest legacy, started in early 1874. It cost $5 million, and opened for business in October 1875, six weeks after Ralston's death. He wanted a truly grand hotel, one that would stand as a symbol of San Francisco's having come of age, and he got it. It had 800 rooms, and its seven stories towered above its neighbors. Until 1906 it was San Francisco's most notable landmark.

Ralston spared no expense in either the building or the furnishing of the hotel. To guard against earthquake, iron reinforcing bolts were used throughout the two-foot-thick walls. To guard against fire, storage reservoirs containing over seven hundred thousand gallons of water were installed under the hotel and on the roof.

Inside the hotel, the seven floors, each with its own gallery and promenade, looked down upon a central marble-paved courtyard and carriage turnaround surrounded by potted plants and trees. Directly above, an elaborate domed ceiling of amber-colored glass bathed the hotel in soft, natural light. The rooms, which could receive messages via pneumatic tube and which also received filtered air from a primitive air-conditioning system, were furnished with highly polished mahogany, teak, ebony, and rosewood.

Such an opulent hotel naturally attracted royalty and the leading businessmen, artists, and politicians of the day. Among the famous guests who stayed there were Prince Louis Napoleon Bonaparte, J. P. Morgan, Oscar Wilde (who registered as "O. Wilde and servant"), and President Teddy Roosevelt. Two of the country's heroes, Generals Sherman and Grant, were feted at separate banquets in the 1870s and treated like native sons. Both men had spent time in San Francisco earlier in their careers. Sherman had been a banker, and Grant, when a junior officer, had been stationed at the Benicia arsenal for a time.

In the thirty-one years of its existence the Palace Hotel was the "prestige" place to stay and to be seen. Anybody who was anybody (or wanted to be somebody) went to the Palace.

Alas, in 1906, the original Palace, despite having its own reservoirs, perished in the holocaust of flame. Gone were the seven tiers of galleries, the polished wood, the amber skylight. All but the memories were turned to ashes.

The eight-story Palace on the site today, opened in 1909, and has since been refurbished several times. One important change took place before 1906. Around the turn of the century, with the automobile beginning to replace the horse-drawn carriage, the cul-de-sac was torn up. Horses had earlier been barred because their hoofs made too much noise clip-clopping on the marble flagstones. The turnaround was replaced by a lounge furnished with overstuffed chairs and couches, and potted palm trees and other plants.

The Garden Court today occupies the site of the old courtyard. Surrounded by potted palms and covered by a decorative glass skylight, it retains the grace and charm of the earlier era. It is a great place to enjoy a leisurely Sunday brunch, and to imagine what the Palace was like in the golden years of the Victorian Age.

Ralston Hall – Notre Dame de Namur University.
Location: 1500 Ralston Avenue, Belmont. **Phone:** (650) 508-3501. Docent-led tours weekdays by appointment only. Call Monday – Friday, 9 a.m. to 5 p.m. to make reservations. **Admission:** $5.00 per person. **Website:** www.ralstonhall.com.

Of all William Ralston's major edifices—the Palace Hotel, the California Theatre, his Nob Hill mansion—only his country estate in Belmont survived 1906. The main house stands today; much of the interior, especially, still looks like it did in Ralston's heyday.

The original building came from Italy. It was actually a villa owned by an Italian count who, worried about the unreliability of American workers and the uncertainty of finding the requisite materials in California in 1852, had it taken apart, crated, and shipped to San Francisco. It was then hauled down the peninsula to Belmont where it was uncrated and reassembled. Ralston, casting about for a country estate, bought it in 1864. Sparing no expense, he immediately began expanding the modest dwelling into a sprawling mansion of over eighty rooms, making it, at the time, the largest private residence on the West Coast. Surrounding the main house were acres of landscaped grounds and a number of satellite buildings, including greenhouses, a bowling alley, and a Turkish bath. Servants lived in a fifty-room house of their own half a mile away.

Ralston entertained on a grand scale, sometimes hosting dinner parties for a hundred or more guests. After he died, William Sharon continued the tradition. In 1876, Sharon hosted an extravagant dinner for William Tecumseh Sherman, and topped that three years later with a tribute to Ulysses S. Grant. On the latter occasion 1,800 guests enjoyed 15,000 oysters and 100 cases of champagne. Dancing went on into the early hours of the morning; special trains left at one, three, and five o'clock in the morning for San Francisco, where horse-drawn carriages and their liverymen awaited their owners. (General Grant, shy and never a social lion, was overwhelmed by his reception and retreated early.)

Despite the splendor and the grand events Ralston Hall hosted over the years, the striking thing about visiting it today is how tasteful and elegant it is. This is partly due to Ralston's haphazard additions to the original villa and partly due to his distaste for the gaudy Victorian architecture that enlivened Nob Hill a short time later.

If William Ralston were to return today he might not initially recognize the exterior of his house, since stucco has replaced the wooden clapboard he knew. But inside, the main rooms would surely look familiar. The two rooms on either side of the front hall are all that survive from the 1852 house. Beyond those the Ralston additions begin. Of particular note is the ballroom with its polished wood parquet floors—resembling the Hall of Mirrors at Versailles —and the beautiful loge upstairs modeled after the much larger one in the Paris Opera. Notice the silver rails and fittings, emblematic of Ralston's Nevada silver fortune. (In Ralston's day, every interior doorknob was of solid silver.) In the loge are photographs of the Ralstons and their children, and a few remaining pieces of their personal furnishings.

The house, now a National Historic Landmark, passed through numerous hands after the Ralston/Sharon era, and the estate and grounds today are greatly reduced from their former size. Of the once seemingly ubiquitous outbuildings only a stone carriage house is left. In 1922, the Sisters of Notre Dame de Namur bought the property, restored it, and run it still, opening the main building for various functions and public tours.

San Mateo County History Museum.
Location: 2200 Broadway, Redwood City. **Phone:** (650) 299-0104. **Hours:** Tuesday – Sunday, 10 a.m. to 4 p.m. **Admission:** Adults, $4.00; Students, Seniors, Children, $2.00. **Website:** www.sanmateocountyhistory.com.

The museum has a few artifacts from the Ralston mansion, some of which are displayed from time to time, including a painted plate embroidered with gold trim and a big "R," a salt cellar, and some silverware. Ralston's Bank of California partner, Darius O. Mills, built an estate in Millbrae (named for Mills). On display from his mansion is an elaborate inlaid rosewood curtain tie-back.

The museum also has a number of late 19th century coaches including a Spider Phaeton, a ladies Brougham, and a beautifully restored Park Drag—all fine examples of how the wealthy got about just before the advent of the automobile.

The Silver Age

The Old Mint.
Location: Fifth and Mission Streets, San Francisco. The Old Mint currently is **closed** but plans to reopen as a museum of San Francisco history at some unspecified date after refurbishing. **Website:** www.sfhistory.org.

The silver boom of the 1860s and 1870s quickly taxed the facilities of San Francisco's Commercial Street mint, built in 1854. Construction of a new, larger mint began at Fifth and Mission streets in 1869. It was completed and opened for business in 1874, and quickly became the busiest mint in the country, surpassing Philadelphia, New Orleans, and Carson City.

The building is a beautiful example of the Greek Revival style then in vogue for federal government buildings; it is the only such structure on the West Coast. The front and north façades have recently been refinished. The other sides, all made of the same crumbling limestone, are also due for resurfacing.

The old museum had a number of exhibits and artifacts related to the silver era. One of them was the superintendent's office,

The Old Mint, shortly after its completion in 1874.

re-created to its nineteenth-century appearance with most of its original furnishings. Some of the nearby offices were incongruously furnished as domestic bedrooms and living rooms of the Victorian era.

In the basement, the exhibits had more to do with money than with San Francisco history. But at the south end, in a glass case, were several chunks of unprocessed silver ore from Virginia City mines and some of the end product of the "The Big Bonanza"—a pile of Liberty Head silver dollars. Next to these were two drafts, dating from the 1870s, drawn on Virginia City banks. There were also strange markings on the surrounding walls. They were caused by silver dollars pressing through the canvas coin bags that once filled that room.

You also used to be able to get a stamped coin souvenir of your visit. For one dollar, employees would stamp a souvenir medal from a large brass slug.

Rand Richards

The Sub-Treasury Building—now the Pacific Heritage Museum.

Sub-Treasury Building – Pacific Heritage Museum.
Location: 608 Commercial Street (between Montgomery and Kearny), San Francisco. **Phone:** (415) 399-1124. **Hours:** Tuesday – Saturday, 10 a.m. to 4 p.m., except holidays. **Admission:** Free. **Website:** www.ibankunited.com.

The Sub-Treasury Building stands on the site of the first San Francisco branch mint (1854–74). It was built between 1875 and 1877 to serve the federal government as a branch of the treasury after a larger mint had been constructed at Fifth and Mission streets in 1874. The sub-treasury's function was to handle transactions between the government and private individuals, and to store coin and bullion used in those transactions. This was originally a four-story structure, but the top three floors, which were made of wood, burned in the 1906 fire. The ground floor and basement contained the bullion vault, and were constructed of steel beams covered by corrugated iron. These two levels survived the 1906 disaster, and preserved their contents of $13 million in gold and silver.

The building now houses the Pacific Heritage Museum, which primarily features changing exhibits related to Pacific Basin culture. There is, however, a permanent display on the history of the sub-treasury building. You can also look down into the vault and see replicas of strong boxes and coin bags.

Virginia City.
Location: On Highway 341 in western Nevada, twenty miles southeast of Reno.

Virginia City is where the great silver rush began. In its heyday it was the largest city between St. Louis and San Francisco, and its dateline was familiar to newspaper readers in major U.S. cities and in the capitals of Europe. The more than $300 million of Comstock treasure created Virginia City and helped to build San Francisco. Today San Francisco is a major metropolis, while Virginia City is nearly a ghost town that is kept alive only by tourism.

The silver is long gone and Virginia City is off the beaten path, but the old town is still rich in nostalgia. Mine tailings dot the surrounding landscape, and from May to October a ceremonial engine and a few cars from the Virginia & Truckee Railroad haul visitors on a short run from the depot to the edge of town and back. You can also see Mark Twain's desk in the basement of the *Territorial Enterprise,* the local paper where he got his start as a writer.

The Transcontinental Railroad

> ## The Golden Spike – Cantor Arts Center at Stanford.
> **Location:** Museum Way and Lomita Drive, Stanford University campus, Palo Alto. **Phone:** (650) 723-4177. **Hours:** Wednesday – Sunday, 11 a.m. to 5 p.m.; (Thursday to 8 p.m.). Closed Monday, Tuesday, and major holidays. **Admission:** Free. **Website:** www.museum.stanford.edu.

After being closed for nearly ten years due to the 1989 earthquake, this refurbished museum reopened in January 1999.

Among Stanford family memorabilia is the gold spike used in the historic 1869 ceremony at Promontory, Utah. The spike looks much like any other railroad spike except that it is made of gold. It is engraved on all four sides with the names of Stanford, his partners, and various other dignitaries. It lists the date of the ceremony as May 8, which was the date originally chosen, but due to a delay in the arrival of the Union Pacific train, the driving of the spike was postponed until May 10.

The spike was one of several brought to the ceremony. Also on view is another spike, this one made of pure Comstock silver. These spikes were ceremonial; none was actually driven into a tie. They were, instead, dropped into prepared holes. The gold spike, however, does show small indentations on its head. It is thought that a few of the Army officers at the scene may have done their own "driving of the spike" with the hilts of their swords as it lay in its hole.

The spikes rest today on a stand in a lucite box in the gallery outside the Stanford Family Memorabilia Room. The historic rail line at Promontory is no more. The Southern Pacific built a new main line across Great Salt Lake in 1903 and 1904, and the Promontory route became a branch line. In 1942 it was abandoned, and its rails were torn up for wartime scrap.

The museum also houses a couple of other artifacts associated with the rail line: the silver-plated maul used in the "driving" of the spike, and the shovel used in the ground-breaking ceremony of January 8, 1863, when construction started.

The Oakland Museum – History Gallery.

Location: 1000 Oak Street (two blocks from Lake Merritt), Oakland. **Phone:** (510) 238-3842. **Hours:** Wednesday – Saturday, 10 a.m. to 5 p.m.; (First Friday to 9 p.m.); Sunday, Noon to 5 p.m. Closed holidays. **Admission:** Adults, $8.00; Seniors, Students, $5.00; Children (under 5), Free. **Website:** www.museumca.org.

On display are objects related to the Bonanza Kings and to the transcontinental railroad.

Foremost among the artifacts illustrating the lifestyle of the silver barons are a silver service and dinnerware—cutlery, napkin rings, teapots, and a serving bowl—made from Comstock silver. On the surrounding walls are photographs of the four Bonanza Kings and views of the interiors of the Mark Hopkins mansion on Nob Hill and that of James Ben Ali Haggin, another leading citizen of the era. Rounding out the display are pictures of the Palace Hotel in Virginia City in its heyday, and mining stock certificates from defunct silver mines. There is also a beautifully detailed scale model of an engine and a tender car of the Virginia & Truckee Railroad.

Of the few items pertaining to the completion of the transcontinental railroad, the most memorable is the celebrated photo of the meeting of the Central Pacific and Union Pacific locomotives at Promontory on May 10, 1869. One of the most widely published photos of the nineteenth century, it is almost more interesting for what it does not show: despite the indispensable contribution of the Chinese to building the Central Pacific Railroad, not a single Chinese appears in the picture.

Accompanying this exhibit is a map showing the route of the completed transcontinental railroad, featuring all the stops along the way, and in one of the standing floor displays are some Central Pacific Railroad rate sheets and handbills.

The Chinese

Chinese Historical Society of America Museum.
Location: 965 Clay Street, (between Stockton and Powell), San Francisco. **Phone:** (415) 391-1188. **Hours:** Tuesday – Friday, Noon to 5 p.m.; Saturday, Sunday Noon to 4 p.m. **Admission:** $3.00; Students and Seniors, $2.00; Children (6–17), $1.00. Free first Thursdays. **Website:** www.chsa.org.

This museum documents the Chinese experience in America. Most of the artifacts come from the Bay Area, however, and the emphasis is on Chinese life in and around San Francisco.

The artifacts graphically convey the way life must have been for the Chinese in their adopted home. Among the items on display are a gold miner's rocker, an ancient handmade wheelbarrow, an altar from a Chinese temple, an opium pipe, and a grain fan used to separate shrimp from their shells.

Enlarged historical photographs line the walls, a number of them showing Chinese at work shoveling dirt, sawing lumber, and laying railroad track—just a few of the jobs Chinese performed in contributing to the early California economy.

A section is also devoted to the racial hostility the Chinese faced. There are various 19th-century books, pamphlets, and ads that portray the Chinese as less than human—as bogeymen and as rat-eaters, and there is one illustration that depicts Chinese as being descended from apes and then being transformed into pigs.

China Camp State Park.
Location: On the Marin shoreline outside San Rafael. From Highway 101 in San Rafael, exiting at either North San Pedro Road or at Third Street—which leads into Point San Pedro Road—will bring you to the park and fishing village. It is an eight-mile drive. **Phone:** (415) 456-0766. **Hours:** The park is open daily from 8 a.m. to sunset, and the visitors center and museum from 10 a.m. to 5 p.m. **Admission:** $5.00 per car. **Website:** www.parks.ca.gov.

In the nineteenth century, San Francisco Bay teemed with shrimp. Chinese fishermen, who pioneered the local shrimp fishing industry, soon dotted the bay shoreline with shrimping camps. Settlements such as China Camp were once a hive of activity, with workers laying nets, bringing in the catch, saving the bigger shrimp to be sold live at local markets, and drying and packing the rest for export. At its peak, in the 1870s, China Camp was actually a small town of almost five hundred people, having its own school, stores, a barber, and a doctor. But by the 1880s, as a result of a declining harvest and increasingly restrictive laws aimed at the Chinese, the fishing camps started to disappear.

Today, a much reduced China Camp is the last survivor. One lone shrimper, Frank Quan, a descendant of the village's early pioneers, carries on. He can sometimes be seen in his small boat, reeling in his nets. In summer, if he has had a good catch, he sells fresh shrimp to visitors—although most of them are sold to fishermen for bait.

The main attraction at China Camp, beside the obvious beauty of the setting—in a secluded cove on the shore of the bay—is the visitors center and museum, which is located in an open-air weathered board shed jutting out over the water. The exhibits, which are attractively arranged and supplemented by photographs, detail the history of the camp and the regulatory discrimination that hastened its decline. Among the artifacts is a re-creation of a storage area from a century ago. Baskets of shrimp, nets, rope, and oilskin jackets hanging from pegs on the wall make it look as if their owners would be back any minute to take up where they left off.

Despite China Camp's location at a distance from city conveniences, there is a small cafe on the site that looks as though it's straight out of the 1930s. It serves breakfast, lunch, and Frank Quan's fresh shrimp when available.

Courtesy, the Oakland Museum

Leland Stanford.

7

The Gilded Age (1880–1906)

The last two decades of the nineteenth century and the first years of the twentieth century are sometimes referred to as the Gilded Age, because for some it was an era of opulence. In California, four Sacramento merchants known as the Big Four amassed vast fortunes and built lavish homes on Nob Hill. Down below the hill, however, others were not so fortunate, since they inhabited a sinkhole of depravity called the Barbary Coast.

But despite the social inequities, San Francisco had a substantial middle class supported by an expanding and increasingly diversified economy based on shipping, fishing, agriculture, and manufacturing. With the fading in importance of gold and silver, the export of wheat and many other commodities provided a sound base for continuing prosperity.

The City grew physically as well in the 1880s and 1890s as cable car lines spread far from the city center, opening up new areas for development. Nor did the city fathers neglect the beautification of their growing metropolis as Golden Gate Park was developed and attracted larger and larger crowds.

The Big Four and the Southern Pacific

The Big Four—Charles Crocker, Mark Hopkins, Collis P. Huntington, and Leland Stanford—were relatively obscure Sacramento merchants when fate tapped them for something better. Persuaded by a fanatic railroad visionary named Theodore Judah that a transcontinental railroad could be built, the partners founded the Central Pacific Railroad. After six years of arduous labor, and aided by generous government subsidies, they eventually triumphed. The driving of the golden spike marked their victory.

They were generously rewarded for the risks they took. Not only had the federal government granted them outright a generous subsidy of lands rich in timber and agricultural promise, but the four partners piled up additional wealth through another stratagem. Rather than solicit bids from independent contractors to build the rail line, the Big Four created their own construction company, and then proceeded to charge $120 million for a job that should have only cost $58 million. Armed with this extra $62 million—in essence stolen from the federal treasury—the former Sacramento shopkeepers created a business and financial empire that a Donald Trump or a Henry Kravis could only envy.

Their path to unbridled wealth lay in creating something that subsequent reforms sought to prevent: monopoly. They built a transportation monopoly that soon had the state of California in a stranglehold. They started by buying small railroads that linked the San Francisco Bay Area with the surrounding timber, agricultural, and mining regions. Since rail heads terminated on the shores of the bay, the Big Four, to complete their lock on transportation, also bought as many ferry, riverboat, and steamship lines as they could. Those railroads or waterborne transportation lines that resisted soon found themselves driven out of business by rate wars initiated by Central Pacific-owned companies.

What made the Big Four so powerful was that by controlling transportation lines, and thus freight rates, they effectively controlled any business that had to ship its products to another location. So wheat growers, vegetable farmers, and mine owners, for example, soon found themselves paying freight rates set by the rule of "all the traffic will bear." With competition eliminated, rates were set at such a level that shippers would earn just enough to stay in business. Any "excess" profits were thus transferred from the producer to the railroad. Rates were so high that it cost less to ship goods from Liverpool to San Francisco via New Orleans than from Bakersfield to San Francisco.

The tentacles of the Big Four's empire extended so far and gripped so tightly that the Southern Pacific (as it was named from 1884 on) was called "The Octopus." And although it held sway over much of the state, it had its opponents. San Franciscans, in general, had always opposed the S.P., and most of the city's newspapers— except those in the pay of the railroad—editorialized against it. The San Francisco *Examiner,* in particular, delighted in needling the S.P. by charging that its trains ran so late "the passengers were exposed to the perils of senility." But despite the opposition, the Southern Pacific, with its monopoly kept intact by judicious bribes to various politicians in Sacramento and Washington, D.C., retained its grip on the state from the 1870s into the first decade of the twentieth century.

Collis P. Huntington, the last survivor of the Big Four, died in 1900. In that same year a competing railroad established a terminus on the shore of San Francisco Bay, an event that began to loosen the S.P.'s stranglehold on the state. But it was not until 1910, when a reform state government was elected, that the S.P.'s hold was finally broken. The Southern Pacific, which recently merged with the Union Pacific (and now carries that name), is very much in business today, and although it is no longer the power it once was, the company is still one of the biggest owners of agricultural land in California—a legacy of its early land grants.

The Barbary Coast

San Franciscans today take a secret pride in The City's legendary wicked and licentious past, but the truth is that the Barbary Coast— named after the pirate-infested North African coastline— was home to a nest of criminals, petty and otherwise, and the scene of some truly sordid incidents.

San Francisco's Barbary Coast origins go back to the 1850s and the waterfront hangouts of Sydney Town. It was an area rife with low dives and grog shops, populated by muggers, thieves, and murderers. Typical of the sort of joint found there were The Boar's Head, a "dance hall" whose main stage attraction consisted of a woman having sex with a boar, and a bar called The Fierce Grizzly, so named because a live grizzly bear was chained beside the door.

Another attraction of the time was a character known as "Dirty Tom" McAlear, a filthy beggar who never bathed and who earned his living by charging a few cents and then eating or drinking any object or liquid offered, no matter how foul. This behavior was too much for even the usually tolerant San Franciscans: Dirty Tom's career came to an end when he was arrested and jailed for "making a beast of himself."

A Barbary Coast dance hall, in the 1870s.

The heart of the Barbary Coast was centered around lower Pacific Avenue and Broadway, but as the decades passed it expanded west to encompass Chinatown and south into what is part of today's financial district. Pockets of vice could even be found near Union Square on Morton Street—now the ironically named Maiden Lane—which in the late nineteenth century was lined on both sides with nothing but brothels. In addition to prostitution, the principal forms of recreation in the district were drinking, gambling, and varieties of low entertainment. Opium smoking was also available in Chinatown. A survey there in 1885 counted at least twenty-six opium dens open to the public.

Two types of criminal activity predominated on the Barbary Coast during its heyday: prostitution, and the shanghaiing of the unwary into maritime service.

Prostitution

Prostitution was for many years the lifeblood of the Barbary Coast. There were three main types of establishments: dance halls, parlor houses, and cribs. The dance halls were semi-legitimate businesses offering variety entertainment and employing "pretty waiter girls" who offered sexual services on the side. The floor duty of these hostesses consisted of getting their male clientele to consume as much of the house's watered down whiskey as possible before adjourning to the basement or stalls on the floor above for erotic play.

Most of the women sipped cold tea instead of whiskey while loosening the inhibitions of the patrons, but in one particularly rank spot called the Bull Run, on Pacific Avenue, the women were required to drink liquor along with their customers, because the management felt that their drunken antics enlivened things. Women who passed out were spread on a mattress, and sexual favors were then sold for between a quarter and a dollar, depending on the woman's attractiveness. For payment of twenty-five cents a man could watch his predecessor in action.

Not all the debauchery was so crude. At the upper end of the scale were the parlor houses. These were generally two- or three-story residences that had once been private homes. They were elegantly furnished, if a bit heavy on the red plush and velvet. Rates in these establishments ranged from two dollars to ten dollars and up. This is where "gentlemen" and others who could afford these steeper tariffs came.

At the bottom of the scale for sheer sexual dissipation were the cribs. These "cowyards" were composed of narrow stalls, just wide enough to hold a cot and maybe a chair, and were separated by cheap partitions. Sometimes even the partitions were dispensed with, leaving no room for privacy of any sort. Sex here was quick and cheap, averaging twenty-five to fifty cents.

Whether dance hall, parlor house, or crib, the turnover rate for the women was high. Beauty was paramount, but that faded quickly under the nightly onslaught experienced on the Coast. Those with special sexual talents sometimes outlasted their looks, but with some women entertaining fifty or more men a night, they too eventually departed—only to be replaced by newcomers.

Waterfront Shanghaiing

While the temptations of the Barbary Coast were evident, the perils for unwary sailors and other incautious revelers were not as obvious. One of the most widespread sidelines for owners of the more wretched waterfront dives was `crimping,' the forced recruitment of deckhands for outbound ships.

San Francisco, offering the attractions it did, made it hard for departing sea captains to maintain or recruit seamen for long ocean voyages. The crimps filled the need. The usual payment for supplying a live body to a ship was the victim's first two or three months' wages.

The cycle actually began as soon as incoming ships sailed through the Golden Gate. Because competition was keen among the waterfront bars and boarding houses for customers and possible shanghai victims, as soon as a ship appeared in the bay, "runners" from the various Barbary Coast dives would row out, board the vessel, and entice the crew into their boats with free swigs of liquor and pictures of women in alluring poses. After long sea voyages, most sailors needed little persuading, but others, fearful of forfeiting their wages (sailors were only paid at the completion of a voyage), resisted the entreaties, only to sometimes find themselves clubbed unconscious and dragged off their ships anyway.

Once ashore, the mark was plied with drugged liquor and soon relieved of his cash, jewelry, and other valuables. Those who avoided the Mickey Finns sometimes literally fell victim to trap doors found in certain Barbary Coast saloons. An unwary patron at the bar might instantly find himself in the basement and soon on board a ship, "shanghaied" and on his way out through the Golden Gate. ("Shanghai," as a verb, is credited with having originated in San Francisco. It was probably derived from Shanghai being an exotic destination and a long voyage from San Francisco. Any victim kidnapped and shipped out on an uncertain journey to China or any other foreign land was said to be "shanghaied.")

The End of the Barbary Coast

During the fifty some years of the Barbary Coast's heyday—the second half of the nineteenth century—vice of all kinds flourished unchecked and in the open. Many San Franciscans deplored the depravity and the more outrageous excesses, but periodic attempts at reform met with little success, partly due to protection from corrupt officials who received payoffs or shared in the profits from various establishments.

The Coast started its decline after the 1906 earthquake. While the rebuilding was going on, the feeling arose that the rude Barbary Coast was too low brow for an increasingly important city. More importantly, a reform movement finally gained momentum when a corrupt political boss named Abe Ruef, and his colleague, Mayor Eugene Schmitz, were ousted from power. The final blow came in 1914 when the Red Light Abatement Act, designed to close the brothels, was passed by the state legislature. When the law was upheld by the California Supreme Court in 1917, the area's main attraction and source of revenue was cut off, and the once raucous Barbary Coast faded into history.

San Francisco's Maritime Heritage

In these days of daily airplane and automobile travel it is easy to forget how vital seaborne transportation was in the recent past. Although San Francisco's port activity today is only a shadow of what it was, much of The City's history has been closely tied to shipping, fishing, or local shore-to-shore travel. Up until as recently as the 1950s San Francisco Bay was plied by commercial vessels of all kinds. Besides major ocean-going ships delivering passengers and freight, the bay was home to military transports and warships, ferries serving more than two dozen cross-bay routes, and paddle-wheel steamboats plying the rivers to inland ports such as Sacramento and Stockton. Also to be seen on the bay for many years were exotic fishing boats—feluccas manned by Italians and junks navigated by Chinese—both of these immigrant groups having brought the designs of their boats from their native lands. Today, however, with the bridges having virtually shut down the ferries, and with local fishing waters depleted, almost the only commercial vessels to be seen on the bay are the periodic Marin ferry bound for Sausalito or huge container ships steaming through the Golden Gate on their way to Oakland. The bay sees more use now from weekend sailors and pleasure boaters.

But for San Francisco, especially in its first few decades, the sea was its lifeline. Until the transcontinental railroad was completed in 1869, virtually all of The City's imported goods came by ship from places as far distant as Liverpool and Sydney.

One of the most storied sailing vessels ever constructed, the clipper ship, was built for the run to California. Clipper ships had their heyday in the 1850s, when speed of delivery was more important than cargo capacity on the San Francisco run, since a slow ship might find that it was carrying a cargo of worthless surplus if another ship with similar goods arrived before it. Even with shipping rates at a premium, some clipper ships still paid for themselves in a single trip. One ship, the *Flying Cloud,* set the record for the fastest voyage by a sailing ship from the East Coast around Cape Horn to San Francisco, making it in only eighty-nine days in 1851 and again in 1854, a record that stood until 1989. The same journey around the Horn by ordinary ships took almost twice as long. But as the gold rush economy—and mentality—of the 1850s gave way to the less frenzied 1860s and 1870s, speed of delivery was no longer the prime consideration, and clipper ships gave way to other deep-water sailing vessels.

San Francisco's economy had by this time broadened beyond the export of gold to include many other commodities and products. The most important of these in the late nineteenth century was wheat. The fertile interior San Joaquin Valley, for a time, served as the breadbasket of Europe. Huge grain harvests regularly made their way to San Francisco docks for export. In 1881, for example, 559 ships loaded with grain sailed through the Golden Gate bound for European ports.

The City also served another important market. From 1882 to 1908 San Francisco was "the whaling capital of the world." After the traditional whaling waters off the New England coast diminished in importance in the mid–nineteenth century, the action shifted to the Arctic Ocean and the North Pacific, where the humpback and other whales were abundant. San Francisco was home port for these whalers, and many a pier could be seen with whalebone drying in the sun, waiting to be made into corset stays and other goods popular during the Victorian era. Whaling declined in importance as kerosene replaced whale oil as a fuel and as spring steel superseded whalebone corsets, but despite these changes whaling by Americans in the Pacific continued well into the twentieth century. It was only in 1971 that Point Richmond, the last whaling station in the U.S., closed.

The Cable Cars

Another form of transportation—the cable car—also grew to maturity in the late nineteenth century. Andrew Hallidie, a Scots-descended immigrant and wire rope manufacturer, is usually

Marilyn Blaisdell collection
Birthplace of the cable car—Clay Street. Portsmouth Square is at the right.

credited with inventing the cable car. In truth, although Hallidie had a lot of experience in cable rope technology, patents on cable transportation devices had been issued earlier to others. Hallidie's achievement was to take a wire cable transport system that heretofore had only been used to carry ore or goods, and apply it to moving people up San Francisco's steep hills. Horse-drawn cars were the main mode of urban public transportation prior to the development of the cable car, and Hallidie was allegedly motivated by the difficulty the horses had (and the maltreatment they sometimes received in the form of lashings) in pulling their loads up The City's steeper hills.

Despite his background and his experience at operating cable transport devices in the Mother Lode mines, Hallidie's initial attempt to build a cable-operated streetcar line was greeted with skepticism. But on August 1, 1873 he gave the first public demonstration of his device, taking a passenger-filled car down Clay Street from the crest of Nob Hill to Kearny Street.

The cable car proved a tremendous boon to San Francisco. With this new public transportation, costing five cents a ride, now able to reach any part of the city, new areas were opened to development. Property values tripled wherever the lines went. By the time cable cars in San Francisco reached their zenith, in the 1880s, as many as eight different lines, extending 112 miles, sent cars up Telegraph, Russian, and Nob hills, out to the Presidio, to Golden Gate Park, and even to the Cliff House at Land's End.

With the coming of electricity in the 1890s, cable cars were gradually replaced by electric street cars and trolley buses, and, in the twentieth century, by gasoline powered buses. The cable cars held on until 1947, when they were nearly phased out entirely by the authorities in the name of "progress." The outcry from San Franciscans was such that after a long political struggle, ending in 1955, with only a few miles of track left, they were saved from oblivion. The cable cars received their official seal of approval in 1964 when they were declared a National Historic Landmark.

Golden Gate Park

Golden Gate Park, another San Francisco landmark, came into being about the same time as the cable cars. By the late 1860s, after two decades of unparalleled growth, it became clear that San Francisco, with only a few public squares to break the monotony of the grid pattern, needed a major park to provide a refuge from the growing urban density. In 1868 the Board of Supervisors approved a measure setting aside a strip of blowing sand and dunes, three miles long and a half mile wide, at the western edge of the city. This area, part of what was known as the "Outside Lands," was chosen because it was sparsely populated, and thus it would be easy and relatively inexpensive to settle claims of title with the few squatters who had built rude homes there.

Work began on the eastern end of the park in 1870. Planting trees, shrubs, and other greenery proved a daunting task, since the windblown shifting sands made it difficult for seedlings of any kind to take root. A local newspaper at the time derisively captured the essence of the problem by editorializing that "a blade of grass cannot be raised without four posts to keep it from blowing away." Nevertheless, the park's early gardeners persisted, and the park soon started to take shape.

From the beginning, the guiding principle of Golden Gate Park's creators was that it was to be a "woodland park," as natural in appearance as possible. In keeping with this concept, the early park's bridges were to look "rustic," and were thus made mostly of logs and unfinished lumber. Park roads were laid out curved and winding rather than straight in order to avoid formality, to promote the growth of vegetation, and to discourage carriage owners from driving too fast. Urban features, particularly buildings, were to be kept out of the park. This latter goal was impossible to meet, but over the decades, buildings within the park have been kept to a minimum and restricted to certain areas.

Despite its unpromising beginning, as the vegetation took root and as public transportation became more widespread, Golden Gate Park soon became an immensely popular attraction and destination. Isolated as they were on the tip of the peninsula, and without the range of leisure-time choices available today, San Franciscans of the late nineteenth century flocked to the park to picnic, to play sports, to socialize, and to have fun. The wealthy came in their luxurious carriages, while the middle class and the poor either took public transportation, rode their bikes (bicycle-riding was all the rage in the 1890s), or walked. But come they did. In 1886 one San Francisco newspaper reported that on a given day over fifty thousand people entered the park, most of them coming by streetcar. This was at a time when the city's population was only 250,000.

The 1894 Midwinter Fair

Golden Gate Park was also the site of California's first "world's fair," the Midwinter Exposition of 1894. It's purpose was to showcase San Francisco's mild winters and the state's abundance.

Marilyn Blaisdell collection

The Midwinter Fair of 1894, held in Golden Gate Park.

The fair was conceived by M. H. de Young, publisher of the San Francisco *Chronicle* and a director of the Columbian Exposition of 1893. That year was one of nationwide recession, and in an attempt to boost San Francisco's fortunes de Young proposed the idea of a similar fair for his own city. The fair opened in January 1894, and by the time it closed in July of that year more than 2.5 million people had passed through its gates. Thirty-seven foreign countries had displays, as did every California county and most of the states.

Aside from the usual pavilions depicting man's technological progress, in terms of both architecture and entertainment the emphasis was on the exotic. The major buildings were either East Indian or Egyptian in design. To maintain the interest of fair-goers, there were re-creations of a Hawaiian Islanders' camp, a Cairo street scene, and an Eskimo village complete with a small pond upon which native Alaskans paddled around in skin-covered kayaks. Perhaps the favorite attraction was Boone's Arena, a sideshow where trained animals performed. Attendance increased markedly after one of the lions killed its trainer during a performance.

The early 1890s was also the time when the latest marvel of technology—electricity—was making its presence felt. The Midwinter Fair celebrated this with a Tower of Electricity, situated in the middle of the fairgrounds. At night a beam of light, which could be seen for miles, emanated from the top of the structure, and lit up nearby landmarks.

End of an Era

As the nineteenth century came to a close, San Francisco could look at its past with pride. In only fifty years the city had grown from an isolated, sleepy, backwater village to a major metropolis. At the dawning of the twentieth century, San Franciscans felt confident that their future was bright. Little did they realize, however, that just a few years into the new century, a cataclysm would strike that would drastically alter the city they knew.

Leland Stanford (1824–1893)

"Big Four Railroad Baron"

Leland Stanford was born in 1824 near Albany, New York, the son of an innkeeper and one of eight children. He was a mediocre student in his youth, but by apprenticing at a law firm he was admitted to the bar in 1848. He practiced law only a short time, and in 1852 left for California to join two of his brothers, who had a thriving wholesale grocery business in Sacramento. When the brothers moved to San Francisco, Leland stayed behind and took over the business.

Leland Stanford might have remained an obscure, moderately prosperous grocer if one of his customers had not gone bankrupt. To satisfy his obligation, the debtor paid Stanford with shares in a gold mine. The mine soon started producing, netting Stanford over half a million dollars.

In 1859 Stanford got the break that would soon make him one of the state's richest men. He and a few other Sacramento merchants—including three who, with Stanford, would become known as the Big Four—attended a presentation by a railroad engineer named Theodore Judah. Judah persuaded them to invest in a railroad to be built through the Sierra foothills to the mines, a proposition that seemed dubious at the time due to the difficult terrain that would have to be crossed. Stanford and the others bought a modest number of shares, probably little suspecting that this was the beginning of a railroad empire that would make them all rich.

The transcontinental railroad was completed in 1869. Stanford and his partners, using the Central Pacific Railroad as the foundation, soon built a lucrative transportation network that extended throughout California.

Stanford's wealth enabled him to indulge his love of politics and his desire to be in the limelight. He served a two-year term as governor of California during the Civil War years, and two decades later served as U.S. Senator, an office he effectively purchased through donations to state legislators who then voted to send him to Washington (this was before senators were elected by popular vote).

In 1884, tragedy struck. Leland Stanford Jr., Leland and Jane Stanford's only child, died of typhoid at age fifteen. Casting about for a fitting memorial they eventually settled on a coeducational university to be located on Stanford's stock farm at Palo Alto. Building a university from scratch was a herculean task, but Leland Stanford Jr. University opened in 1891.

Stanford died two years later, and his university almost died with him because of his free-spending ways. He lavished money on numerous projects, including showplace mansions in San Francisco and Sacramento, his Palo Alto farm, and a 55,000-acre orchard north of Sacramento. Stanford University was built with $5 million of borrowed money. When Stanford died, and his estate became tied up in court, the school nearly closed for lack of operating funds. Jane Stanford managed to keep it open after her husband's death, thus preserving what turned out to be the finest legacy that any of the Big Four left.

Courtesy, California State Library

The Leland Stanford mansion.

Sites and Attractions

The Big Four, Nob Hill, and Victorian Homes

A Walking Tour of Nob Hill.
Location: For the purposes of this walk, Nob Hill is the area bounded by the following streets: Powell, Pine, Jones and Sacramento. Start the walk at the corner of California and Powell streets.

The Stanford and Hopkins Estates

The Big Four and the Bonanza Kings, despite their dominating presence, large fortunes, and impact on San Francisco in the late nineteenth century, left little in the way of productive, continuing legacies. Most of them concentrated their energies on building ego-gratifying mansions atop Nob Hill, which replaced South Park as the location of choice after the invention of the cable car in 1873.

Leland Stanford was the first to build on the hill, constructing an elaborate Italianate villa in 1876 where the Stanford Court Hotel stands today. The interior of the Stanford mansion was a showplace that boasted the largest private dining room in the West. In the center of the house a two-story rotunda was supported by giant red granite pillars. Overhead was a roof of amber glass. Other rooms on the main floor included an East Indian parlor, a Pompeiian drawing room, and an art gallery.

The cut stone façade of the building was equally impressive. This was partially an illusion, however, since only the first floor was of stone while the upper stories were redwood covered by plaster and scored to imitate stone. The house went up in flames during the 1906 fire. And, with the exception of the Flood mansion, whose exterior walls were entirely of stone, so did all the other Nob Hill palaces. Still, there are a few remnants from that era.

The place to start a walking tour of the area is at the southwest corner of California and Powell streets. Look diagonally across the intersection to the northeast corner where the red-brick University Club stands. This was once the site of Leland Stanford's stable. The stable's interior was more elegantly furnished than many San Francisco homes of the time.

Walk south down Powell Street. The faded, coal-black, rough-hewn stone walls you see are from the original mansion, having survived the 1906 earthquake. Stanford and Mark Hopkins, who built his home next door up the hill, employed laborers from their railroad to prepare the site and put up the retaining walls. The work crews used stone from the same quarry at Rocklin, near Sacramento, to build these walls that the Southern Pacific used to build its train tunnels and bridges.

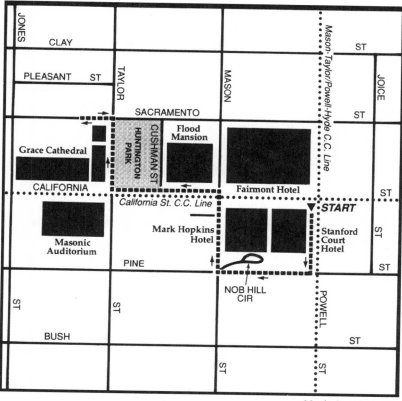

Map by Larry Van Dyke

Nob Hill Walking Tour.

Walk west on Pine Street, and halfway up the block to Mason you will see a decorative medieval tower atop the wall. This little flourish marks the dividing line between the Stanford and Hopkins properties. This turret, and others like it that once adorned this wall, were the inspiration of Mark Hopkins' wife, Mary, who was a voracious reader of historical romances. Not satisfied with being a dutiful Victorian housewife, content to be seen and not heard, she goaded her parsimonious husband into building a hilltop mansion worthy of his station. Once construction got underway she took charge, and gave free rein to her imagination. The Hopkins home went from what was planned as a rather modest dwelling to an almost whimsical fairy castle of wooden towers, Gothic spires, and ornamentation run riot—a dwelling equal to those inhabited by her fictional heroes and heroines. When finished, the home overshadowed the not insignificant Stanford mansion next door.

Both Stanford's and Hopkins's tenures in their luxurious homes were brief. Hopkins, in fact, died in 1878 before his house was completed. His wife finished the job, and married her interior decorator. By the time of the 1906 fire both homes had been converted to other uses: the Stanford mansion was turned over to Stanford University, and the Hopkins estate became the home of the Hopkins Institute of Art, which was administered by the University of California. The Mark Hopkins Hotel now occupies the latter site.

Continue up Pine Street and then take a right at the corner, which will bring you up the hill past more of the original retaining wall. When you reach the top of the hill, cross Mason and California streets to the northwest corner of the intersection. Here you will be standing at the edge of the Flood mansion. Across Mason Street is the venerable Fairmont Hotel, named for Bonanza King James Fair. Fair had plans to build a home of his own on this site, but a divorce, and his death not long afterward, put an end to them. Considering that he was worth $45 million when he died, in 1894, any house he built surely would have rivaled or surpassed the others in the neighborhood. When he died the property went to his two daughters, one of whom was largely responsible for building the Fairmont Hotel. The hotel was under construction and nearly complete in 1906 when the earthquake hit. The foundation and walls were undamaged, but the interior was gutted by the ensuing fire.

The Flood Mansion

James Flood was one of the four Bonanza Kings. He built both this Nob Hill home and a much grander country estate—Linden Towers—down the peninsula in Menlo Park. Each was appointed with the finest furnishings of the age.

The Flood mansion is the only survivor of the grand houses that adorned Nob Hill in the late nineteenth century. Although the interior was gutted in the 1906 fire, the exterior walls, made of Connecticut sandstone, proved sound and were saved. The other Nob Hill palaces, all made of wood, and most of them covered with flammable Victorian decorations, burned to the ground.

Rand Richards collection

The Flood mansion in 1904.

Flood purchased the California and Mason street property in 1882, and constructed this Italianate brownstone during 1885 and 1886. That Flood chose a New York-style brownstone over the prevailing wooden High Victorian designs of his neighbors likely stems from his desire to imitate New York's Fifth Avenue nabobs.

Cornelius Vanderbilt and others had constructed magnificent brownstone mansions just prior to this.

Among the Flood mansion's forty-two rooms were a Louis XV drawing room and a Moorish smoking room with a domed skylight. Surrounding the house was a bronze fence, which still stands. Amid Flood's platoon of servants was one grounds keeper whose sole task was to keep this rail polished and shiny. The rail polisher is long gone, and the lace-patterned fence has mercifully been allowed to corrode to a soothing green.

The building today looks much like it did a century ago, although a few unobtrusive changes have been made. The most notable are the two semicircular wings, one on each side, which were designed by the noted local architect Willis Polk. Other changes include the installation of a third floor between the second floor and the roof (notice the windows in what looks like a half story), and the enclosing of what was the carriage portico on the Sacramento Street side. The central tower in front has been lowered about ten feet to meet the roof line. All these changes were made after 1906. The building currently houses the Pacific Union Club. It is not open to the public.

The Huntington and Crocker Estates

Walk west one block on California to Taylor Street. Next door to the Flood mansion, separated by a narrow one-way street, is Huntington Park, a small, green common with a children's playground. Prior to 1906 this was the site of the Huntington mansion, a white, two-story neoclassical house—built by David Colton, the Big Four's business manager—that was relatively tasteful and restrained for the times. After Colton died it became the residence of Collis P. Huntington, the behind-the-scenes leader and real brains of the Big Four. Huntington rarely lived in the house; he spent most of his time in Washington, D.C., greasing palms and lobbying Congressmen for more favorable treatment for the Southern Pacific Railroad and the other companies he and his partners controlled. After the fire of 1906, Huntington's widow, rather than rebuild, donated the land to the city, which then created the park.

The Crocker mansion (left) and the Huntington mansion (center). Note Crocker's huge "spite fence" just beyond the Huntington residence.

Across Taylor Street from Huntington Park, where the mammoth Grace Cathedral now rises, is where the Crocker mansions once stood. Charles Crocker was the Big Four's construction chief during the building of the transcontinental railroad. In 1877, after purchasing most of the block bounded by California, Taylor, Sacramento, and Jones, he built a huge, Second Empire-style mansion on the southeast corner facing California Street. Eleven years later

Crocker built a similarly grand villa next door on the southwest corner as a wedding present for his son William.

One of the curious incidents involving the senior Crocker and this piece of land was his building of a "spite fence" at the rear of his house. When Crocker bought all the lots on the block, every homeowner would sell to him except one, a German undertaker named Nicholas Yung who owned a small house on the Sacramento Street side just off the southwest corner of Taylor Street. Crocker became enraged by Yung's refusal to sell, and to get even he built a forty-foot-high fence around the three sides of the poor man's house shutting off the natural light and the views from the house, save for those from the entrance on Sacramento Street. Yung, a combative sort, did get a measure of revenge. On the roof of his house he constructed a ten-foot-high coffin, adorned it with a skull and crossbones, and pointed it toward the Crocker mansion. Charles Crocker's reaction was not recorded.

After a couple of years, Yung moved his house off the lot to another part of town, but Crocker left the spite fence standing. It was only after both men died that the dispute was finally settled, with Yung's heirs selling the land to the Crocker family.

Cross Taylor Street to its west side, and walk one block north to Sacramento. On the south side of Sacramento Street, a few yards up from Taylor, are markers showing where the Yung house once stood. Look for the six-inch-wide granite stones laid from the fence to the curb. They are easy to find, since one extends from each of the major pillars between the corner and the entrance to the parking lot—which originally was the carriage entrance to the Crocker grounds.

Walk back down Sacramento Street, turn right on Taylor, and stop as soon as you round the corner. Look carefully at the sidewalk next to the corner granite pillar and you will see some faint, hard to read letters stamped into the concrete. It is the sidewalk manufacturer's mark, and it reads:

CALIFORNIA ASP Co.
SCHILLINGER PATENT
Pat July 19th 1870
Reissue May 2nd 1871

ASP stands for Artificial Stone Paving, the name of the local contractor who paved the sidewalk. By comparing the sidewalk panel containing this legend to the surrounding surfaces you can see that about half of the Sacramento Street sidewalk is still original, laid down in the late 1870s.

The iron fence around the property dates from 1876–77. The black patina of the fence's granite base, and the flecks and chips missing from the wall, were caused by the heat of the 1906 fire.

Stanford University.

Location: Stanford University is located in Palo Alto. The campus is bounded by El Camino Real on the east, Interstate 280 on the west, Willow Road on the north, and Page Mill Road on the south.

Except for their names attached to Nob Hill hotels, the Big Four and the other nabobs did not leave much of anything of permanence to posterity. The notable exception was Leland Stanford, who, after his son, Leland Jr., died of typhoid fever at age fifteen, decided to establish an institution of higher learning in his memory.

Stanford's first choice was to found a technical school that would adjoin the University of California at Berkeley. He accordingly had himself appointed to the board of regents by the governor, but he became embroiled in a political dispute, and the appointment was not confirmed by the legislature. Rebuffed, Stanford decided to found a separate college, and thus Stanford University was born.

The site chosen for the campus was Stanford's Palo Alto stock farm, an eight-thousand-acre spread thirty miles south of San Francisco. Leland Stanford did things in a large way, and his stock farm, where he bred and raised prize-winning trotting horses, was no exception. In the 1880s it had the largest and finest stable in the world, boasting stalls for six hundred horses. Sixty acres of carrots were planted yearly just to feed the colts. Stanford himself would sometimes sit for hours in his carriage by the oval track, watching his trainers put his horses through their paces.

The horse farm was also the site of an experiment that was an early forerunner of motion pictures. A common belief at the time was that an animal on the run had to have at least one foot on the ground at all times. Stanford thought otherwise, and to prove it he hired the celebrated photographer Eadweard Muybridge to photograph his horses at a gallop.

Muybridge's initial attempts were failures, since his camera was too slow to provide the necessary stop action. After further experimentation, he set up a battery of twenty-four sequentially-timed cameras that enabled him to freeze-frame the action. It did indeed show that a horse at a gallop was at times completely off the ground. The twenty-four-frames-a-second speed developed by Muybridge is today the standard for motion pictures.

One of the stock farm's original red barns, dating from about 1878 and once part of a cluster of similar structures, still stands on the northern edge of campus just off Electioneer Drive. Even now it is a working horse farm, owned by the university and leased to a private individual who stables horses and gives riding lessons. A state historical stone marker and plaque a short distance away on Campus Drive West provides the details of the farm's connection to the development of motion pictures.

The campus itself, whose initial buildings surround the main quad and are a combination of Richardson Romanesque and Mission Revival styles, was designed by Frederick Law Olmsted, creator of New York's Central Park. The school opened its doors in 1891, but went through difficult times after Leland Stanford died in 1893. The university was nearly insolvent at the time of his death from his prodigious spending on various projects, and his widow Jane was left to shoulder the burden of establishing what was to become one of the country's great universities.

When Jane Stanford died in 1905 she was interred in the mausoleum containing her husband and son. The granite-faced structure, flanked by sphinxes, is located on the campus in a grove bounded by Quarry Road, Campus Drive East, Palm Drive, and Arboretum Road.

Cantor Arts Center at Stanford University.

Location: Museum Way and Lomita Drive, Stanford University campus, Stanford. **Phone:** (650) 723-4177. **Hours:** Wednesday – Sunday, 11 a.m. to 5 p.m. (Thursday to 8 p.m.) Closed Monday, Tuesday, and major holidays. **Admission:** Free. **Website:** www.museum.stanford.edu.

The university's art museum contains the previously mentioned golden spike and other Stanford family memorabilia. Among these items are a book of Muybridge's photographs of trotting horses in motion. The book is closed but a nearby illustration shows a horse with all four feet in the air—exactly what Stanford was trying to prove. Other photographs include shots of all three Stanford family homes in California: on Nob Hill in San Francisco, in Sacramento, and in Palo Alto. Several Muybridge's photos of the opulent interiors, including one of Stanford's private art gallery in his Nob Hill home, are also on view.

The Haas – Lilienthal House.

Location: 2007 Franklin Street (near Jackson), San Francisco. **Phone:** (415) 441-3004. **Hours:** Sundays 11 a.m. to 4 p.m., Wednesdays and Saturdays, Noon to 3 p.m. Docent-led tours. **Admission:** Adults $8.00, Children and Seniors, $5.00. **Website:** www.sfheritage.org.

The Haas-Lilienthal House is the only Victorian house in San Francisco with its original furnishings that is open to the public. The City is fortunate to have it, not only because the descendants of the original owners donated it to a local preservation group in 1973, but because the 1906 fire was halted at Van Ness Avenue, only a block away. Made of redwood, the house surely would have gone up in flames had not the fire been stopped where it was.

The house was built in 1886 by William Haas, a German immigrant who created a successful wholesale grocery business in San Francisco. (Haas's descendants today are part owners of Levi Strauss & Company and formerly owned the Oakland A's baseball team.) It is a prime example of a late nineteenth century upper-middle-class house. It cost more than eighteen thousand dollars, which certainly is not in the million-dollar-plus range of the Nob Hill mansions but is still a tidy sum when you consider that the average house of the time cost about two thousand dollars.

Architecturally, the house combines elements of both the Stick style, with its characteristic rectangular bay windows, and Queen Anne Tower style—distinguished by the rounded corner tower— popular during the 1880s and 1890s. Except for the chimneys and fireplaces on the south wall, which were added about 1900, the exterior of the house looks the same today as when it was built. Even the gray paint is believed to be the same as the original color.

Inside the house are to be found most of the original furnishings. Although some of the furniture was updated as the twentieth-century inhabitants decorated to suit their needs and the changing times, the interior still strongly reflects the Victorian era and its emphasis on propriety. Rooms on the main floor are divided by sliding doors to keep out kitchen smells and small children. Heavy drapes and formal furniture still decorate the high-ceilinged rooms paneled in golden oak and mahogany. Upstairs, in the family quarters, a real highlight is the master bathroom with its elaborate plumbing, including a bidet, gas fixtures, and antique glass medicine bottles.

Barbary Coast Vice

The Barbary Coast.

Location: The Barbary Coast initially was centered around lower Pacific Avenue and Broadway, and included the area east of Kearny Street to the waterfront. Later it expanded west toward Chinatown and south toward the financial district.

Not much remains of the once notorious Barbary Coast. Its descendants—the handful of topless clubs clustered near the intersection of Broadway and Columbus—bear little resemblance to their perverted and depraved ancestors. There is still plenty of flesh on display in the few remaining clubs, and they seem to draw their share of sailors, Japanese tourists, and fresh-faced youngsters just turned twenty-one with their ID's to prove it. But a few scantily clad females bumping and grinding to canned music doesn't compare to the early days when stage attractions sometimes featured women having sex with animals. Any nineteenth-century habitué of the Coast who returned today would find the current scene tame indeed. Pacific Avenue, between Kearny and Montgomery streets, once the raucous heart of the district (it was called "Terrific Pacific"), is now a quiet, treelined thoroughfare of law firms, antique dealers, and other small businesses.

The only building remaining that provides even a hint of the neighborhood's old character is the former Hippodrome bar and dance hall at 555 Pacific Avenue, off Kearny Street. It dates from after 1906, and is the third Hippodrome to occupy the site. Long shuttered, its carnival-like bulb lighting and friezes of naked maidens are the only visual reminders of the Barbary Coast's heyday.

A Walking Tour of Historic Chinatown.

Location: The main body of Chinatown, which is sandwiched between Nob Hill and the financial district, is encompassed by California, Stockton, Broadway, Columbus, and Kearny streets. The spine is Grant Avenue, which runs through the middle of Chinatown from Bush to Broadway. This walk will take you from the corner of Jackson and Stockton, three blocks to Sacramento via several alleys, and then will turn back one block to finish at Grant and Clay streets.

Chinatown, which adjoined the Barbary Coast, also had much to offer those looking for vice. The district, like the rest of downtown, was leveled by the 1906 earthquake and fire.

The origins of Chinatown go back to The City's early days. Chinese had been in San Francisco since the gold rush, but they did not congregate in any particular area until the late 1850s and early 1860s, when Western merchants started moving from the Portsmouth Square area to the new shopping districts emerging on Market Street and at Union Square. As the whites departed, the Chinese moved into the buildings they abandoned. By the 1870s and 1880s, faced with increasing hostility toward them by the white majority, the Chinese withdrew into that portion of the city bounded by California, Stockton, Broadway, and Kearny streets, creating the predecessor of today's larger Chinatown.

Despite the lack of tangible remnants from the earlier era, a walk through the district can provide a glimpse of what pre-1906 Chinatown was like. It can also offer a look not only at what replaced it, but it will give you a sense of the Chinese and their enclave, which is so thoroughly entwined with The City's history.

Chinatown's alleys, which were carved through city blocks in the 1870s to create more space in this densely populated quarter, were the scene of some of the more abhorrent incidents in San

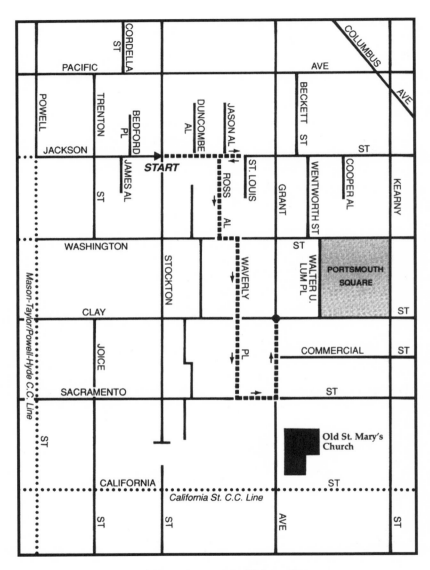

Chinatown Walking Tour

Francisco's history. Inasmuch as the residents of nineteenth-century Chinatown were overwhelmingly male—men intending to make their fortunes and then either send for their families or return to China—it is not surprising that illicit services flourished. Gambling, prostitution, and drugs such as opium were rife. And although such establishments abounded throughout the area's confines, much of the activity clustered in these alleys.

The place to start a walking tour of Chinatown's alleys and streets is at the northeast corner of Stockton and Jackson streets. Walk east—downhill—on Jackson toward Grant Avenue. About mid-block on the left is a narrow dead-end, Duncombe Alley. In the 1870s and 1880s this crevice was lined with opium dens, some of them underground in the cellars. Today, the spaces are occupied by Chinese seamstresses, hunched over their sewing machines, doing piecework for local clothing manufacturers.

Cross over to the other side of Jackson and walk a few steps farther down to St. Louis Alley. This cramped walkway was once the site of a notorious slave market, where young Chinese girls were stripped naked and auctioned off to begin a life of involuntary prostitution. Now only the clatter of mah-jong tiles echoes down this path.

Walk back up Jackson a short distance on the same side and enter Ross Alley. This inviting thoroughfare, which leads to Washington Street, was once known as the "Street of the Gamblers," because it housed no fewer than twenty-two gambling dens. Each entry door was fortified with iron boiler plate to thwart police raids.

At the end of the alley go across Washington, turn to the left, and then take the first right, which is Waverly, a two-block-long street. In April 1879, Waverly Place (then called Pike Street) was the scene of a bloody battle between two tongs that fought over ownership rights to a Chinese slave girl. Over fifty participants engaged in hand-to-hand combat, and at least four were killed.

Waverly Place today is a placid corridor lined primarily with the offices of various Chinese associations. On the west side, only a few doors from Washington Street, is one of several temples in Chinatown open to the public. Called the Tin How, which is an Anglicized version of Tien Hau, the goddess of sailors and sojourners, it provides an evocative look at the age-old Chinese form of worship. (Unlike the organized group worship familiar to Christians, Chinese faithful pray privately to individual gods.) The temple is located on the top floor of 125 Waverly, up a good three flights of stairs from the street. It is open seven days a week, 10 a.m. to 4 p.m. Admission by donation.

Waverly Place is also a good spot to see some of the more elaborate chinoiserie façades that have been added to what are relatively plain Edwardian buildings put up after 1906. The west side of Waverly abounds with examples of this ornamental decoration. Also look back toward Washington Street, where the three-story building and its even more striking neighbor just to its right provide additional architectural riches.

Pre-1906 Chinatown was composed of the same Italianate-style buildings as the rest of the city. It was only the decorations, such as red paper lanterns hanging from balconies, and sign boards, and wall posters with Chinese characters, that set the area apart. It was after 1906, and particularly during the 1920s, that the pagoda roofs and other colorful embellishments were added. This remodeling effort was primarily the idea of the local merchants association, which thought it would promote tourism and erase Chinatown's opium den and slave girl image.

Proceed down Waverly to Sacramento Street, turn left to Grant Avenue, and then left again. Grant Avenue's original name was Dupont Street, after naval officer Samuel F. DuPont. The name was changed to Grant Avenue in honor of President Ulysses S. Grant after his death in 1885, although the Chinatown portion was not renamed until 1908, after the earthquake.

Go north on Grant half a block until you see Commercial Street on the right side. This modest street sits virtually in the shadows of the financial district. Yet the first block, extending down to Kearny Street, still retains the scale and much of the flavor of nineteenth-century San Francisco. Many of these buildings housed brothels in the decade after 1906.

Continue north on Grant half a block and stop at the corner of Clay Street. The little open-air shop on the northwest corner selling T-shirts, and knickknacks from foldout wooden benches and boxes recalls Chinatown before the 1906 earthquake and fire, when this type of sidewalk vendor was common.

San Francisco's Maritime Heritage

> ### The Hyde Street Pier.
> **Location:** 2905 Hyde Street (on the bay at the foot of Hyde Street), San Francisco. **Phone:** (415) 561-7100. **Hours:** Open daily Memorial Day to mid-October, 9:30 a.m. to 5:30 p.m.; mid-October to Memorial Day, 9:30 a.m. to 5 p.m. You can board the *Balclutha,* the *C. A. Thayer,* and the *Eureka* ferryboat for self-guided tours. There are ranger-guided tours of the *Balclutha,* and periodically of the *Eureka* (of the engine room only). **Admission:** The pier itself is free, but it costs $5.00 for Adults (16+) to board the ships. Children 15 and under are free. **Website:** www.nps.gov/safr.

The Hyde Street Pier (or San Francisco Maritime State Historic Park, as it is officially known) has one of the finest collections of historic ships in the world. You can read books, look at photographs, and visit museums, but nothing evokes the great era of sail more than actually being aboard a sailing ship. The Hyde Street Pier has several fine examples, as well as other vessels and maritime artifacts. Among them are the following:

The *Balclutha*

This three-masted square rigger was one of the last sailing ships built; steam-powered vessels soon thereafter replaced the graceful windjammers. She was built in Scotland in 1886 and made her maiden voyage to San Francisco, which soon became her home port and remained so for the rest of her service.

During her career the *Balclutha* journeyed to ports such as Antwerp, Capetown, and Melbourne, carrying such diverse cargo as grain, coal, guano, and jute gunny sacks. She rounded Cape Horn seventeen times. But her main duty in her last few decades was on the salmon run, visiting Alaskan ports and returning to San Francisco loaded with cases of canned salmon. In 1930, after the end of her active service, she was purchased and then renovated by a promoter who put in at various West Coast ports and touted her as a pirate ship, based on a bit part she played in the 1934 movie *Mutiny on the Bounty.* In 1954 she was purchased for a modest sum, restored, and preserved as a historic ship.

Although the permanently moored *Balclutha* can no longer raise her sails, to walk her decks today, feel her gently sway beneath your feet, and admire her brass fittings and polished woods, is to invoke the spirit of the golden age of sail.

Inside the vessel, below the main decks, are a number of exhibits and nautical artifacts. One of the highlights is the captain's cabin in the aft of the ship. This cozy Victorian sitting room, with its comfortable sofas and settees surrounded by highly polished bird's-eye maple and mahogany walls, provided the captain and his wife

Rand Richards

The *Balclutha* at Hyde Street pier.

(captain's wives, more often than not, accompanied their husbands on these voyages) with a measure of comfort in what was essentially a harsh environment. Also note the gas-fueled brass hurricane lamp, and the small bar, suspended from the ceiling, containing liquor bottles and stemware.

Back on deck, in the forward part of the ship, is the forecastle. This small, cramped room with its hard wooden bunks gives an idea of how the ordinary sailors lived and relaxed in between their backbreaking chores. It also graphically illustrates the contrast between their lot and that of the captain.

Scattered throughout the rest of the ship are displays of nautical gear along with descriptive boards that provide historical background and explanations of how the gadgets worked. Also of interest, on the lowermost deck is a recreated cargo hold stacked with replica cases of wine, olive oil, and mustard, furniture in crates, jute gunnysacks, and boxes of Alaskan salmon.

The *C. A. Thayer*

This three-masted schooner, built in 1895, at first carried lumber from the redwood forests north of the bay down the coast to San Francisco. Later she served the fishing industry in Alaska and the North Pacific, bringing salmon and salted cod through the Golden Gate to Bay Area consumers. When the *C. A. Thayer* made her final voyage in 1950, it was the last by a commercial sailing ship on the West Coast. After her retirement, she too was put on display as a "pirate ship" before being rescued and saved for posterity.

On board the *Thayer*, period artifacts strongly convey what a no-frills, workaday windjammer this once was. Near the entry is the galley with its utensils and plain white dishes. Around the corner in the donkey room is a large boiler that would have been used as an auxiliary while the ship was in port.

Also on the main deck, at the after end, be sure to see the small but charming captain's cabin. Not as luxurious as the one on the *Balclutha*, it nonetheless is fitted with the homey touches of a late Victorian parlor: a hardwood couch covered in red satin, a claw-footed table and stool, a child's chair, a brass bird cage, and a rolltop desk—since the cabin served as the captain's office as well as living quarters. (Note: some of these items may not be on display at the time of your visit.)

Below the main deck, in the dark underbelly of the ship, are more panels with photos providing greater detail on the *Thayer's* career. Up in the forecastle are the hard, wooden slat berths of the sailors and fishermen, a graphic illustration, once again, of the crews' subservience to the captain and his officers.

The ferryboat *Eureka*

Across the dock from the *Balclutha* and the *C. A. Thayer* is a vessel of much different shape, but one that also got its start on San Francisco Bay about the same time as her two neighbors. The *Eureka* is a steam-driven paddle-wheel ferryboat. Originally named the *Ukiah*, she was built in 1890 and served during her early years as a combination railway car and passenger ferry. In 1920, as the automobile gained ascendancy, she was converted to an auto and passenger ferry and renamed *Eureka*. She made the San Francisco to

Sausalito run for many years, and docked daily at the very pier that is her permanent home today.

On the lower deck of the *Eureka* there is an evocative lineup of 1920s and 1930s vintage autos, looking as though they are ready to be driven off on to city streets as soon as the boat docks. You can also visit one of the two wheelhouses, examine the bay depth charts, and imagine that you are piloting one of these monsters through the bay. For those who are mechanically minded, park rangers give below-decks tours of the engine and boiler rooms.

Despite the advent of the Golden Gate and Bay bridges in the 1930s, the *Eureka* continued her ferry duties until 1957, when in mid-voyage an engine crank pin snapped, putting her out of service. She was virtually the last survivor of a continuous bay ferry tradition dating back to the early days of the gold rush. Regular service on the bay ended in 1958. In 1970, limited commuter ferry service using sleek diesel-powered boats connected Marin County to San Francisco; it continues today, with an expanded schedule.

Besides the three vessels mentioned above, the Hyde Street Pier has other attractions as well. Bobbing on the water near the *C. A. Thayer* are replica feluccas of the type used by Italian immigrant fishermen; they were quite common on the bay from 1850 to about 1920. Also of interest on and around the pier are a turn-of-the-century houseboat, the wheelhouse of a tugboat, and the scow schooner *Alma*, a shallow-draft boat that once plied the bay's inland waterways carrying bricks, bundles of hay, and similar cargo.

Visitor Center, Haslett Warehouse.
Location: 499 Jefferson Street, corner of Hyde. **Phone:** (415) 447-5000.
Hours: 9:30 a.m. to 5 p.m., with extended summer hours. **Admission:** Free. **Website:** www.nps.gov/safr.

Just across from the Hyde Street Pier, the Visitor Center contains detailed scale models of all the major vessels on the Pier. An array of artifacts provide evidence of what life was like on board such vessels. On view is a holystone—a heavy block of pumice used for scrubbing ships' decks, a belaying pin, leg irons, and a medical kit a captain would have used to treat shipboard injuries. There is also a 1919 photo of two sailors in the forecastle of a ship that strongly resembles the *Balclutha*.

The National Maritime Museum.
Location: At the foot of Polk Street adjacent to Aquatic Park, San Francisco. **Phone:** (415) 561-7100. **Hours:** Open daily, 10 a.m. to 5 p.m. **Admission:** Free. **Closed** until 2009 for renovation. **Website:** www.nps.gov/safr.

On the second floor of this building, which is around the corner from the gold rush exhibit mentioned in Chapter 4, are objects illustrating this particular period of San Francisco history. On view are a few artifacts from The City's days as a whaling port: a model of a whaling ship, photos and lithographs, and several harpoons, including a mean-looking exploding harpoon. There are also displays on shipbuilding in the Bay Area, yachting on San Francisco Bay, riverboats on the inland waterways, and on the local fishing industry. The latter is supplemented by many photographs, including one of Fisherman's Wharf in the early days, and several of feluccas and Chinese junks fishing in bay waters. There are also several photos of the *Balclutha* (at that time named the *Star of Alaska*) and her crew, including a fine one of her under sail off the Golden Gate in the 1920s.

The Cable Cars

The Cable Cars.
Location: See the map on page 162 for the cable car routes. **Hours:** Cars start running about 6 a.m., and make their last run between 12:30 a.m. and 1 a.m. Signs at the embarkation point and at most intersections provide exact times. **Admission:** $3.00 per ride. $1.00 from 9 p.m. to 7 a.m. for Seniors (65+) and the disabled. All day passes cost $11.00 apiece, and provide unlimited rides on cable cars and on the Muni's buses and streetcars. **Website:** www.sfmta.com.

The cable cars are one of San Francisco's trademarks and, with the possible exception of the Golden Gate Bridge, symbolize San Francisco more than any other attraction. At one time many American cities, including New York, Chicago, Denver, and even

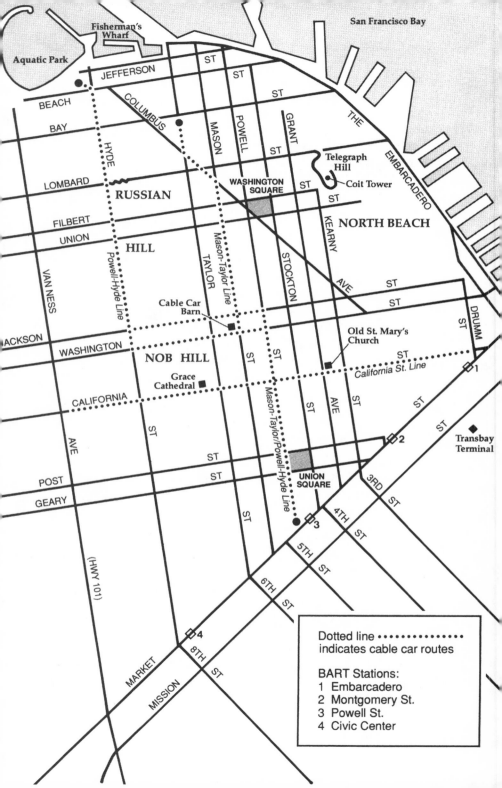

Oakland, had passenger cable cars; so did cities in Europe, Australia, and New Zealand. San Francisco now has the only surviving cable car system.

A few modifications have been made in the design since the first car was put into operation in 1873, but the basic method of locomotion has remained largely unchanged. The operating principle is quite simple. Beneath the slots in the streets where the cable cars run is a continuously moving woven steel cable that wraps around huge wheels in the powerhouse (where the cable car museum is) forming a complete loop. A car moves when a "gripman" on board pulls the lever that engages a steel grip, like a giant pair of pliers, which clamps on to the moving cable, propelling the car along at a maximum speed of nine and a half miles an hour. To take on and let off passengers, the grip is released, the gripman hauls on the brake lever, and the car comes to a stop.

Because of stress and friction, cables wear out quickly and have to be replaced several times a year. The steel dies or clamps, which are the only parts that grip the cables, have an even shorter life. They typically last only three to four days before being replaced.

At one time almost a dozen different cable car lines—and as many companies—operated in San Francisco, with routes extending a total of 112 miles over city streets. Today, three city-owned lines cover just 10.5 miles, all in the northeast corner of town.

There are two types of cable car: single-ended and double-ended. Single-ended cars only go in one direction and are reversed on turntables at their terminuses to make the return journey. Double-ended cars have controls at both ends and do not need to be turned around. The Mason-Taylor and Powell-Hyde lines use single-ended cars, while the double-ended cars are on the California Street line.

The Cable Car Barn and Museum.

Location: 1201 Mason Street (at Washington), San Francisco. **Phone:** (415) 474-1887. **Hours:** Open daily, April thru September, 10 a.m. to 6 p.m.; October thru March, 10 a.m. to 5 p.m. Closed Thanksgiving, Christmas, and New Year's Day. **Admission:** Free. **Website:** www. cablecarmuseum.org.

This unique museum is housed in the cable car barn, which dates from 1909. The previous building was built in 1887, but like almost everything else in the area it suffered major damage in the 1906 earthquake and fire. Amazingly, except for the loss of a few bricks from the crown on top, the chimney at the rear survived the disaster. Until 1911 the cable machinery was powered by steam from giant boilers; the steam was vented through this chimney.

The museum inside houses Andrew Hallidie's original 1873 cable car. It, along with at least twenty-seven other cars, managed to escape the conflagration of 1906. (The 1873 car was in Baltimore for an exhibition and thus escaped destruction, while the others were on lines outside the fire-consumed downtown area.) Two other antique cars, dating from 1876, are on view, as are scale models of a variety of other cable cars that have appeared on city streets in years past. Also on display are a couple of grips and related machinery. The exhibits are supplemented by photographs and descriptive panels. From both the museum deck and from a room in the basement you can watch the steel cables come winding in and out of the building—truly a one-of-a-kind attraction.

Golden Gate Park and
The Midwinter Fair of 1894

Golden Gate Park.
Location: The park extends from the Great Highway, at the Pacific Ocean, three and a half miles inland to Stanyan Street, its eastern border. The half-mile-wide park is bounded by Fulton Street on the north and Lincoln Street on the south.

One of the finest urban parks in the country, Golden Gate Park has a wealth of inviting sights and attractions. Several of those remaining from the Gilded Age are the Conservatory of Flowers, which was California's first municipal greenhouse, the music concourse, and the Japanese Tea Garden; the latter two are survivors from the 1894 Midwinter Fair.

Courtesy, the Oakland Museum
Golden Gate Park's Conservatory of Flowers in 1887.

The Conservatory of Flowers.

Location: Off John F. Kennedy Drive at the east end of Golden Gate Park, San Francisco. **Phone:** (415) 666-7001. **Hours:** Open Tuesday - Sunday, 9 a.m. to 4:30 p.m. Closed Mondays. **Admission:** Adults, $5.00; Youth (12–17), Students with ID and Seniors (65+), $3.00; Children (5–11), $1.50; under 5, Free. **Website:** www.conservatoryofflowers.org.

Erected in 1879, the Conservatory is the oldest building in Golden Gate Park. It might not have ended up there had James Lick, its owner, not died in 1876 before he could construct it on his San Jose estate. Lick was one of San Francisco's first millionaires, and he had ordered the conservatory for the grounds of his South Bay home. The structure was left to the Society of California Pioneers, who sold it for $2,600 to Charles Crocker and a group of other prominent businessmen who had agreed in advance to donate it to the park.

The building is modeled after one in Kew Gardens, London, and is made of wood with the exception of the columns, which are of iron. The central dome was severely damaged by a fire in 1883, but was reconstructed within a few years. The structure came through the 1906 earthquake almost unscathed, suffering only a few shattered panes of glass. At the beginning of each summer the exterior is whitewashed to protect the plants from sunlight.

Inside, one is reminded of *The Little Shop of Horrors,* since upon entering you are immediately overwhelmed by towering Amazon-like plants with leaves the size of elephant ears. With the filtered sunlight and a fine mist sprayed every few minutes from pipes strung throughout, plants thrive in the pampered environment. Even ordinary house plants such as pothos and Swedish ivy grow to huge dimensions here. But despite the sense of being engulfed by foliage, a stroll around reveals nature's botanical richness in all its variety, sheltered under the Gothic tracery of the Conservatory.

The Music Concourse

Location: In Golden Gate Park half a mile west of the Conservatory.

Where the Music Concourse and the various museums are today is where the Midwinter Fair of 1894 was held. The shallow, flat valley and the sculptured embankments between the museum buildings were created for the fair. The area, called the Grand Concourse at the time, was renamed the Music Concourse after the Spreckels band shell was built in 1900. The groundbreaking for the fair was held in August 1893 at the spot where the bronze statue, Roman Gladiator, stands today, across from the de Young Museum. About 150 yards farther east on Tea Garden Drive (the roadway in front of the de Young) is another statue, called Apple Cider Press, which dates from the fair. Across from it are two concrete sphinxes marking what was the entrance to the fair's fine arts museum, one of five major buildings put up for the exposition.

After the fair closed, in July 1894, the fine arts museum was the only one not torn down. Although heavily damaged by the 1906 earthquake, it was repaired and continued in use until its descendant, the M. H. de Young Memorial Museum, opened in 1919. Three years earlier, the California Academy of Sciences North American

Hall had opened. These two buildings were the nucleus of what has become a cluster of further halls and additions (and remodelings) to both museums over the ensuing years.

The 1919 de Young was torn down in the early 21st century and replaced with an all new structure in 2005.

The Japanese Tea Garden.

Location: On Tea Garden Drive across from the Spreckels band shell in Golden Gate Park, San Francisco. **Phone:** (415) 752-4227. **Hours:** March to October, Tea Garden open daily, 9 a.m. to 6 p.m.; November to February, 9 a.m. to 4:45 p.m. **Admission:** Adults, $4.00; Seniors, $1.50; Children (6–12), $1.50; under 6, Free. Free admission Monday, Wednesday, and Friday, 9 to 10 a.m.

The Japanese Tea Garden, which was originally called the Japanese Village, was the most popular concession at the 1894 fair and is its only survivor. It was first operated by a peripatetic Australian named George Turner Marsh, who had lived in Japan before emigrating to San Francisco. (Marsh, who was born in a suburb of Melbourne called Richmond, once owned a house among the sand dunes at Twelfth and Clement streets. He named the surrounding locality after his birthplace, which is why the area north of Golden Gate Park is today known as the Richmond district.)

Marsh also had an estate in Mill Valley, where he employed a number of Japanese to build a garden and a large Oriental gate. When he was awarded the Tea Garden concession, he shipped the gate and his workers across the bay to construct the Japanese Village for the fair. The present main entrance gate is a made-in-Japan replica that was put up in 1985 to replace the deteriorating original. The teahouse is also a reconstruction.

When the exposition ended, Marsh sold the concession to the park's commissioners. They hired a native Japanese, Makoto Hagiwara, to tend the gardens and operate the teahouse. Hagiwara and his descendants ran the tea garden almost continuously until 1942, when grandson George, his family, and all other resident Japanese-Americans were sent to detention camps. Since then the Tea Garden has been operated by the City and County of San Francisco and maintained by the park's gardeners.

Makoto Hagiwara, incidentally, is usually credited with being the inventor of the fortune cookie, a product which he served in his teahouse. It was a popular novelty, which Hagiwara unfortunately failed to patent, and it was quickly copied by Chinese restauranteurs in San Francisco, who went on to make it a world-famous staple of every Chinese meal.

The Japanese Tea Garden today is a sylvan retreat of bonsai trees, azaleas and Japanese exotics. It is pleasant to meander along its tranquil pathways, and soothing to pause for quiet reflection.

Sutro Heights

Sutro Heights, The Cliff House, and Sutro Baths Ruins.
Location: All these sights are located on Point Lobos Avenue at Ocean Beach, where San Francisco meets the Pacific Ocean. Sutro Heights is a public park, part of the Golden Gate National Recreation Area, as are the Sutro Baths ruins below the Cliff House. U.S. park rangers periodically give tours of both sites. **Phone:** (415) 561-4323 for tour information. The park's visitor center has closed and will reopen in the future in a new home on Merrie Way, above the Sutro Baths ruins. **Website:** www.nps.gov/goga.

At the westernmost edge of San Francisco sits the Cliff House, Sutro Heights Park, and the ruins of the Sutro Baths. In the 1890s, all three were the property of Adolph Sutro, one of The City's leading citizens. (He was also mayor of San Francisco from 1895 to 1897.) Sutro was a German immigrant who made his fortune on the Comstock by building a drainage tunnel to siphon ground water that was hampering operations at the lower levels of the mines. With perfect timing, he sold the tunnel in 1880, just before the Comstock was found to be depleted, and invested his profits in San Francisco real estate. Among his acquisitions was the land at Ocean Beach. San Franciscans considered him a fool when he bought it, since it was mostly sand and dunes at the time, but he proved them wrong by successfully developing the property.

By the 1890s Sutro had ensconced himself in a cliff-side home with sweeping views down the beach and out over the ocean. A parapet, used as an observatory, rimmed the western edge of the property and the grounds were studded with life-size copies of ancient Greek and Roman statues. Although Sutro died in 1898, his daughter, Emma, lived in the house until her death in 1938. The land was then donated to the City and County of San Francisco. The house and other structures were razed in 1939, and most of the statuary was carted off. The grounds were turned into a public park. Only the stone lions at the front gate, a statue of Diana on the

Marilyn Blaisdell collection

Interior of the Sutro Baths.

grounds, and part of the parapet survive from Sutro's time.

Directly below his estate, on the edge of the Pacific Ocean, Sutro also built what was the third of six Cliff Houses to occupy the site. It was constructed in 1896, and was a grandiose imitation German castle. It survived the 1906 earthquake and fire only to succumb to a separate fire in September 1907. A smaller and more modest Cliff House, has since replaced it.

But of the three projects Sutro undertook on his ocean front land, his greatest achievement was the Sutro Baths. Only the ruins remain; the cement foundations can be seen on the beach north of the Cliff House. The Baths opened to the public in 1896. At a time when public bathhouses were common, it was the largest such facility in the world. It boasted seven swimming pools—six saltwater and one fresh-water—and five hundred dressing rooms. Its several stories, including promenades and spectator galleries, could accommodate more than twenty thousand people at a time. The whole complex was covered over by a two-acre roof made of 100,000 panes of glass.

The entrance to this pleasure palace was a Grecian temple replica that stood at the curve on Point Lobos, midway between the Cliff House buildings and the free-standing restaurant to the east. Once inside, visitors could swim, just watch, visit the gymnasium, or stay for a stage production in the theater. There was also a museum housing what Sutro referred to as "bric-a-brac": stuffed wild animals, suits of medieval armor, Egyptian mummies, some of the midget Tom Thumb's personal effects—even a carnival made of toothpicks.

The Sutro Baths was a popular attraction for the first few decades after it opened, but as times changed, attendance dwindled, and, in 1954, with the baths themselves needing much work, they closed. An ice-skating rink, converted from one of the pools, remained open until early 1966, when it closed for good. On June 26, 1966, when the building was in the process of being demolished, a fire of undetermined origin finished the job, burning it to the ground.

8

Earthquake and Fire (1906)

In the early morning of April 18, 1906 San Francisco was struck by one of the largest earthquakes ever recorded in North America. At first, the loss of life seemed to be light, and the damage moderate. But a crippling blow had been struck when the quake severed The City's water mains. Small, scattered fires soon grew into one huge conflagration, and without adequate water to fight it, much of San Francisco was consumed by the time the fire was finally brought under control three days later.

The 1906 fire, which was more destructive than both the great London fire of 1666 and the Chicago fire of 1871, was the greatest natural calamity ever to befall a major American city.

The Earthquake

The earthquake struck at 5:12 a.m.; it was preceded by an audible rumbling. Other than a few newsboys, deliverymen, and police officers who were already up at that hour, most San Franciscans were still in their beds when the first big jolt hit.

The first tremor lasted forty seconds. It was followed by a ten-second respite, which was succeeded by another, even stronger twenty-five seconds of vibrations. The Richter scale had not yet been invented, but most subsequent evaluations have rated the temblor at about 7.9 (on a scale of 10), giving it an explosive force of almost thirty times greater than the 6.8 magnitude quake of October 1989—which only lasted fifteen seconds. The April 18 tremor was so powerful—the equivalent of close to 15 million tons of TNT—that its vibrations were recorded as far as away as Birmingham, England.

The quake emanated from the now famous San Andreas fault. The fault had only been discovered in 1893 by a geologist named

Andrew Lawson, who found it by noticing similarities between the valley beneath which it lay and neighboring valleys where faults were known to exist. He named it for San Andreas Lake in San Mateo County, under which it runs.

The 600-mile-long fault is formed at the juncture of two tectonic plates deep in the earth's crust. In northern California the San Andreas fault roughly parallels the coastline but does not lie under San Francisco proper; it dips underwater at Daly City and reemerges on land at Point Reyes, north of the Golden Gate. East of the fault is the North American Plate, upon which rests much of the American land mass. Composed primarily of sandstone and serpentine rock, it is moving south. Abutting it to the west is the Pacific Plate, which is composed of granite and marble. It is moving north.

The plates shift on an average of two inches a year, although the movement varies widely from year to year. Years or even decades can pass with little movement, as the two plates become locked together. But then the stored energy is abruptly released in a violent earthquake, and the two plates will lurch past each other by fifteen or more feet, as they did on the San Andreas fault in April 1906.

The earthquake's epicenter was offshore, just a few miles south of the Golden Gate. The huge shudder originating there affected cities and towns along a two-hundred-mile stretch, from Fort Bragg on the Mendocino coast to San Juan Bautista near Monterey Bay.

North of The City, Santa Rosa was hit hard; most of its downtown buildings collapsed. To the south, the Stanford University campus suffered heavy damage. Several of the recently completed structures were reduced to piles of rubble, while others, although still standing, were so badly damaged that they were later torn down. San Jose also received its share of death and destruction. Over one hundred people were killed—trapped under collapsed buildings or killed by falling debris. Curiously, although the quake caused harm as much as forty miles inland, Oakland and Berkeley, just across the bay, were little affected.

In San Francisco itself, eyewitnesses reported seeing the ground undulate in waves as high as two or three feet. In some places tears in the earth ripped through streets, shifting and twisting streetcar rails. Elsewhere, sidewalks buckled and split; fire hydrants were knocked loose, spilling precious water. In the city's cemeteries, at least five hundred tombstones toppled over. They all fell toward the east.

Buildings on landfill, particularly those made of unreinforced brick and mortar, suffered heavy damage. But even structures on solid ground felt the brunt. Thick wooden beams sometimes splintered. More vulnerable brick and stone veneers peeled away, falling in clumps, shattering in the streets, blocking access, and leaving their structures looking like dollhouses with their interiors exposed. Inside dwellings, pictures were thrown off walls, plaster showered down, and chimneys toppled, collapsing through roofs— in a few cases killing people sleeping in their beds.

Marilyn Blaisdell collection

Buildings on landfill suffered heavy damage.

Courtesy, California State Library

A crowd watches the Call Building burn.

The Fire

The earthquake was highly destructive in San Francisco and elsewhere in and of itself. But the tearing of the earth had sown the seeds for a tragedy of much greater proportions. In the initial minutes after the tremor, as people collected their thoughts, they spoke in whispers, seemingly as though afraid that loud speech or noise would trigger more shocks. But the momentary lull was soon replaced by an eruption of noise: the further collapsing of shaky walls, the cries of the injured, and the sound of wailing fire engines leaving their stations to combat a number of scattered fires.

In the wreckage brought about by the quake there were plenty of causes of fires: fractured gas mains, crossed electric wires, broken chimneys, overturned stoves, the spilled contents of bottles of chemicals. Soon there were at least fifty separate fires underway in San Francisco. It would have been a heroic task to put them all out under the best of circumstances. But when firemen hooked up their hoses to fire hydrants, they found in almost every instance that the water trickled out, then stopped. The main water pipes leading from San Francisco's two biggest reservoirs had been fractured in many places. Both basins, Crystal Springs and the Pilarcitos, were located in San Mateo County, and their conduits either originated at or stretched across the San Andreas fault on their journey to The City. Even if they had somehow been made secure, it is doubtful whether the water they transported could have prevented the holocaust: there were more than three hundred breaks in the water mains within the city limits alone.

To compound the problem of the lack of water, the earthquake had severed almost all telephone and telegraph links, not only within the city but to the outside world as well. This made coordination between fire, police, and rescue operations virtually impossible, further hampering fire-containment efforts and delaying aid from neighboring communities. Before the advancing fire forced him to flee, a sole Postal Telegraph operator on Market Street did manage to tap out a message alerting the world to San Francisco's fate.

The conflagration, which started in numerous places, had by early afternoon of the first day coalesced into three main fires— south of Market, north of Market in what was then the wholesale district near the waterfront, and in Hayes Valley, west of City Hall. But as the flames ate up block after block the separate blazes soon merged into one and the fire took on a life of its own, becoming a raging, uncontrolled inferno. Temperatures reached as high as 2,700 degrees Fahrenheit. In that extreme heat, iron and steel buckled and twisted, marble melted, sandstone crumbled, dishes and coins fused together in heaps, and glass dissolved into liquid pools. The light from the fire could be seen over fifty miles away. Cinders and dust swirled all around. Smoke rose five miles in the air; sheet music from a Market Street store came down in Marin County.

Courtesy, California State Library

The burning city, seen from a retreating ferryboat.

Faced with all this, and with San Francisco composed largely of wooden buildings standing shoulder-to-shoulder, easily facilitating the spread of flames, no fire-fighting force could have saved the city. Still, The City's firefighters and military personnel, under the command of Brigadier General Frederick Funston, tried valiantly to hold the line. Public and private cisterns were tapped until dry. Then dynamiting of buildings was tried in attempts to create fire-breaks, but this was rarely effective. Such firebreaks might have worked if they had been done in a wide enough stretch and far enough from the flames to keep them from spreading. Instead, the mayor, Eugene Schmitz, wishing to avoid possible political fallout, gave orders to use dynamite only if buildings were immediately threatened. The resulting explosions, so near the source of ignition, only served in many cases to expand the fire into previously untouched areas.

After three days of holocaust it was over. By Saturday morning, April 21, the fire had essentially burned itself out. The unusual easterly winds, which had fanned the flames for several days, subsided. The prevailing westerly winds resumed, and finally—too late—a squelching rain fell.

Refugees and the Aftermath

While a good portion of The City's real estate was going up in smoke, residents watched—first with fascination, then with disbelief, and finally with despair as they saw the fire advance inexorably toward their homes and businesses. Some of those who had not been ordered to evacuate by soldiers or police waited until the flames were virtually at their doorsteps before loading whatever possessions they could salvage into steamer trunks, baby carriages, and wheelbarrows, and then took a last look backward and set off. There were few instances of panic. Most people were calm, resigned to their fate.

Some of the refugees caught ferries to Oakland, but most headed for Golden Gate Park, the Presidio, or the city's other smaller parks and commons out of the fire zone, where they camped out in jerry-built tents. In the weeks after the fire, people cooked outdoors over makeshift grills and stoves, a necessity mandated by the mayor's order not to cook indoors until chimneys had been inspected. Shortly after the fire, construction was begun on one-room "refugee shacks," which were arrayed row upon row in large camps.

Despite the hardships and inconvenience, San Franciscans did not lose their sense of humor. One photographer captured several smiling couples lounging in front of their tent. A sign posted on the flap said: "Furnished Rooms with Running Water, Steam Heat and Elevator." Painted on the side of a sidewalk kitchen was: "Eat, Drink and Be Merry, for Tomorrow We May Have to Go to Oakland."

Although individual San Franciscans put the best face on it, the scope of the disaster could not be denied. Somewhat more than three thousand people are now believed to have perished—a remarkably low figure, considering the magnitude of the damage. The number of homeless, however, was staggering: 250,000, or roughly two-thirds of the city's residents.

Property damage in the area where the fire raged was virtually total. Almost every structure from the waterfront north to North Beach, west to Van Ness Avenue, south to Townsend Street, and southwest as far as Twentieth Street in the Mission, was consumed. A few key buildings, such as the mint and the main post office, were saved, and small enclaves on Russian Hill, Telegraph Hill, and the area now known as Jackson Square were spared. But the rest of the city looked like Dresden after it had been destroyed by incendiary bombs during World War II—block after block of rubble and soot, with an occasional chimney still standing. Five hundred and fourteen city blocks, or over four square miles, were reduced to ashes. More than twenty-eight thousand buildings burned—four-fifths of the property value of San Francisco. Estimates of the value of the loss range up to $500 million—the size of the federal budget in 1906.

In short, it was a catastrophe. But despite the devastation, the loss was not total. As one chronicler of the events of 1906 put it: "The wound was deep, but the patient would live."

Courtesy, California State Library

The aftermath: Chinatown in ruins.

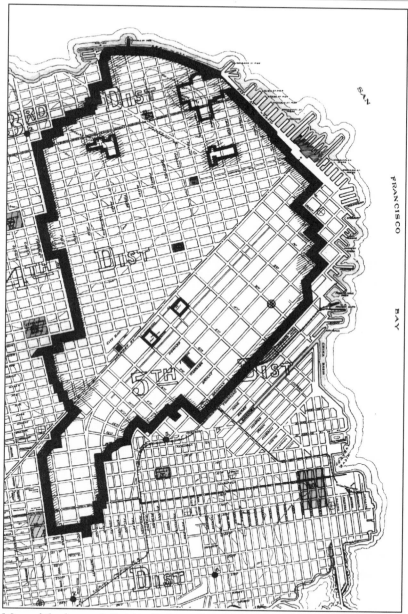

Map of the burned district. Jackson Square and parts of Telegraph Hill and Russian Hill plus the post office and the mint escaped the flames.

Frederick Funston (1865–1917)

"Fearless Freddie"

Frederick Funston was born in Ohio, the son of a Congressman. He was raised in Kansas, but he soon headed west where he embarked on a life of adventure. By the time he was thirty he had sailed solo down the Yukon River, joined a survey party mapping Death Valley, and had run a coffee plantation in South America.

San Francisco Public Library
Frederick Funston

Red haired, hot tempered, and slight of build—he was just over five feet tall and weighed only 120 pounds—he quickly earned the moniker "Fearless Freddie." Working as a train conductor on the Santa Fe Railroad, he once threw a drunken, much bigger man, off the train. When the drunk retaliated by throwing a rock through one of the train windows, Funston halted the train and chased him down.

Seemingly destined for a military career, he was at first thwarted when he failed the West Point entrance exam. Lusting for action, he joined insurgent forces in Cuba as a guerilla fighter against the Spanish occupiers. Although lacking any artillery experience, he rose through the ranks to become Chief of Artillery for the Cuban Army.

Funston returned to Kansas in 1898, and joined the Twentieth Kansas Regiment as a colonel, at the invitation of the governor. When the Spanish-American War broke out, the Twentieth was called up, and Funston found himself where he had always wanted to be—an officer on active duty in the U.S. Army. He was sent to the Philippines, where he quickly established his courage. In 1899 he was awarded the Congressional

Medal of Honor for leading a charge against the enemy through point-blank fire.

Funston was promoted to Brigadier General, and came to San Francisco in 1901 in a peacetime role as second in command of the military department of California, a position requiring diplomatic and social skills. It was a hard task for Funston who, despite his bravery, was shy and lacked small talk. He faced further difficulty in his role of army liaison to the mayor's office. From the outset he distrusted the corrupt mayor, Eugene Schmitz, and detested his limp handshake.

When disaster struck on the morning of April 18, 1906, Funston, without consulting the mayor, ordered his troops into action to help the beleaguered city. Schmitz became testy about this skirting of his authority, but the two soon smoothed over their differences. What was perhaps even more remarkable was that Funston acted without his superiors' prior approval. (It was later given.) Funston's soldiers generally performed creditably during the crisis. The general took an active role in directing their efforts in dynamiting buildings, in protecting property from looting, and in providing tents, rations, and other army supplies to the civilian populace.

Despite his de facto and temporary usurpation of power, Funston's career prospered after 1906. He soon succeeded his boss, General Adolphus Greeley—who had been in Washington, D.C. at the time of the quake—as commander of the U.S. Army's Pacific Division, then went on to service in Hawaii and the Philippines. He was appointed military governor of Vera Cruz in 1914, promoted to Major General, and led the hunt for Pancho Villa. It was his last burst of glory. "Fearless Freddie" Funston died suddenly and prematurely of a stroke at age 51 in San Antonio, Texas in 1917, while sitting in a hotel lobby. He is buried at the Presidio in San Francisco.

Sites and Attractions

The Earthquake and Fire

The 1906 Earthquake Trail – Point Reyes.
Location: Point Reyes National Seashore in Marin County. The park's entrance is just north of the town of Olema, which is situated at the juncture of Highway 1 and Sir Francis Drake Boulevard. The earthquake trail starts across the parking lot from the Bear Valley Visitor Center. **Phone:** (415) 464-5100 (visitor center). **Hours:** The earthquake trail is open for self-guided tours daily from sunrise to sunset. The visitor center is open weekdays, 9 a.m. to 5 p.m.; weekends and holidays, 8 a.m. to 5 p.m. **Admission:** Free. **Website:** www.nps.gov/pore.

The best place to learn about the great earthquake that devastated San Francisco is at Point Reyes, where a paved "Earthquake Trail" half a mile long will show you some of its startling effects. It begins near the restrooms across from the parking lot.

About halfway around you will find yourself standing almost right over the San Andreas fault—a line of blue posts marks the fault line—and looking at dramatic evidence of the earth's displacement. What was once one continuous fence is now two fences sixteen feet out of alignment.

Along the trail you will see several descriptive boards on earthquakes in general and on Bay Area faults in particular. The first panel shows how the California coast straddles two major tectonic plates moving in opposite directions and how Point Reyes, separated from the mainland, is moving northward. Twenty million years ago it was just north of Los Angeles, having traveled over 300 miles since then.

The last panel on the trail has a large full-color map showing the geology and the active faults of the San Francisco Bay Area. Different colors show the various soils that comprise the land surrounding the bay, ranging from bedrock to mud to fill. Much of the bay's shoreline is fill, and the map provides a sobering look at just where the areas of heaviest damage are likely to be in the next big quake. On this map you can easily see that coastal areas of the bay such as San Francisco's Marina district and the Cypress section of the Nimitz freeway in Oakland—two of the places hardest hit by the October 1989 earthquake—were built on landfill.

The Old Hospital – Former Presidio Museum.
Location: Lincoln and Funston streets in the Presidio, San Francisco. No phone. Interior not open to the public.

Rand Richards

The refugee cottages behind the Old Hospital.

Located behind the old hospital are two one-room, wooden cottages with hipped roofs. As tent living gave way to the need for temporary but solid housing, more than five thousand of these simple, shed-like cabins were built to house refugees. These two, which still have their original doors and three quarters of their original lumber, were moved to this site in 1986 from a lot at

Thirty–fourth Avenue and Geary Boulevard, where they had been joined together as an addition to an existing dwelling.

These cottages were initially located at Camp Richmond, one of the largest refugee camps, which occupied twenty-four city blocks between Cabrillo and Lake streets and Eleventh and Fifteenth avenues. Although they were designed as basic, temporary housing, quite a number survived, possibly due to the fact that their inhabitants could get their two dollar a month rental fees refunded if they arranged to tow the cottages to their own lots. Researchers believe that fewer than twenty such cabins remain in private hands and are still in use. Most are located in the Richmond district.

San Francisco History Room – New Main Library.
Location: Civic Center, Larkin at Grove streets, San Francisco. **Phone:** (415) 557-4567. **Hours:** Tuesday – Thursday, 10 a.m. to 6 p.m.; Friday, Noon to 5 p.m.; Saturday, 10 a.m.to 5 p.m.; Sunday, Noon to 5 p.m. Closed Monday. **Admission:** Free. **Website:** http://sfpl.lib.ca.us.

The San Francisco History Room on the sixth floor of the new main library has an extensive collection of material on all periods of The City's history. It is primarily used by students and researchers, but is open to the general public. The glass display cases around the room contain a variety of historical artifacts. These are changed from time to time, but there usually are numbers of relics from the 1906 disaster, especially when April 18 rolls around.

Items recently seen here include some charred tea saucers fused together by the fire's heat as well as several hand-colored postcards showing various aspects of the fire's aftermath: pedestrians and people in carriages fleeing the fire; Union Square aswarm with refugees; men in bowler hats sifting through the rubble.

The fire spared the few blocks of downtown now known as Jackson Square. Among the buildings saved was the A.P. Hotaling liquor warehouse. A printed card repeats a famous ditty penned after the fire: "If, as some say, God spanked the town/For being frisky/Why did he burn the churches down/And save Hotaling's whiskey?" To prove the point, next to the card stands a mint-condition—and empty—bourbon bottle with an A.P. Hotaling label.

The Old Mint

Location: Fifth and Mission streets, San Francisco. The Old Mint currently is **closed** but plans to reopen as a museum of San Francisco history at some unspecified date after refurbishing. **Website:** www. sfhistory.org.

The mint was one of the few buildings in the downtown area to survive the 1906 earthquake and fire virtually unscathed. Structural damage was limited to a small crack that opened in an interior wall in the west wing. (In the basement, the foundation's massive granite blocks kept damage to a minimum.) The subsequent fire surrounded the mint, destroyed every neighboring building, and melted the mint's windows. But the depository was spared further harm due to a heroic effort by its employees, who tapped cisterns in the basement to keep the roof and the exterior walls wet.

The saving of the mint proved to be of great value. Immediately after the disaster it not only sheltered refugees, but it also helped The City get back on its feet by using its reserves to honor drafts and by acting as a ready source of coin.

The mint continued in operation until 1937, when the present mint was constructed at Market and Duboce streets. The Old Mint, as it then became known, was subsequently used by other government agencies, was temporarily abandoned, then restored, then closed. It is now a registered National Historic Landmark.

The old museum had numerous photographs of the mint, including several showing it as it looked after the fire—a lone sentinel in a landscape of destruction.

San Francisco Fire Department Museum.

Location: 655 Presidio Avenue (between Bush and Pine), San Francisco. **Phone:** (415) 563-4630. **Hours:** Thursday – Sunday, 1 p.m. to 4 p.m. Closed the rest of the week and on holidays. **Admission:** Free. **Website:** www.sffiremuseum.org.

Here you will find several items that give an idea of the tremendous heat generated by the fire. Among them are two glass bottles melted and twisted into strange shapes, and a blackened pile of Indian head pennies fused together by the heat that was found in the ruins of the Emporium department store on Market Street.

On the wall in the same glass case holding those relics is a framed color map of the downtown area that shows, by means of a superimposed red border, where the fire was finally stopped. The map also shows where some of the principal water mains were located—and broken—and a few spots where the earthquake ripped open city streets.

Another map illustrates the four stages of the fire, while a third map shows the main water conduits that fed San Francisco from its peninsula reservoirs—the ones that ruptured the morning of April 18. On the same wall is a vivid full-color lithograph showing the city aflame.

In the same glass case is a fire station logbook open to April 1906. Earlier pages are filled line-by-line with details of fire-fighting activities. April 18 has but a few entries, mainly describing injuries to firemen. The overwhelming battle the fire fighters faced, however, is reflected in the terse sole entry for April 19: "Worked at Various Fires."

The Oakland Museum – History Gallery.

Location: 1000 Oak Street (two blocks from Lake Merritt), Oakland. **Phone:** (510) 238-3842. **Hours:** Wednesday – Saturday, 10 a.m. to 5 p.m.; (First Friday to 9 p.m.); Sunday, Noon to 5 p.m. Closed holidays. **Admission:** Adults, $8.00; Seniors, Students, $5.00; Children (under 5), Free. **Website:** www.museumca.org.

The centerpiece of the Oakland Museum History Gallery's collection of 1906 memorabilia is a beautifully restored, gleaming American-LaFrance steam-powered fire engine that saw action in San Francisco that April. All its polished fittings proved useless, however, since there was virtually no water to be had, and it was returned by ferry to Oakland. But the sight of it must have at least given beleaguered City residents hope that the fire could be stopped.

There is a display of fire department relics of the era, including badges and speaking trumpets. There are also some melted and blackened objects fished from the ashes, including a stack of plates fused together and some charred silverware.

Wells Fargo History Museum.

Location: 420 Montgomery Street (between California and Sacramento), San Francisco. **Phone:** (415) 396-2619. **Hours:** Monday – Friday, 9 a.m. to 5 p.m. Closed bank holidays and weekends. **Admission:** Free. **Website:** www.wellsfargohistory.com.

This museum, which has artifacts from most periods of San Francisco history, also has a number of things from the 1906 disaster. Like the other museums mentioned above, it has some charred remnants recovered from the ruins—in this case some blackened china fragments, scorched coins and spoons, and a blackened ledger book.

Other items include a rare panorama.of the burnt district taken from the roof of the Kohl Building and a note handwritten in pencil dated 4-18-06 from a man to his brother and sister that captured the immediacy of the danger: "We are all alive. Home not burned yet. Going to the hills as fire is coming this way fast."

Courtesy, Park Archives, GGNRA.
The Palace Hotel and Lotta's Fountain (at right) after the 1906 quake.

The Annual 1906 Anniversary Celebration
Location: Held at Lotta's Fountain, at the intersection of Market, Kearny, and Post streets in downtown San Francisco.

It only happens once a year, but every April 18 at 5:12 a.m. a dwindling number of survivors of the 1906 "Big One" gathers to reminisce and give interviews. Their stories about that fateful day are sometimes moving, sometimes funny. It has been an annual event since 1924, and usually draws a crowd of several hundred, some wearing period clothing. A few antique fire engines usually put in an appearance, and the gatherings always conclude with everyone joining in to sing a rousing rendition of "San Francisco."

If you can get yourself out of bed early enough to be there at that hour it is an event worth experiencing for the warmth, fellowship, and commemorative spirit generated.

Courtesy, California State Library
The Panama Pacific International Exposition's glittering Tower of Jewels.

9

A New Century (1906–1941)

San Francisco rebuilt quickly after the earthquake. Although constructed along the same lines as the old city, the new metropolis incorporated a grand new civic center with a classically inspired city hall. The City celebrated its rebirth with a world's fair—the Panama Pacific International Exposition of 1915.

Two decades later, in the midst of the Great Depression, "the city that knows how" brought to fruition a century-old dream by spanning the bay with two bridges—the Golden Gate and the Bay Bridge. This provided an excuse for another world's fair—the Golden Gate International Exposition of 1939–40—more popularly known as "Treasure Island."

Two other bay islands saw activity of a very different sort. Angel Island served as the landing site for Chinese and other immigrants, and Alcatraz gained a lasting notoriety when the federal prison opened its doors in the 1930s and housed Al Capone and other leading criminals of the day.

The City Rebuilds

The ashes from the 1906 fire were barely cold when the immense cleanup task began. Some of the heavy stone, brick, and mortar chunks were loaded onto ore carts brought in on temporary rail lines routed into the heart of the destroyed area, but most of the debris was hauled away by horses pulling drays. The work load proved so taxing that an estimated fifteen thousand horses died during the cleanup. Much of the debris was dumped in Mission Bay at the foot of King and Townsend streets, and when that was filled in the rest was towed in barges outside the Golden Gate and dumped into the ocean.

News of the devastating earthquake and fire in San Francisco quickly reached other U.S. cities and other countries, many of which responded with donations of food, medicine, and other forms of aid. Japan, in particular, contributed generously, providing almost a quarter of a million dollars for relief, more than all other foreign countries combined. In the months following April 1906, $9 million was raised, most of that coming in the days immediately following the earthquake and fire. While not an insignificant sum, it was dwarfed by the size of the loss—nearly $500 million. Fortunately, insurance paid most of it, enabling The City to start reconstruction quickly.

The Burnham Plan

San Francisco had been the premier West Coast city ever since its founding. But around the turn of the century, civic leaders became concerned for the first time about the competitive threat of faster-growing Los Angeles. The city fathers looked at their densely packed city, spread over its inflexible grid, and decided that San Francisco needed a master plan that would transform it into a physically more beautiful city and confirm its preeminent stature.

The man they chose to draw up such a plan was Daniel Burnham, a noted Chicago architect who had been chief of construction for the Columbian Exposition of 1893. Burnham was a graduate of the Ecole des Beaux-Arts in Paris, the foremost architectural school of its day, one whose instructors drew their inspiration from the models of ancient Greece and Rome. This was also the era of the "City Beautiful" movement, in which the nascent idea of city planning incorporated classical buildings into city plans featuring parks and boulevards.

With his background and training, it was almost foreordained that Burnham would choose Paris as his model for revamping San Francisco. His plan, copies of which had already been distributed to the Board of Supervisors when the earthquake struck on April 18, showed a San Francisco of wide, tree-lined boulevards, some that were mere expansions of current city streets, and others that were carved across the existing grid pattern to link nonexistent plazas.

But Burnham's plan went even further, calling for one–way streets and a network of subways. He also envisioned classical colonnaded temples looking down upon the city from the peaks of prominent hilltops, and he planned a park several times the size of Golden Gate Park for the area west of Twin Peaks. The pièce de résistance was to be a new city hall and civic center located in a semicircular plaza that would radiate from the intersection of Van Ness Avenue and Market Street.

Courtesy, California State Library

Burnham's plan proposed a redesigned civic center.

The earthquake and fire that devastated the city would, at first, have seemed to provide an ideal opportunity to institute the sweeping changes Burnham envisioned. But Burnham's plan would have required the politically difficult measures of condemning property to widen city streets and the selling of municipal bonds to raise revenues for the proposed civic improvements.

While the plan was initially praised by most, opposition soon developed. Property owners resisted the street widening idea, and San Franciscans were in no mood to incur bonded indebtedness on top of what it would take to rebuild. The final blow came from The City's business community, which opposed any delay in rebuilding for fear of losing business to Oakland and Los Angeles. So Burnham's ambitious and visionary plan for San Francisco never came to be. The impatience to rebuild, to get back to business, won out; the new city went up along the lines of the old.

The New City Hall and Civic Center

In only three years, much of San Francisco's downtown had been rebuilt. The city hall, however, whose graft-influenced shoddy construction had left it a ruin after the 1906 tremor, had been razed and not replaced. (The mayor and other city officials operated out of a temporary building and the repaired Hall of Records, which adjoined City Hall.) With a crying need for a new city administration building, Daniel Burnham returned to San Francisco in 1909 and submitted a refined sketch for a civic center that would fan out from the point suggested in his original plan—the intersection of Van Ness Avenue and Market Street. A bond issue to fund the project was submitted to the voters but it was defeated, failing to reach the two-thirds majority needed for approval. The last bit of Daniel Burnham's grand plan thus came to naught, still leaving San Francisco without a city hall.

Despite this final rejection, Burnham's efforts cannot be said to have been in vain. Although none of his plan was executed as he envisioned, City Hall and the Civic Center clearly show his influence and that of the City Beautiful movement he championed. Some of his more radical ideas, such as one-way streets and subways, were ahead of their time and were implemented later. One-way streets were introduced to San Francisco in 1942, and limited subway service in the form of the Bay Area Rapid Transit came in 1974.

Not long after the electoral defeat of Burnham's revised Civic Center plan, a similar measure put to the voters passed by a ten to one margin. The dramatic shift in public opinion was caused by the construction of the Panama Canal, which would open in 1914. Several major U.S. cities had coveted the honor of being the official host for a fair to celebrate its opening. In January 1911 Congress approved San Francisco's bid. Suddenly there was an urgent need for an impressive civic center and city hall as a place to welcome visiting dignitaries.

With the funds needed thus assured, the only question remaining was to choose a site for the new civic center. Several leading architects favored Burnham's Market/Van Ness location but the old city hall grounds located at Larkin and McAllister streets, four blocks to the northeast, won out. It was an area already established as a governmental hub, and it had another big advantage in that there would be no need to rearrange such streets as Market and Van Ness. A few changes were made at the old site, however. The former city hall had stood where the old main public library is today. It was decided that the new city hall would be situated a block away, between Van Ness Avenue and Polk Street. Across the plaza from it, facing Larkin Street, were to be the main library and the opera house. The old library stands today on its planned site, but the opera house, which was to occupy the lot directly across Fulton, where the New Main Library is, was not built due to a squabble between Mayor James Rolph, Jr. and opera boosters. The opera house was eventually constructed two decades later across Van Ness Avenue, on the other side of City Hall.

Once the new civic center site plan was approved and the City Hall design finalized, construction began. But despite the best efforts to have everything completed by the opening of the Panama Pacific International Exposition, only the Exposition Auditorium—on Grove Street facing Civic Center Plaza—was ready when the fair opened, in February 1915. City Hall was dedicated shortly before the fair closed, in December 1915, and the dedication of the old Main Library came early in 1917.

The Panama Pacific International Exposition

The idea for an international fair to celebrate the linking of the Atlantic and Pacific oceans via the Panama Canal first surfaced in 1904, when construction on "the big ditch" started. San Francisco's plans to bid for the fair were set aside in 1906, when the earthquake struck, but by 1909, with much of the city rebuilt, they were revived with enthusiasm. The City was anxious to put behind it a messy graft scandal and trial involving the mayor and other officials, and eager to show the world the new city that had risen so quickly from the ashes of the old.

After San Francisco's bid was approved, the question became where to stage the exposition. Three possible locations were proposed: the Lake Merced oceanfront, the western half of Golden Gate Park, and Harbor View (now called the Marina district). At first it was felt that the fair should be citywide, linking all three spots. President Taft, during a visit to San Francisco in October 1911, officially broke ground for the exposition in Golden Gate Park. But it was decided soon after his visit that attendance would probably be greater if it was held in one location; Harbor View was selected. At that time the area was undeveloped and had a ragged shoreline. A seawall was built, and by 1913 the expanse had been filled with sand dredged from the bay. Landscaping of the grounds and construction of the buildings then proceeded rapidly.

Despite the outbreak of World War I and the subsequent pullout of a few foreign country participants, the Panama Pacific International Exposition (PPIE) opened on schedule, February 20, 1915, with twenty-nine U.S. states and twenty-five foreign countries participating. The fair covered 635 acres of San Francisco's northern waterfront—all of the present day Marina district and portions of U.S. Army land at Fort Mason and the Presidio. The southern boundary extended to where Lombard and Chestnut streets are today.

In addition to the state and foreign country pavilions, there were eleven major buildings, many designed by noted architects of the day. The graceful exposition halls, done in the Beaux-Arts style, were tinted in pastels and earth tones suggestive of the surrounding Bay Area landscape, and were accented by indirect lighting, an innovation at a time when naked bulb illumination was the norm. The PPIE seemed almost a fantasy city—one whose overall ambience was heightened by San Francisco's coastal fogs, which, when shot through with searchlights from machines placed on the grounds, created a play of light and shadow that further enhanced the whole effect. The result was a fair of such beauty and harmony that author Gray Brechin likened it to "a miniature Constantinople at the base of Pacific Heights."

The main area of the fair was a large rectangle covering the Marina. At the east end stood Machinery Hall, a building so vast that an airplane flew through it, while on the west stood the Palace of Fine Arts. Between the two rose the attention-getting highlight of the fair, the forty-three story Tower of Jewels. This glittering edifice literally shimmered, because attached to it were over one hundred thousand colored, cut-glass beads suspended by wires so that they would flutter in the breeze. The effect was further enhanced by tiny mirrors placed behind each bauble, which made them glint and flash in the light. Rounding out the main fair area at the eastern edge was "The Zone," the location of the amusement arcades, food and beverage stalls, and panoramas of various kinds. Here also was to be found a working scale model of the Panama Canal, the ostensible reason for the fair.

San Francisco Public Library
The Panama Pacific International Exposition of 1915.
The Tower of Jewels is at the right.

The Exposition was an aesthetic and financial triumph. When its gates closed on December 4, 1915, after ten months, nearly twenty million people had attended. The most successful of San

Francisco's three fairs, it earned a profit for its backers above and beyond the $1 million they spent on building the Civic Center's Exposition Auditorium.

In hindsight, the PPIE, despite its emphasis on the future and the promise it held, proved to be more a last farewell to the conformity and established social order of the nineteenth century. World War I was in progress. The twentieth century, with its upheavals, rapid change, and increasing complexity, would soon transform everything.

Chinese Immigration

In 1906, Chinatown, like the rest of The City's business district, was reduced to ruins. But despite some talk by white community leaders of moving the Chinese to Hunters Point, their enclave was quickly rebuilt in the same location.

Ironically, while this new Chinatown was being raised from the ashes of the old, its population was dwindling. The Exclusion Act of 1882, which severely proscribed Chinese immigration and restricted entry to a few occupational categories such as teachers, students, and government officials, was tightened even further in the early twentieth century, so that only those claiming citizenship or a family tie to a U.S. resident could enter. In 1910 a quarantine station was established on Angel Island to determine who qualified. It was here that "paper brides" and "paper children"—Chinese attempting to enter illegally by claiming kinship with U.S. citizens—coming from mainland China spent weeks, months, and occasionally a year or more while trying to land in San Francisco.

Alcatraz

Alcatraz Island, with its famous cellblock and other prison buildings clearly visible, is the most celebrated landmark in San Francisco Bay. It is not called "The Rock" for nothing. A jagged, essentially barren knob sitting in the middle of the bay, it was first referred to as a "rock island" by the Spanish in 1770. A home only for birds until the gold rush populated the Bay Area, the island was not even tagged with a name until 1826, when an English sea captain, drawing a map of the bay, mistakenly transferred the name given to Yerba Buena Island—"Isla de Alcatraces" (Pelican Island)—to the guano-covered isle. The name was later misspelled Alcatrazes, and then shortened to the present version in 1851.

Alcatraz's human history dates from 1850, when President Millard Fillmore set aside the island as part of a strategic network of defense sites ringing the entrance to the bay. By the late 1850s military fortifications had been built and the first guns installed. From 1859 to 1907 Alcatraz served primarily as a U.S. Army fort, and secondarily as a military prison. During the Civil War, Confederate sympathizers were held on the island, and in the decades following, Indian "troublemakers" such as Captain Jack of the Modoc tribe and several of Geronimo's lieutenants were also confined there.

From 1907 to 1933 Alcatraz was solely a military prison, holding mainly deserters and other military offenders. In 1934 the army yielded title to the island. On January 1 of that year Alcatraz opened as a "maximum security, minimum privilege" federal prison. Notorious criminals such as "Machine Gun" Kelly, Al Capone, and Robert Stroud, "The Birdman of Alcatraz," were soon transferred here from other federal prisons. The cellblocks where these prisoners were kept are the primary attraction for visitors.

Alcatraz was closed by Attorney General Robert Kennedy in 1963 after a congressional committee determined that the costs to maintain prisoners on Alcatraz equaled those of guests staying at New York's Waldorf Astoria. After an occupation by native Americans from 1969 to 1971, Alcatraz was opened to the public in 1973 as part of the Golden Gate National Recreation Area, a network of Bay Area parks and green areas forming what is the largest urban park in the world.

San Francisco's Two Bridges

Proposals to span both the bay and the Golden Gate go back as far as 1851, when William Walker, editor of a San Francisco newspaper—and later a notorious adventurer in Nicaragua—lobbied for a pontoon bridge that would connect San Francisco to the east shore of the bay. Over the decades many other plans to span the bay, some serious, some frivolous (including one by San Francisco's favorite nineteenth-century eccentric, the Emperor Norton), were put forth. None was given serious attention until about 1920.

The real reason it took so long (besides the obvious one of the relatively primitive pre-twentieth century bridge-building technology) is that the need just was not great enough until the twenties. What created the need was the advent of the automobile. The bay's ferries, which had served as San Francisco's link to most of the Bay Area's other communities ever since The City's founding, naturally also served to transport autos. In the year 1921, the ferries handled more than eight hundred thousand cars. By 1930 that figure had become six million. At that volume, ferries were being taxed to their limit. Bridges to span both the bay and the Gate could wait no longer.

By the early 1920s no fewer than thirteen different plans for linking the shores with bridges were under serious discussion. Several bridges were, in fact, built before construction even started on the Golden Gate Bridge or Bay Bridge. Both the Dumbarton Bridge across the southern end of the bay, and the Carquinez Bridge across Carquinez Strait, opened to vehicular traffic in 1927. The San Mateo Bridge came next, in 1929. The two major bridges were soon to get underway.

The Golden Gate Bridge

The man chiefly responsible for building the Golden Gate Bridge was Joseph Strauss. A diminutive outsider (he was from Chicago), Strauss burned with the ambition typical of someone driven by a need to overcome his insecurities and make his mark. He built more than four hundred bridges in his lifetime, including the workaday Fourth Street Bridge at China Basin in San Francisco, but he saw the Golden Gate Bridge as his crowning achievement, his assurance of a place in history.

He was a tireless promoter of the bridge, speaking to dozens of civic groups to drum up support throughout its long gestation period. This promotion was necessary, because the proposed

Golden Gate Bridge was the subject of attack from many directions. During much of the 1920s and into the early 1930s, the start of construction was delayed due to litigation from a number of groups. Some did not want to see the natural beauty of the majestic entrance to San Francisco Bay despoiled; others were afraid that the bridge might not be earthquake proof. The Southern Pacific was in opposition, since it controlled the steamship and bay ferry lines, and obviously had a lot to lose if a bridge was built.

There were other obstacles. Approval of the War Department was necessary, since the army owned the land on both sides of the Gate. The War Department, once it was assured that the army would control the bridge in the event of war, and that government vehicles could cross free of charge at all times, gave its consent.

The bridge's engineering proved to be quite a challenge. Many of the details relating to the loads, wind stresses, and so forth were successfully worked out through complex mathematical equations by Charles Ellis, an engineering professor. Ellis spent three years working tirelessly on the problems posed only to find himself unjustly fired by Strauss, who accused Ellis of wasting time and money.

Financing was another problem. The voters had approved bonds to raise the necessary working capital, but by the early 1930s, with the Depression deepening, the market for the bonds had nearly dried up. Only a pledge from A. P. Giannini, founder of the Bank of America, to guarantee the sale of the first $6 million worth of bonds kept the project from stalling.

Courtesy, California State Library

Strauss's original design for the Golden Gate Bridge. It was ridiculed as looking like "two grotesque steel beetles crawling out from either shore."

Although the opposition and delays were frustrating to Strauss they actually proved highly beneficial in one regard. His initial design for a suspension bridge—the one used to promote it—could only be described as ugly. But during this period Strauss hired a young East Bay architect and assistant named Irving Morrow. Strauss's drawing was scrapped, and it was Morrow who produced the inspired design for the bridge that was built.

The construction bids to contractors were let in 1931, and after a last burst of litigation attempting to block the bridge, work finally got underway. Construction on the Marin tower anchorage began on January 5, 1933.

The actual construction proved to be a herculean task. The bridge required two main towers. The one on the north shore proved to be relatively easy, because it could be anchored to bedrock just offshore. The southern pier, however, was a tremendous challenge. The specifications called for it to be built 1,100 feet offshore in water 100 feet deep. The work here was some of the most hazardous of the whole project, because divers had to work in the treacherous currents flowing in and out of the Gate and because the pier's foundation of steel pilings had to be blasted thirty-five feet deep into sloping bedrock on the floor of the bay.

Once the south pier's toehold was established, the concrete foundation for the tower resting on it could be poured. To build what was essentially a concrete tower underwater, a breakwater—or fender—was completed around the site. The still water inside, which covered an area the size of a football field, was then pumped out to allow concrete to be poured into the resulting empty space.

Once the towers were complete the last major job was the spinning of the cables between them. This was accomplished by means of shuttles, which moved from each anchorage to mid-span and back. By the time this task was complete, enough pencil-thick wire had been spun to circle the earth three times.

During the four years of construction the bridge had a remarkable safety record. It would have been almost perfect had it not been for an accident that occurred just a few months before the bridge was completed. Twelve men were working on a scaffold beneath the span, stripping away the forms for the concrete roadbed, when a corner bracket snapped. The rest of the platform quickly gave way, spilling its human cargo and what remained of the scaffold into the safety net below. The net, not designed to hold that much weight, tore, plunging the men into the water below. Only two of the twelve survived the fall.

Despite this tragedy there was much celebration three months later, when on May 27, 1937 the bridge was dedicated and opened for a special "pedestrians only" day. More than two hundred thousand people walked across. They and other northern California residents had much to be proud of. This beautiful bridge, which cost $35 million, was brought to fruition during the depths of the Great Depression. An aesthetic delight and an engineering marvel, it remains today—seventy years after it was built—a prime example of a rare perfect marriage of art and science.

The Bay Bridge

The San Francisco-Oakland Bay Bridge, more commonly shortened to The Bay Bridge, experienced far less opposition when it was first proposed than did the Golden Gate Bridge. With heavy ferry commute traffic already existing between San Francisco and the East Bay, a bridge connecting the two shores was assured of eventually paying for itself through tolls. Financing the cost of construction, therefore, proved to be much easier than it was for the Golden Gate Bridge. Unlike the latter, which was financed solely through the sale of bonds to public and private investors, the $77 million cost of the Bay Bridge was advanced by the federal government in the form of a loan. President Herbert Hoover, an engineer and a Stanford grad, took a personal interest in the project and was instrumental in securing federal approval.

Although the choice of where to build the Golden Gate Bridge was never an issue, the location of a San Francisco to East Bay crossing was. The route from the Alameda shore to Yerba Buena Island to Rincon Hill seems today to be a logical choice for conducting traffic in and out of San Francisco. But what dictated the Yerba Buena to Rincon Hill connection was the existence of an underwater ridge of bedrock spanning the bay along that line. On both sides of the ridge the water was many feet deeper, making the construction of a bridge elsewhere less likely since it would need an underwater concrete pier just as the Golden Gate Bridge had.

The Bay Bridge, although one continuous roadway, is actually two different bridges connected at Yerba Buena Island. The original bridge from the Alameda shore to the island is a traditional cantilever-truss structure, like a typical railroad bridge. This isn't surprising when you realize that for roughly the first two decades of its existence, half of the lower deck of the Bay Bridge was given over to interurban electric commuter trains. The other half was reserved for trucks. Initially, the upper deck carried two-way automobile traffic—three lanes in each direction. But in 1958 the train tracks were removed and the bridge was converted to vehicular traffic only—the lower deck five lanes eastbound, the upper deck five lanes westbound.

The bridge from the island to San Francisco is a suspension bridge (necessary because of the deeper water), like the one spanning the Golden Gate. Building the Bay Bridge entailed greater

California Toll Bridge Authority/San Francisco Public Library
The Bay Bridge and the Yerba Buena tunnel under construction in 1935.

difficulties than those faced by its more illustrious neighbor. The Golden Gate Bridge, at approximately one mile in length, is perfect for a single complete suspension span. But the distance from San Francisco to Yerba Buena is two miles—too long for a single span. What this necessitated, therefore, was the building of a huge stanchion—in effect another island—midway between the two points of land in order to provide an anchor to absorb and contain the stresses the steel suspension cables would deliver. This concrete tower, or pylon, proved to be as much of a construction nightmare as was the south tower of the Golden Gate Bridge.

Unfortunately for the Bay Bridge builders, the Golden Gate method of pouring concrete into a hollowed-out fender could not be used. Their pylon would be anchored farther below the surface, in water too deep for divers to work in for the time necessary to secure a footing. So instead of pouring cement from the bottom up, strange as it may seem, they built the pylon from the top down. To do this they towed a huge steel box, or caisson, to the site and, gradually filling it with cement, lowered it below the surface. As it sank, the sides of the caisson were built up to keep the water from spilling into it. When it reached the bay floor, at a depth of 200 feet, steel rods were inserted into preset hollow tubes, the pylon was anchored to bedrock, and the cement was poured. Although this gray-painted stanchion midway between San Francisco and Yerba Buena Island looks deceptively small, it is actually the height of a forty-eight story building, or almost as tall as the Bank of America tower in San Francisco's financial district.

The final obstacle to the completion of the bridge was carving a four-story tunnel through Yerba Buena Island. When completed, it was the largest diameter vehicular tunnel in the world and it remains so today.

The eight-and-a-half-mile-long bridge was completed two months ahead of schedule after three and a half years of construction, and was opened to traffic on November 12, 1936. Twenty-seven men had died during the construction, nearly three times as many the number killed while working on the Golden Gate Bridge. Despite the tragic loss of life, the bridge's completion provided a much-needed lift to the Depression-ravaged Bay Area.

The Golden Gate International Exposition "Treasure Island"

With the two bridges completed, San Francisco decided to celebrate, and to invite the world. As the 1930s drew to a close, The City held its third world's fair in less than fifty years. The site chosen for the Golden Gate International Exposition, as the fair was officially called, was the Yerba Buena shoals, a four-hundred-acre site just north of Yerba Buena Island. The location was easily accessible from all parts of the bay, which gave it an added advantage since it was agreed that the property would serve as the new San Francisco airport once the fair closed. With construction mostly financed by the Works Progress Administration (WPA), 300,000 tons of boulders were used to build a seawall around the roughly one-square-mile area, and the resulting lagoon was then filled in.

In February 1939, after three years of dredging, filling, and construction, "Treasure Island" opened for business. The fanciful name, a press agent's tag, resulted from the claim that soil pumped from the bay to fill the island contained Mother Lode gold washed down from Sierra streams. This was true enough, but any amounts of gold dredged up would have been minuscule. Nevertheless, an early publicity shot showed "miners" panning for gold on Treasure Island.

Among the fair's landmark structures were the Tower of the Sun, the Court of the Moon, and a statue of the goddess Pacifica

San Francisco Public Library

The Golden Gate International Exposition of 1939–40.
Notice the Pan American Clipper resting on the water.

surrounded by a cascading fountain. The Pan American Clipper was another attraction, taking off from an adjacent lagoon for distant Asian cities (the exposition's theme was peace and unity among the peoples of the Pacific Basin).

Some of the fair's exhibits, such as the $40 million worth of art by European masters, were designed to be uplifting and educational, while others provided pure entertainment. Masters of a contemporary art form of the day, swing music, also performed. Benny Goodman, Eddie Duchin, Count Basie, and others appeared at various times. Sally Rand, the famous fan dancer, provided art of a different sort: her Nude Ranch drew men in steady numbers during both years of the fair. And, like the Panama Pacific International Exposition before it, Treasure Island had a separate area set aside as an amusement zone. Called the Gayway (this was before "gay" connoted something different than lighthearted and happy), it was home to carnival Ferris wheels, roller coasters, and a variety of lowbrow entertainments, including an automobile racetrack for monkeys, flea circuses, and a miniature Wild West village with midgets dressed as cowboys.

For all of its attempts to enlighten and entertain, Treasure Island was not a financial or artistic success. It lost money, and it was criticized on aesthetic grounds for its mostly lackluster architecture and for its confusing motifs, which varied from tropic isle to Old West to South Seas pirate.

The fair's main architect was Arthur Brown, king of the Beaux-Arts classicists, who had designed City Hall and portions of the PPIE a generation earlier. But Modernism was dawning, leaving most of the major buildings looking dated. So despite its attempt, like all world's fairs, to predict the future and project a vision of a better life, Treasure Island looked backward more than forward.

Like the PPIE, which took place during World War I, the Golden Gate International Exposition coincided with another world war. A few months after Treasure Island opened, Hitler invaded Poland. By the time it closed, in September 1940, France had fallen to the Germans. Six weeks after Pearl Harbor, Pacifica, the fair's symbol of peace, was dynamited. The U.S. Navy swapped land it owned at Mills Field in San Mateo County—where San Francisco International Airport was eventually built—for Treasure Island, and converted it to a naval base.

James Rolph, Jr. (1869–1934)

"Sunny Jim"

James Rolph, Jr. was born in San Francisco in 1869 to a British father and Scottish mother who had emigrated to The City the year before. He grew up at Twenty-first and Guerrero streets, a working-class neighborhood in the Mission district. As a youth he worked as a newsboy, clerk, and messenger. After finishing school, Rolph and a classmate started a shipping company, which grew and became quite successful. Rolph, expanding his interests, started a bank and soon had made his first million.

He came to public prominence as head of a relief committee after the 1906 earthquake. Although he turned down an offer to run for mayor in 1909, he was persuaded to run in 1911 and was elected by a landslide. He took office in January 1912, was reelected four times, and served for nineteen years—far longer than any other San Francisco mayor before or since. His tenure was a productive one. During his time in office the new city hall and the rest of the civic center was built, the Panama Pacific International Exposition was held, and the Hetch Hetchy water system, which supplies most of The City's water, was launched. Numerous bridges, tunnels, and other public works came to fruition while he was mayor.

"Sunny Jim's" success can largely be traced to his personality. He was the Ronald Reagan of his day: not an intellectual, and bored by the details of administration—but likeable, personally generous, and a man of cheerful good humor. All these traits made him immensely popular; he was reelected by wide margins in all his campaigns. Photos of the time invariably show him with a smile on his face, greeting dignitaries, or appearing at various groundbreakings, shovel in hand.

He was known as the "Mayor of All the People," a title he earned partly because he was such a contrast to the political hacks, corruption, and special-interest favoritism that had preceded him, but mostly he deserved it on his merits. He had a remarkable ability to relate to people of all races, religions, and political persuasions. He once invited Communist demonstrators outside City Hall into his office for a chat—this at a time when they were being clubbed by police in other major cities.

Rolph might have succeeded as mayor in any era, but he had the good fortune to have had most of his political career when times were good. The two decades he served as mayor were mainly ones of optimism and prosperity. But in 1931, Rolph became governor of California, and his luck started to sour. The Depression was on, times were different, and an aging "Sunny Jim" was not up to the task. His praise of a lynch mob in San Jose hurt him politically, and he died shortly thereafter, in 1934, of a heart attack. San Francisco, where he was much loved, mourned him, and responded with one of the biggest funerals it has ever given.

International News Photo/San Francisco Public Library

James "Sunny Jim" Rolph, Jr.

Sites and Attractions

The Panama Pacific International Exposition

The Palace of Fine Arts.
Location: 3601 Lyon Street (between Bay and Jefferson), San Francisco. The main pavilion is outdoors and is open to the public free of charge.

Of the resplendent 1915 Panama Pacific International Exposition, only the Marina Green, the yacht harbor, and the Palace of Fine Arts remain. The latter, purposely designed to look like a ruin, ironically was the only building to survive when the fair was bulldozed.

The Palace of Fine Arts was widely considered to be the most beautiful building of the PPIE; it was saved simply because fairgoers and San Franciscans were loath to tear it down. Fortunately it was on U.S. Army land, and thus there was not a pressing need to raze it. The land on the other side of Lyon Street was owned by private developers, who, once the fair ended, quickly proceeded with demolition to make way for the present-day Marina residential district.

The Palace of Fine Arts, which was intended as a paean to art and artists, was designed by noted local architect Bernard Maybeck. Maybeck cited two influences as the inspiration for his design. One was a nineteenth-century Romantic painting called "The Isle of the Dead," which depicted a royal body being borne on a barge toward its final resting place, a tomb on an island. The other influence was the eighteenth-century artist Giovanni Piranesi, the creator of grand yet fanciful engravings. The impact of these two influences can be seen in such touches as the large funeral urns, the staircases leading nowhere, and the large, empty planter boxes on top, with weeping maidens peering into them. (During the fair these boxes were meant to hold California live oak trees, but this never happened.)

The lagoon in front of the main temple was originally a frog pond, where neighborhood children caught frogs and sold them to fishermen for bait. The initial plan called for filling in this pond, but Maybeck decided to save it. He used it to great advantage, superbly integrating it into the building. The western shore practically leads

Rand Richards

The main rotunda of the Palace of Fine Arts today.

into the edifice itself. The overall harmony of the two together is such that one local architect described the Palace of Fine Arts as the only building where the ducks—who inhabit the lagoon's placid waters—are an integral part of the architecture.

The original structure, which like all the fair's other buildings was meant to be temporary, was made of staff, a mixture of burlap and burlap-type fiber over a wood frame. Not surprisingly, some fifty years later the Palace of Fine Arts looked like a *real* ruin. In the mid-1960s casts were made of the original, which was destroyed and then replaced by a reinforced concrete copy.

The structure in place now looks much as it did at the time of the PPIE, but it is not as colorful. The 1915 rotunda, for example, had supporting columns that were painted dark red and topped with gold capitals. The priestesses, or women figures, surrounding the top—which look small from the ground but are actually much larger than life-size—had red lips and blue eyes. The columns on the arcade surrounding the rotunda were a dark green. The rotunda's top, however, is close to the original burnt orange. The Shed, the semicircular building behind the rotunda, which houses two fourteen-foot-high angels from the original Palace of Fine Arts, has also been altered since 1915. At that time it, like the main portion, was dark red and covered with architectural details and planter boxes, but after the reconstruction of the main building there was no money left over to restore these.

The Palace of Fine Arts today retains the sense of "timeless melancholy" that its designer intended. It stands as a reminder of the most magnificent world's fair San Francisco ever staged, and is a wonderful place for quiet contemplation or a tranquil walk.

The Oakland Museum – History Gallery.
Location: 1000 Oak Street (two blocks from Lake Merritt), Oakland. **Phone:** (510) 238-3842. **Hours:** Wednesday – Saturday, 10 a.m. to 5 p.m.; (First Friday to 9 p.m.); Sunday, Noon to 5 p.m. Closed holidays. **Admission:** Adults, $8.00; Seniors, Students, $5.00; Children (under 5), Free. **Website:** www.museumca.org.

The Oakland Museum's History Gallery has a number of unique items from the PPIE. The most distinctive is the collection of statues such as the water sprite, which stood near the entrance to the Court of Abundance, and a figure known as The Philosopher, which adorned the colonnade atop the Tower of Jewels. These three-foot-high plaster and resin figurines are actually maquettes, or studio versions, used as models for the much larger originals, which were auctioned off after the fair.

Other artifacts include a souvenir official guide, medallions, a fine, decorative commemorative plate, and from the Japanese pavilion, furnishings and life-size statues. There are also several large, framed architectural renderings in color that show the major buildings and the fairgrounds.

Wells Fargo History Museum.
Location: 420 Montgomery Street (between California and Sacramento), San Francisco. **Phone:** (415) 396-2619. **Hours:** Monday – Friday, 9 a.m. to 5 p.m. Closed bank holidays and weekends. **Admission:** Free. **Website:** www.wellsfargohistory.com.

On view here is a good selection of Tower of Jewels baubles in colors of emerald, canary, and ruby, which are increasingly hard to find.

The Bank of California Museum.

Location: In the basement of the main branch of Union Bank of California, 400 California Street (between Sansome and Montgomery), San Francisco. There is no phone or website for the museum. **Hours:** Monday – Friday, 9 a.m. to 4:30 p.m. Closed bank holidays and weekends. **Admission:** Free.

In keeping with this museum's focus on money, the display related to the PPIE consists of several beautiful gold commemorative coins, ranging in value from one dollar to fifty dollars. There are also a few silver half-dollar pieces.

Sidewalk Stamp – Fillmore Street Steps.

Location: Fillmore and Vallejo streets, northeast corner.

One quirky and seldom noticed legacy of the PPIE is the ladder of steps that cascades from here down to Green Street. The top step bears an incised inscription of three lines:

PRESENTED TO THE PEOPLE
1915
FILLMORE STREET IMPROVEMENT ASSOCIATION.

What makes this noteworthy is, first, Pacific Heights made a great vantage point for viewing the entirety of the fair and several grand homes, including James Leary Flood's stunning palazzo just a block up the hill, were completed in time to take advantage. Second, civic improvements were being made all over town. One was these steps, which were likely one of the first to pave the way for similar transformations nearby thus aiding pedestrians in navigating San Francisco's steep streets.

San Francisco's Beaux–Arts Civic Center

City Hall, the New Main Library, and the Civic Center.
Location: The city government's complex—the Civic Center—is bounded by Van Ness Avenue, McAllister, Hyde, and Grove streets. City Hall's main entrance faces Polk Street. The New Main Library is on Larkin Street, across the plaza from City Hall. **Hours:** City Hall is open weekdays, 9 a.m. to 5 p.m. The Library's hours vary. Call (415) 557-4400 for information on the latter.

San Francisco's Civic Center is thought by many architects and historians to be the premier example in the United States of a Beaux-Arts municipal government complex. It is also one of the few examples of the City Beautiful movement of the early twentieth century that was ever brought to fruition. In recognition of the Civic Center's unique status, it was entered on the National Regis- ter of Historic Places by the federal government in 1987.

San Francisco Public Library
City Hall and the Civic Center Plaza, as they looked in the 1920s.

The centerpiece is City Hall. The design resulted from a local competition that was won by the firm of Bakewell and Brown, which was awarded a first prize of $25,000 by a panel of judges composed of Mayor James Rolph, Jr. and other city officials. The structure, faced with California granite, cost $3.5 million, and opened for business on March 1, 1916. Mayor Rolph, beaming with pride, loved to point out to visitors that the dome, extending to a height of 308 feet, was sixteen feet higher than the U.S. Capitol.

The building, the epitome of Classical Revival architecture that was so integral to the Beaux-Arts style, projects a Renaissance air—particularly the dome, which is reminiscent of St. Peter's Basilica in Rome. The whole effect, as seen from the outside, is one of imperial grandeur. City Hall's interior, as beautifully proportioned as its exterior, projects an aura of rhythm and substance. The main staircase, leading to the Board of Supervisors chambers on the second floor, has been the scene of several movies and numerous wedding pictures.

The other major building of the same period is the old main public library, which is situated across the plaza from City Hall. It was completed in 1917 at a cost of $1 million. It was also faced with California granite, and echoes the Beaux-Arts style of City Hall, but in a less elaborate manner. The interior once housed two color murals from the Panama Pacific International Exposition, "Pioneers Leaving the East" and a matching panel entitled "Pioneers Arriving in the West." They were removed when the building was remodeled into the Asian Art Museum.

Facing the Civic Center plaza on the other sides are the Exposition Auditorium on Grove Street, completed in 1915 in time for the PPIE's opening, and across from it on McAllister Street is the California State Building, completed in 1926. The Opera House, originally intended as a matching twin for the old library, was supposed to be situated across from it to the south, on Fulton Street. Instead, it was built on Van Ness Avenue across from the west entrance to City Hall, and then not until the early 1930s.

Although the Civic Center is now a historic district, meaning that prior approval is required for modifications or alterations within its boundaries, changes are occurring. In April 1996 the library moved into a new Beaux-Arts style building (but featuring state-of-the-art amenities) that was constructed across Fulton Street on Marshall Square. The old library is now occupied by the Asian Art Museum, which was formerly located in Golden Gate Park. Plans are for the Civic Center Plaza itself to one day to be reconfigured to its original design. This would reestablish an open center, anchored on the north and south sides by individual fountains, rather than the recent setup of one long rectangular fountain (recently converted to a stretch of green lawn) leading from City Hall to Larkin Street.

Immigration Station

Immigration Station – Angel Island.

Location: Angel Island, the largest island in San Francisco Bay, is located off the Tiburon peninsula. Immigration Station is on the northeast side of Angel Island in the Winslow Cove (North Garrison) area. There is a visitor center at Ayala Cove that can provide maps. **Phone:** (415) 435-3522. Public access to the island is by ferry only. Primary points of departure are San Francisco and Tiburon. The Blue & Gold Fleet, **Phone:** (415) 705-5555, located at Pier 41, San Francisco, and the McDonough ferry, **Phone:** (415) 435-2131, which departs from 21 Main Street, Tiburon, both serve the island daily during the summer. Call the above numbers for departure times and the winter schedule. **Admission:** Angel Island itself is free. The ferry tolls on the Blue & Gold Fleet are: Adults, $14.50; Children (6–12), $8.50; under 6, Free. The McDonough ferry: Adults, $10.25; Children (5–11), $8.00; Bicycles, $1.00. Immigration Station is **closed** until 2008. **Websites:** www.angelisland.org and www.parks.ca.gov.

Immigration Station opened in January 1910 as a detention center for immigrants awaiting entry papers and the outcome of medical exams. It was intended as an "Ellis Island of the West," and was meant to serve arrivals from Europe coming through the Panama Canal as well as Chinese and other Asians. World War I and tightened national immigration laws, however, blocked European emigration. So during its thirty-year life, 97 percent of the newcomers processed through Angel Island were Chinese.

Despite the heightened restrictions, overseas Chinese quickly discovered that the one relatively easy way to land in San Francisco was by claiming kinship with a current California resident, since the exclusion laws permitted U.S. citizens to bring in their families. But with all records having been destroyed in 1906, and thus with no method of verifying citizenship or familial ties, the Bureau of Immigration decided that interrogating new arrivals in detail was the best way to separate those with legitimate claims from those with spurious ones. Those Chinese who falsely claimed blood or marriage ties were known as "paper children" or "paper brides." Many of these paid fees to brokers in exchange for study booklets, from which they would memorize the answers to such questions as "How many houses in your village?" or "Which direction does the family altar face?" Those whose answers did not match those of their sponsor were sent back to China.

Notwithstanding the fact that during its existence the island depot processed 175,000 Chinese, Immigration Station never proved very satisfactory. The facilities were cramped, the buildings were firetraps, and it was an inconvenient boat ride from the

Courtesy, California State Library

The Administration Building at Immigration Station. It may look like a resort, but it was a dreaded destination for Chinese immigrants.

mainland. But it was not until November 1940, when a fire destroyed the administration building, that the Angel Island station was closed. Processing of Chinese immigrants shifted to San Francisco proper. In 1941 the U.S. Army took over the former detention center, and soon was using the barracks that once held Chinese immigrants to house German, Italian, and Japanese prisoners of war.

By 1970, the barracks, abandoned by the army and in disrepair, were about to be razed, when a park ranger noticed Chinese ideographs, some carved, others written in pencil, on the walls. These turned out to be poems penned by the Chinese detainees, recording their loneliness, anger, and misery while they awaited their hoped-for clearance to enter San Francisco. Because the poems were deemed to be historically significant, the California legislature appropriated funds to preserve the building as a museum.

A visit to the barracks is a moving experience. Except for a representative sample of the steel mesh cots the detainees used to sleep on, all the furnishings, including the plumbing, have been removed, leaving on the bare walls the poems themselves—faint echoes of their authors' despair.

San Francisco's Two Bridges

The Golden Gate Bridge.

Location: The Golden Gate Bridge spans the entrance to San Francisco Bay, connecting The City to Marin and the other northern counties. The single deck bridge provides for six lanes of vehicular traffic. There are ten-foot-wide walkways on each side of the bridge. Generally, pedestrians are allowed on the east side and bicyclists on the west side. Access is from the parking lot next to the toll plaza on the San Francisco side, and from Vista Point on the Marin side. **Website:** www.goldengatebridge.org.

The Golden Gate Bridge is said to be the most photographed man-made structure in the world. It is easy to see why. Spanning the entrance to one of the world's great harbors, the bridge enhances the natural beauty of the site. It is graceful, uncluttered, beautifully proportioned—a bridge of timeless design. Even modest details such as the vertical fluting on the towers, which capture the rising and setting sun, providing alternative light and shadow, enhance the bridge's atmospherics. It is a small thing, but it's one of the little touches that, in combination with the span's other parts, adds up to a perfect whole.

The rust-red color has also been widely hailed as an inspired choice. Silver and black were the traditional bridge colors at that time, and still are, but Irving Morrow, the principal designer, felt that the international orange color finally selected would not only complement the red rocks of the Marin hills in the background, but would also provide a contrast to the blue sky above and the silver-gray fogs swirling through. The choice of color was sealed when a red lead primer coat was applied as the bridge neared completion, and many people wrote to say how beautiful it looked.

The initial coat of international orange, applied in 1937, was only the first of several. The bridge today requires ongoing maintenance and painting to guard against the continual wear brought about by salty air, fog, sun, wind, and rain.

One of the finest ways to experience this magnificent bridge is to walk across it. But if you want to view it from a distance there are many good vantage points, both in San Francisco and around the bay. Two of the best places for taking in its sweep—and for taking photographs—are the parking lot just east of the toll plaza (take the last San Francisco exit if heading northbound on Highway 101) and the scenic viewpoint at the north end of the bridge in Marin County (take the Vista Point exit).

The San Francisco – Oakland Bay Bridge.

Location: The 8.4-mile-long Bay Bridge extends from the Alameda shore to (and through) Yerba Buena Island, and feeds into San Francisco in the Rincon Hill area south of Market Street. It is a double-deck bridge: the lower deck has five lanes of automobile traffic eastbound, the upper deck five lanes westbound. Like the Golden Gate Bridge, it never closes (an exception was for four weeks after the October 1989 earthquake). Unlike the Golden Gate Bridge, there is no pedestrian access.

In the mid-1980s, visitors to San Francisco were asked in a survey to name prominent landmarks. A substantial 50 percent named the Golden Gate Bridge but only 1 percent cited the Bay Bridge. If a similar study was done today the lesser known Bay Bridge would surely rank higher, although not perhaps in a favorable manner. For as virtually everyone knows, the earthquake that struck northern California on October 17, 1989 made the bridge headline news when one section of the upper deck of the truss- cantilever portion collapsed onto the lower deck. Television broadcast the image into every home, including the unforgettable footage of a car driving into the gap, killing its driver.

The Bay Bridge's lack of respect versus the Golden Gate Bridge also partly stems from its less "artistic" design. The X-bracing of the former's suspension towers provide a more traditional look than the sculpted art deco rectangles of the Golden Gate Bridge's towers.

From a spectator's point of view, among the best places to see the Bay Bridge are from atop major hills in San Francisco. There are several good spots on Russian Hill, such as the Vallejo Street dead-end just east of Jones Street. Another vantage point, albeit from farther away, is from the Twin Peaks overlook. Closer up, you can see the bridge in all its glory from Treasure Island in the middle of the bay. Another good spot is from along the Embarcadero promenade south of the Ferry Building on the San Francisco waterfront.

The best way to appreciate this underrated bridge is by driving across it, preferably late at night when traffic is minimal. Drive west on the upper deck toward San Francisco. Gliding down the highway under the arc of lights above—added to the suspension cables in 1988—and seeing San Francisco illuminated before you on a clear night is to experience a little magic.

Alcatraz Island

Alcatraz.
Location: Alcatraz Island is located in San Francisco Bay just south of Angel Island. It can only be reached from San Francisco, by booking a trip on Alcatraz Cruises (Hornblower) at Pier 33 on the Embarcadero. There is service daily except for major holidays. **Phone:** (415) 981-7625. Ten departures daily starting at 9:30 a.m. Reservations are recommended, especially during the summer. **Admission:** Call for prices or see their **Website:** www.alcatrazcruises.com.

Alcatraz is one of San Francisco's most popular attractions, drawing over one million visitors a year. It is about a ten-minute boat ride from the Embarcadero to the island. When you dock at the island a park ranger, or volunteer, will give a brief orientation, which includes such useful information as where to find restrooms and departure times for the mainland. Before setting off to explore, you might want to purchase, for one dollar, the informative map/guide about Alcatraz and its history.

To tour the island you can take ranger-led tours given periodically on various themes such as movies about Alcatraz, visit the cellblocks with headsets for the audio tour, or you can simply wander about on your own—or any combination of the above.

Start your walk by heading up through the 1857 guardhouse and sally port, the oldest structure on Alcatraz and the island's only remaining intact nineteenth-century building. At the end of the first curve in the path you will pass the former PX and Officers Club (1910) from the island's army days. Beyond that, at the next bend in the path, to your left you will see the former army barracks (1905), which served as housing for prison guards starting in the 1930s.

Keep winding up the trail to the next turn where a sign will direct you to the main prison building, or cellhouse. This contains cell-blocks A through D and a dining hall. It was built between 1909 and 1912 by army prisoners, who then became its first inmates. The audio tour starts here. The narration is by former guards and convicts, who talk about life on The Rock, and comes complete with sound effects such as cell doors slamming.

Within the prison you can roam about the four cellblocks and the dining hall. Along the walls in several locations are mug shots of several of the most notorious criminals such as Al Capone and "Machine Gun" Kelly who were housed within Alcatraz's walls. (The exact location of Al Capone's cell is unknown, since prison officials insist that no records were kept as to which cells held which prisoners.) D Block, which has larger cells because it was modernized in 1940, was the isolation unit where the truly hardcore incorrigibles were housed. "Birdman" Robert Stroud spent much of his time here.

The Golden Gate International Exposition

Treasure Island Museum.

Location: Treasure Island is a man-made appendage on the north side of Yerba Buena Island in the middle of San Francisco Bay. It can only be reached via the Bay Bridge. Going either way on the bridge, stay in the far left lane. Slow to 15 mph as you exit. The museum containing artifacts from the Golden Gate International Exposition is located in the Administration Building to your right as you pass through the gate. **Hours:** Open weekdays, 10 a.m. to 3:30 p.m.; until 4:30 p.m., weekends and holidays. **Admission:** Free. **Closed indefinitely.** Check the website for reopening information. **Website:** www.treasureislandmuseum.org.

The Administration Building, which houses the Treasure Island Museum, is one of only three major structures left from the 1939–1940 Golden Gate International Exposition (GGIE), and is the only one open to the public. (The other two are the large hangar-like buildings directly behind the Administration Building. Originally they served as the fair's Hall of Air Transportation and the Palace of Fine and Decorative Arts.) As you head toward the museum, note the glass control tower on top of the building—a reminder that Treasure Island was supposed to serve as the San Francisco airport when the fair closed.

Six of the surviving sixteen Pacific Unity statues that ringed a fountain near the center of the fair now flank the front doors of the Administration Building. There are plans for all sixteen sculptures to be restored and grouped in a new arrangement in the parking lot in front of the Administration Building. Some of the statues will surround another fountain from the fair—the Pacific Basin fountain—which will also be restored and moved to the parking lot. A scale model in the foyer shows the proposed new configuration.

Once inside the Administration Building, which houses exhibits relating to several periods of military and naval history, turn right. The GGIE exhibit begins at the end of the corridor. The display starts with a brief history of Yerba Buena Island, then proceeds with several photos of the filling-in of the shoals and the creation of Treasure Island.

As you move toward the back wall take a moment to study the color map, which has a key that identifies all the fair's buildings and exhibits. This key is helpful in placing the scenes in the accompanying photographs. Just to the right of this map is a wall full of photos, most of them in color, taken during the fair. The night shots are the most striking, because the buildings and fountains were floodlit in reds, blues, and greens.

The rest of the exhibit contains a generous array of artifacts from the fair: admission stubs, programs, brochures, souvenir towels, drinking glasses, and the like. There are also some sharp black and white photos of the lunch stands, snack shops, and interiors of the exhibits that vividly take you back half a century. Also attention getting is a silent video showing scenes from the fair.

Near the exit is a display of mementoes from the famous China Clipper, which used Treasure Island as its home port. Artifacts on view include a polished metal scale model of the craft, photos of passengers in the roomy interior, and an original, well-worn leather briefcase with the Pan American Airways logo and the words 'China Clipper' embossed on it in gold leaf.

10

Modern Times (1941–1989)

With the bombing of Pearl Harbor and the coming of World War II, San Francisco would begin to change from a basically homogeneous, predominately white, somewhat insular city, to the more international, multiethnic metropolis of today. The war brought with it a huge influx of people—military and civilian—that boosted The City's population to what was unofficially estimated to be more than 800,000—a record high. When the war ended, many of the newcomers stayed on.

As the cataclysmic 1940s gave way to the more settled 1950s, the Bay Area enjoyed the surge in prosperity that prevailed throughout most of the rest of the U.S. But the self-satisfied mood of the Eisenhower years gave way to a counter reaction in San Francisco, where a small group of nonconformists known as the Beats planted the seeds of revolt. The Beats and their movement were short lived, but their influence flowered anew in the 1960s as "hippies" invaded a poor, neglected neighborhood south of the Panhandle near Golden Gate Park. The "Summer of Love" was chronicled the world over, making Haight-Ashbury a household name and a symbol of youthful rebellion of the baby boom generation.

The Haight-Ashbury phenomenon left a legacy of increased tolerance: it was one of the influences that led to gains by gays, women, and ethnic minorities during the 1970s and 1980s. As the latter decade came to a close, San Francisco was sharply reminded of its vulnerability when a 7.1 earthquake, the biggest since 1906, rocked northern California.

San Francisco Goes to War

On December 7, 1941 the Japanese bombed the U.S. naval base at Pearl Harbor, bringing America into the war. Thousands of San Franciscans went to Ocean Beach and, as if they could see Hawaii from there, gazed uncertainly toward the horizon. What was certain was that San Francisco, with its magnificent harbor, was to play a major role in the war effort during the next four years.

Military facilities around the bay began to bristle with activity. Some, such as the Presidio and Fort Mason, which had been around since the days of Spanish rule, already were active posts, and merely heightened their pace of operations. Other little-used forts and bases sprang to life, while still others were created from scratch. Local installations that served the war effort included Forts Barry, Baker, and Cronkhite on the Marin shore, Fort McDowell on Angel Island, Mare Island Naval Shipyard in Vallejo, Camp Stoneman near Pittsburg, Treasure Island, the Alameda Naval Air Station, the Oakland Army Base, and Hunters Point Naval Shipyard in San Francisco. The entire Bay Area was seemingly one big armed camp, as troops and equipment came pouring in.

While the experiences of front-line soldiers and the detailed records of combat have always dominated war histories, what is equally important is the home front effort that provides support and supplies. With battles soon to be waged from Australia to Japan and on numerous islands throughout the vast Pacific, huge numbers of ships would be needed.

In the Bay Area, the prime support contribution took the form of shipbuilding. Two facilities, in particular, dominated. The Bechtel Corporation built Marinship in Sausalito, which, at its height, employed 22,000 workers, while across the bay in Richmond, Henry Kaiser constructed a shipyard that became the world's largest. At its peak, it employed 100,000 men and women, and operated three eight-hour shifts a day, seven days a week. With all this activity, it is not surprising to learn that in 1944 the Bay Area led the world in shipbuilding.

The Liberty Ships

These shipyards built various types of vessels, but what they mostly produced were Liberty ships—cargo vessels built to uniform specifications. They carried a wide variety of supplies to troops overseas, including such diverse items as medicines, blood plasma, munitions, whiskey, and mail.

To support the war effort, hundreds and hundreds of Liberty ships were required, and they were needed as soon as possible. To achieve the original goal of constructing a 7,000-ton ship in only ninety days, an assembly line process much like that used to mass produce automobiles was set up. Through such efficiency the original ninety-day goal was not only met but exceeded, when Henry Kaiser produced one in fifty-six days and then one in forty-two days. To speed things even further, prefabricated parts were used wherever possible, and in a contest with an Oregon shipyard, Kaiser produced a Liberty Ship in an incredible four days. The average time of construction, however, was six to eight weeks. By the war's end over five hundred Liberty ships (out of 2,751 built nationwide) had been launched from the Richmond shipyard alone.

The War's Impact on San Francisco

The shipyards, military facilities, and defense plants that dotted San Francisco and the bay after 1941 led to an insatiable demand for civilian war workers. With every able-bodied draft-age male having been called up for military duty, women and minorities were actively recruited nationwide for the essential home front manufacturing and service jobs. Mexicans and other Latinos came north, and blacks came from the Deep South. Closer to home, Bay Area Chinese went to work supporting the war effort, and women—who comprised one-third of all Liberty ship workers—found meaningful work outside the home for the first time. Every group but Japanese-Americans contributed. They were unjustly interred in camps as alleged subversives. It was this vast in-migration and minority participation that marked the beginning of the change of San Francisco from a predominately white population to the much more diverse multi-racial and ethnic mix of today.

As the population surged, San Francisco and other Bay Area communities became full to bursting, putting a tremendous strain on housing, transportation and government services. Housing in particular was in critically short supply, since with wartime production a priority, the only civilian buildings being built were dormitories and barracks to accommodate defense plant workers. Most of these were temporary structures, but some of the more solidly constructed ones, such as those at Hunters Point in San Francisco, still survive. The housing shortage even extended to the city's hotels, which were often full to capacity, forcing some military personnel in transit to sleep in chairs in the lobbies. San Francisco was so crowded that by late 1943, for what was surely the only time in The City's history, local civic groups discouraged conventions and tourists from coming.

The War's End

The Japanese surrender on August 14, 1945—V–J Day—marked the end of World War II. Celebrating soldiers and civilians caused a near riot as throngs jammed Market Street and the city's downtown. In the following days and weeks, when troopships and supply vessels returned home through the Golden Gate, private boats sailed alongside to greet them, and bands played "California Here

San Francisco Public Library

Celebrants jammed Market Street on V-J Day.

I Come." Fort Mason's hillside was adorned with big white letters that said "Welcome, Well Done." And a huge circular storage tank that stood behind where the Marina Safeway is today (the area was a gasworks at the time) had a big sign that simply said "Thanks."

After the war, many of the civilian workers who had come from other cities, states, and countries stayed on in the Bay Area, as did some of the servicemen and servicewomen who had liked what they had seen when passing through. San Francisco would now be a different place from the city that *San Francisco Chronicle* columnist Herb Caen had, before the war, called an "innocent village."

The Beat Generation

After the turmoil of the war most Americans wanted nothing more than to pursue a career, buy a home, raise a family, and enjoy the prosperity that washed over the country during the next decade. But with everyone pursuing the same goals, a certain sameness and conformity settled in. Even San Francisco, accustomed as residents are today to its polyglot social milieu, was a model of conventional behavior. Ladies in the San Francisco of the 1950s, for example, wore hats and white gloves while on shopping excursions downtown.

Perhaps inevitably, a reaction set in. A small group of bohemians, in opposition to the prevailing mainstream beliefs, clustered in San Francisco's North Beach. They spoke out against the complacency they witnessed in the face of seemingly intractable problems such as racism and the specter of nuclear annihilation.

They became known as the Beats—a term Jack Kerouac derived from his characterizing his as a "beaten" generation, a comparison to the Lost Generation of the 1920s. The seminal event that launched their movement was a poetry reading at the Six Gallery in October 1955. It was here that Allen Ginsberg gave the first public reading of *Howl.* (The long vanished Six Gallery was located on Fillmore Street, in Cow Hollow near Union Street.) Ginsberg wrote this epic work at 1010 Montgomery Street, just off Broadway, where he lived from February to August 1955.

While Ginsberg, Gary Snyder, Lawrence Ferlinghetti, and other poets formed the nucleus of the emerging Beat scene, it was not long before a sort of uniform developed among the camp followers who surrounded them. Sandals, berets, turtlenecks, and dark glasses typified the appearance of these coffeehouse idlers. Herb Caen called them "beatniks," meaning it derogatorily. In 1957 the Russians had launched the first satellite, Sputnik, and Caen, in one of his newspaper columns, added the word to the lexicon when he noted that Sputnik and the Beats were both "far out." Joining the two words at the hip, he created beatnik.

The Beat movement was short lived. By 1958 the beatniks had been covered by the national media and were part of the contemporary scene. Tour buses began runs through North Beach so that tourists could gawk at the Beats. (A group of Beats once responded to this invasion of their turf by marching to fashionable Union Square, playing their bongos, and checking out the "squares.") By the early 1960s the beats were passé. The coffeehouses gave way to topless clubs, and the few Beats remaining found themselves forced to move away from formerly inexpensive North Beach as the tourist boom inflated prices.

Some of the Beats moved to Haight-Ashbury, at that time a somewhat rundown, largely black neighborhood just outside the east entrance to Golden Gate Park. Neglected Victorian houses offered cheap rent, and the Beats, who worshiped jazz and black musicians, felt at home in the black community.

What the Beats also found in the Haight, however, was the genesis of a separate group emerging from the district's youthful population. (San Francisco State University was located in Haight-Ashbury until 1952 when it moved to its Nineteenth Avenue location, but many of its students continued to live in the old locale.) The Beats considered this new gathering not "cool" enough to be hipsters like themselves, so they were belittled as junior grade hipsters or "hippies."

The Beat movement, with its love of jazz and poetry and its interest in Asian culture and Zen Buddhism, passed from the scene in the mid-1960s. But its influence was felt in Haight-Ashbury as the hippies inherited the Beats' sense of political and philosophical alienation from society. The hippies also enthusiastically embraced drugs, and soon would expand beyond the Beats occasional use of marijuana to embrace LSD and other mind-expanding drugs in a big way.

Haight-Ashbury before the Hippies

Haight-Ashbury before the hippie invasion was quite different from what it later became. The district originally was supposed to be a part of what would be Golden Gate Park when the park was being planned in the 1860s. Squatters and land speculators had staked claims in much of the area, however, and proved difficult to dislodge. A compromise was reached whereby in return for clear title to certain parcels, the squatters would give up their claims to a narrow strip at the eastern end of the park. Thus the eastern portion of Golden Gate Park was narrowed to the Panhandle, and the grid pattern of streets was extended to the south of the Panhandle to form the nucleus of what became Haight-Ashbury.

The district did not really start to grow until the early 1880s when a cable car line was put in along Haight Street. By the 1890s, development was in full swing and the Haight had become a fashionable resort area. A number of San Francisco's wealthier families built country homes as weekend retreats. Growth continued into the new century, and picked up even more noticeably after the 1906 disaster, when refugees from downtown migrated to the undamaged Haight.

Beginning with the depression of the 1930s, Haight-Ashbury started on a long decline. The district's once proud Victorians fell into disrepair as their owners either failed to maintain them or else walked away from mortgage payments they could no longer meet. Many blacks who had emigrated to San Francisco during the war to work in defense plants moved into the Haight in increasing numbers in the 1940s and 1950s.

The Hippie Era

The first flowering of the Haight—leading to the Summer of Love in 1967—started in late 1965 when first one and then a second offbeat coffeehouse opened. Beats and hippies now had places of their own to congregate. It was also about this time that funky clothing and most of San Francisco's seminal rock bands made their initial appearance. One of the earliest groups was called The Charlatans; their trademark was the Victorian-era clothes they wore, picked up from local secondhand thrift shops where such articles were plentiful. The Charlatans lasted only a few years, but two bands that also started then—the Jefferson Airplane and the Warlocks (the latter soon mutated into the Grateful Dead, a name they took from an Egyptian tomb inscription)—would endure for decades. Adding to the scene were Ken Kesey and his Merry Pranksters, who gave LSD parties at various Bay Area locations and advertised them by passing out handbills that offered the provocative headline, "Can You Pass the Acid Test?"

In January 1966 the world's first psychedelic shop opened on Haight Street, and, as the year progressed, LSD and other drugs became more prevalent. Hippies chalked color swirls in wild, psychedelic patterns on Haight-Ashbury sidewalks and on the pathways leading into Golden Gate Park—usually just one step ahead of the police, who tried to expunge their art. That year an air of good feeling prevailed; total strangers sometimes hugged one another in stoned fellowship.

Early 1967 saw tens of thousands congregate in Golden Gate Park for a human Be-In, an event presided over by Allen Ginsberg, Timothy Leary, and others in celebration of the new spirit of community that seemed to be enveloping the Haight. More festivals followed. Bands such as the Airplane, the Dead, and Big Brother and the Holding Company—featuring Janis Joplin—played free concerts; LSD tabs were plentiful and were passed out among the revelers like candy. Silly crazes took hold as everyone looked for new drugs and new ways to get high. A rumor spread that bananas, when dried and smoked, produced an hallucinogenic high. Immediately thereafter, every grocery on Haight Street sold out of bananas.

By spring, the word was out that Haight-Ashbury was the place to be. With summer approaching and school letting out, everyone knew that thousands of young people and others wanting to partake of the attractions would descend on the Haight. The throngs soon arrived. For awhile the mellowness continued. But the publicity, the expectations, and the onslaught proved to be too much. Just as the gold rush had started in 1848 in an atmosphere of trust and goodwill, only to turn nasty in 1849 as a coarser element invaded, so it was with Haight-Ashbury. By August 1967 the Summer of Love had turned ugly as drifters, criminals, drug abusers, and opportunists of all kinds arrived (including Charles Manson), looking to take advantage of easily available drugs and sex. Fights broke out, two well-known drug dealers were murdered within a day of each other, and methamphetamine, or "speed," replaced the more benign LSD as the drug of choice.

It was the beginning of the end of Haight-Ashbury's brief golden era of peace and love. Things got worse in 1968; in February a confrontation with police led to a riot. The police tactical squad wielding long batons, swept through the district. In April, after Martin Luther King was assassinated, store windows along Haight Street were smashed. Hard drug usage became widespread when cheap heroin flooded the market, creating a virtual epidemic. By 1969 the Haight had hit bottom; strung-out needle freaks roamed the streets, stealing and robbing to support their habits. Many storefronts along Haight Street became vacant and were boarded up; the remaining shop owners installed protective metal grates.

Haight-Ashbury's Legacy

It took several more years, but by the early to mid-1970s the Haight had turned the corner and was starting to rebound. Escalating real estate prices, as well as a renascent appreciation of The City's Victorians—many of which are located in the Haight—led to the restoration of these noble survivors.

The hippie era left behind few physical signs of its existence. Virtually all of the hippie hangouts, coffeehouses, psychedelic shops, and crash pads are now other businesses, most having changed identities several times since the sixties. One of the few tangible remnants of the time still in place is the Haight-Ashbury Free Clinic, just off Haight Street. Other more mobile survivors include bands such as the Jefferson Airplane and the Grateful Dead; the latter kept on truckin' up until Jerry Garcia's death in 1995. *Rolling Stone* magazine could also be classified a survivor, since it got its start in San Francisco in October 1967, chronicling the Haight-Ashbury scene and the rock groups it spawned.

But the main legacy of Haight-Ashbury and the hippies' penchant (and the Beats before them) to try almost anything, and in the process to tear at the fabric of social conformity, is that it eventually led to a greater acceptance and tolerance on the part of mainstream America. This, in turn, led to greater visibility and gains for gays, women, and minorities in the 1970s and 1980s.

The convulsions of Haight-Ashbury in the 1960s turned out to be a necessary corrective and reminder to the larger society of San Francisco's heritage of tolerance. This tradition of open-mindedness dates back to the area's earliest days of human habitation. The Indians of the region, perhaps by happy accident, presaged this legacy with the harmony of their social relations and a relative absence of conflict and war. They were followed by the easy living Californios, with their noted hospitality toward strangers.

Rand Richards

The Haight-Ashbury Free Clinic.

With the gold rush and the arrival of the Yankees, San Francisco began its life as a wide open city, one without the usual social norms but also without the social taboos and restrictions. While the city developed as a major seaport and became a magnet for sailors and transients, it further expanded the boundaries of tolerance as civic officials cast a blind eye to the vice that developed. The influx of Asians, with their live-and-let-live philosophy, has also contributed to this liberal spirit. The Beats and hippies followed, rebelling against what had become a stratified, complacent society. They reminded the powers that be that San Francisco's legacy, its distinctive difference as a great city, is its willingness to accommodate different voices and lifestyles, however strange they may at first seem.

The 1989 Earthquake

On October 17, 1989 at 5:04 p.m. northern California was hit by a 6.8 earthquake, the biggest since 1906. Sixty-seven people were killed, and damage totaled in excess of six billion dollars. As area residents found out, a killer earthquake affecting San Francisco is major national and international news. Santa Cruz and Watsonville suffered more widespread destruction, but most of the media glare focused on the collapsed Cypress structure portion of the Nimitz freeway, the upper deck section of the Bay Bridge roadway that fell onto the lower deck, and the extensive quake damage and dramatic fire in San Francisco's Marina district.

The earthquake originated on the San Andreas fault and ruptured a twenty-five-mile length of it. As bad as this might sound it was nothing like the estimated 7.9 temblor of 1906, which released more than thirty times the energy, produced more than ten times the ground motion, and ruptured a 250-mile-long section of the same fault farther north.

The epicenter of the 1989 quake was located near Aptos, which explains the greater overall destruction in nearby Santa Cruz and Watsonville. But most of the deaths occurred near the shoreline of San Francisco Bay, where seismic waves permeating mud and bay fill collapsed the structures built on them that were not anchored to bedrock.

The two-tier Cypress structure, whose upper deck pancaked onto the lower one, crushing dozens of cars and killing forty-three people, was erected on soft bay mud. Not far away, a fifty-foot section of roadway in the Bay Bridge's cantilever-truss section, which rests on wooden piles driven into the ooze below, crashed onto the lower deck when the jolt yanked it off its support pins. In San Francisco's Marina district, an area largely built on uncompacted fill put in after the Panama Pacific International Exposition of 1915, many of the homes and apartment buildings suffered damage; a few buildings even telescoped down from four stories to one as the lower floors gave way. None of the Marina's apartment buildings or houses that collapsed was anchored to bedrock, and when the seismic waves reached them the sandy soil experienced a process called "liquefaction," which turned it into a liquid slush and caused the buildings to settle.

Virtually all of the physical evidence of the quake's damage has now been erased. The severely damaged buildings have been demolished and sometimes replaced; affected streets repaired and repaved; building cracks smoothed over and replastered. The Bay Bridge, obviously a priority, was back in business only a month after the quake. The twisted remains of the Cypress structure were carted off by a salvage company; the former stretch of freeway today is nothing more than a dusty, quiet median strip. The Marina, too, shows few scars of the trauma. Lots that stood empty and idle for a time have in recent years sprouted with new apartments and condominiums in response to the need for housing.

Vince Maggiora/San Francisco Chronicle
Shades of 1906: San Francisco's Marina district, October 17, 1989.

Lawrence Ferlinghetti (b.1919)

"The Good Gray Poet"

Lawrence Ferlinghetti's early life could have come straight from a Dickens novel. He was born in 1919 in Yonkers, New York. His Italian immigrant father had died several months before; shortly afterward, his mother was committed to a mental institution, and a great aunt took him to Strasbourg, France. She brought him back to the United States when he was five, and abandoned him. He was sent to an orphanage, and was later taken in and raised by a wealthy Bronxville, New York family. This fortuitous adoption ended his turbulent early years. He enjoyed a normal childhood thereafter, becoming a paperboy, an Eagle Scout, and an amateur sports enthusiast.

© Rob Lee/New Directions
Lawrence Ferlinghetti

Ferlinghetti attended a private high school, and after graduation, inspired by the novels of Thomas Wolfe, he enrolled at the University of North Carolina at Chapel Hill. He graduated with a bachelors degree in journalism in 1941. With war approaching, he enlisted in the navy just prior to Pearl Harbor. He served in both the Atlantic and Pacific theaters and reached the rank of lieutenant commander.

After the war, having previously read and been influenced by some of the great poets and novelists, Ferlinghetti enrolled at Columbia University in New York, where, in 1947, he received his Masters degree in literature. He then went on to Paris and earned a Ph.D. at the Sorbonne.

Lawrence Ferlinghetti first visited San Francisco in 1950. He was attracted by its European feel, and with his new bride he moved to The City permanently in 1951. He continued writing poetry and fiction—which he had for many years—and soon met the poet Kenneth Rexroth and others of the budding San Francisco literary and poetry scene.

Ferlinghetti also met Peter Martin, publisher of a struggling literary magazine named *City Lights,* after the Charlie Chaplin film. The two became partners, and in June 1953, in an effort to help support the magazine, they opened a bookstore of the same name. It was the first paperback-only bookshop in the United States, and was an immediate success. When Martin moved to New York two years later he sold his interest to Ferlinghetti, who soon launched a publishing company under the City Lights rubric as well, and began by publishing the works of local poets.

One day a young poet named Allen Ginsberg came into the bookshop and showed the publisher some of his poems. Ferlinghetti recognized Ginsberg's talent, and after the Six Gallery reading in which the latter delivered his stirring reading of *Howl*—his primal scream of a poem about the evils of materialism, conformity, and war—he knew he had to publish it.

Howl was published in 1957. The captain of the juvenile division of the San Francisco Police Department decided that it was "not fit for children to read." Ferlinghetti and his store manager were arrested on obscenity charges—Ginsberg was out of the country—and copies of *Howl* were seized. After a celebrated trial and a not guilty verdict, in which the poem was ruled to be not obscene, Ferlinghetti found himself a First Amendment hero and a national and international figure.

But despite the notoriety of the *Howl* trial and his subsequent recognition as a poet, publisher, and social activist, Lawrence Ferlinghetti has never received much mainstream media attention. Maybe it is because his benign personality and relatively conventional lifestyle—he is divorced but is close to his two grown children—do not make good copy. Or perhaps it is because the good-natured poet does not fit the image of the tormented, self-destructive artist complete with lurid sex life, as exemplified by Jack Kerouac and Neal Cassady, two leading lights of the Beat movement who burned out early and died young. In any event, the lanky gray-bearded poet can still occasionally be seen today walking the streets of North Beach not far from his Columbus Avenue bookstore.

Sites and Attractions

World War II – The Liberty Ships

> **The S.S.** *Jeremiah O'Brien.*
> **Location**: On the San Francisco waterfront at Pier 45, Fisherman's Wharf.
> **Phone:** (415) 544-0100. **Hours:** Open daily, 9 a.m. to 5 p.m. (6 p.m. in summer), except major holidays. Last admission, one hour before closing. **Admission:** Adults, $8.00; Seniors (62+), $5.00; Juniors (6–12), $4.00; Children (under 6), Free. Family, $20.00. **Website:** www.ssjeremiahobrien.org.

A National Historic Landmark, the *Jeremiah O'Brien* is one of only two surviving, unaltered, and still operable, Liberty ships of more than 2,700 constructed. Although she was built and launched in Port- land, Maine—in one of eighteen shipyards nationwide that built Liberty ships during World War II—the ship is essentially identical to the vessels produced by Bay Area shipyards. Launched in 1943 as part of the U.S. merchant marine fleet ferrying supplies and ammunition to allied forces, she was manned by merchant seamen and U.S. Navy gunners.

The *O'Brien* spent her first year making cargo runs across the Atlantic. She participated in the Normandy landings, arriving on the French coast a few days after D-Day. Later she was shifted to the Pacific. With San Francisco as her home port she delivered cargo to Brisbane, Shanghai, and Manila. After the war ended the *Jeremiah O'Brien*—named for an American Revolutionary War hero—was mothballed at Suisun Bay, where she remained until the late 1970s. Some restorative work was done on her, and she was opened to the public in 1980.

On board, the thing that strikes most first-time visitors is how such a large ship with so many complex and interwoven parts and

The S.S. *Jeremiah O'Brien.*

systems could have been built in fifty-six days. Even more amazing is how other Liberty ships were later built in less than a week.

You are free to tour the ship on your own, visiting all parts of the vessel including the labyrinthine engine room which, with its myriad pipes and staircases, looks like something out of an industrial nightmare. On the upper deck, at the bow, are the chartroom with its gyrocompass and nautical map of San Francisco Bay, and the Master's stateroom (the skipper is called a master on board, a captain on shore). Note how Spartan the stateroom is and how little it differs from those of the other officers' quarters nearby. It's quite a contrast from the nearby *Balclutha,* where the captain lived apart from the rest of the crew and in relative luxury.

A recent addition in Cargo Hold #1 is a wonderful large-scale diorama of the Jeremiah O'Brien unloading cargo onto a barge on the Normandy coast shortly after D-Day.

Marinship – Bay Model Visitor's Center
Location: 2100 Bridgeway, Sausalito. **Phone:** (415) 332-3871. **Hours:** Tuesday - Saturday, 9 a.m. to 4 p.m., with additional summer hours of Saturday, Sunday, and some holidays, 10 a.m. to 5 p.m. Closed federal holidays. **Admission:** Free. **Website:** www.sph.usace.army.mil/bmvc.

The Bay Model building encompasses part of what was Marinship, one of the Bay Area's World War II shipyards. A well laid out and evocative display loaded with historic photographs charts Marinship's history and documents how marsh and tideland along the Sausalito waterfront was transformed almost overnight into a bustling shipyard cranking out Liberty ships, tankers, and oilers. Period artifacts such as clothing and tools nicely complement the photographs.

Beat Era Hangouts

City Lights Bookstore.
Location: 261 Columbus Avenue (near Broadway), San Francisco.
Phone: (415) 362-8193. **Hours:** Open every day 10 a.m. to Midnight.
Website: www.citylights.com.

The City Lights bookstore is one of the few remaining landmarks from the Beat era of the 1950s. It was a magnet for Allen Ginsberg, Jack Kerouac, Neal Cassady and other Beat writers and poets.

Generally considered to be the first paperback-only bookshop in the United States, the original store, which opened in June 1953, occupied just the pie-shaped corner of the 1907 building it inhabits. Later it expanded downstairs and farther across the main floor of the building; recently it added a poetry room at the north end.

City Lights made headlines in 1957 when its owner, Lawrence Ferlinghetti, was arrested by the San Francisco police and charged with obscenity for selling the first American edition of Allen Ginsberg's poem Howl. A local judge acquitted Ferlinghetti, finding that Howl had "redeeming social value." This precedent-setting ruling paved the way for the publication in the U.S. of previously banned works such as *Lady Chatterley's Lover* and *Tropic of Cancer*.

Vesuvio Café.
Location: 255 Columbus Avenue, San Francisco. **Phone:** (415) 362-3370.
Hours: Open daily, 6 a.m. to 2 a.m. **Website:** www.vesuvio.com.

Just across Jack Kerouac Alley (still Adler Place on old maps) is Vesuvio Café. Opened in 1949 by Henri Lenoir, a French émigré, this bar was a favorite watering hole for the Beats. Jack Kerouac, author of the classic *On the Road*, came in for a drink one evening in 1960 before going to Big Sur to meet author Henry Miller, who had admired Kerouac's work and had invited him down to his coastal retreat. Kerouac called Miller several times that night to let him know he was still coming, but instead got drunk and spent the night in San Francisco. The two never did meet.

The Vesuvio today, with its bric-a-brac, antique-shop décor, is little changed from the Beat days. Occasionally some new piece of decoration makes it appearance. A recent addition is a framed copy of an early *San Francisco Chronicle* edition headlining the great quake of 1989.

Across Columbus Avenue from the Vesuvio and City Lights are two other hangouts frequented by many leading literary lights of the 1950s and 1960s—Spec's at 12 Kenneth Rexroth (Adler Place), and Tosca's at 242 Columbus. These two bars, along with City Lights and Vesuvio Café, remain today favorite stops for local and visiting writers, artists, and musicians.

Beat Era/Hippie Artifacts

The Oakland Museum
Location: 1000 Oak Street (two blocks from Lake Merritt), Oakland. **Phone:** (510) 238-3842. **Hours:** Wednesday - Saturday, 10 a.m. to 5 p.m.; (First Friday to 9 p.m.); Sunday, Noon to 5 p.m. Closed holidays. **Admission:** Adults, $8.00; Seniors, Students, $5.00; Children (under 5), Free. **Website:** www.museumca.org.

At the back of the History Gallery in the northeast corner there is a small section devoted to the cultural upheavals of the 1950s and 1960s. The Beat Era is represented by a re-creation of a North Beach coffeehouse/bar of the period. Surrounding a bar set with an espresso machine and pitchers of beer are posters for jazz concerts, bongo drums, and a beret. Nearby are some album covers of combined jazz and poetry events. One features a youthful-looking Lawrence Ferlinghetti.

From the hippie era, a highlight is Country Joe MacDonald's guitar adorned with a peace symbol and the words "Peace, Love." Next to it is a gaudily bejeweled vanity and dresser done by a flower child of the sixties. Other items include hippie clothes such as a tie-dyed T-shirt, candles, incense, wind chimes, and record albums featuring the Beatles, the Grateful Dead, the Jefferson Airplane, and other bands of the period.

Haight–Ashbury in the 1960s

A Walking Tour of Haight–Ashbury.

Location: The heart of Haight-Ashbury is the area south of the Panhandle in the blocks bounded by Oak, Masonic, Frederick, and Stanyan streets. This walking tour starts at the intersection of Haight and Masonic and concludes at the corner of Stanyan and Waller.

Although gentrification has touched the Haight, and real estate is expensive, the neighborhood still retains much of the flavor of its hippie days. Clothing styles have changed since then, but the area still attracts the same kinds of people who would have been seen wearing bell bottoms and love beads a generation ago.

Today's residents also evince the same anti-establishment, anti-corporate views their predecessors did. Several national chains have attempted to open outlets in the Haight in recent years, and have been greeted with hostility. The latest example was Thrifty Drug, which in 1988 started construction of a store at the corner of Haight and Cole, only to have it torched in a huge arson fire that also destroyed several neighboring businesses and apartments. Before that, Round Table Pizza opened an outlet. Petitions to City Hall for its closure did not work, but an informal boycott did. Only McDonalds, which suffered spray-paint attacks at first, has stayed.

To experience the varied character of this unconventional district and to look at the few remaining landmarks from the 1960s, start your walking tour at the northeast corner of Haight and Masonic streets. The ground floor of this building, in 1967, housed a popular café and hippie hangout called "The Drogstore." The owners had wanted to call it "The Drugstore Café" to associate the name with the emerging good-times drug culture that was still prevalent, but the police found the name too suggestive and forced the change. The site now houses a restaurant.

Walk one block south up Masonic to Waller and take a right. Stay on the north side of Waller so that you can view the fine row of large Queen Anne style Victorians on the opposite side of the street. When you reach Delmar Street, just a half block west, take a left and proceed up the street for a block and a half. The sprawling Victorian cottage at 130 Delmar is where the Jefferson Airplane lived in the 1960s. (This, and the former Grateful Dead house mentioned below, are now private residences, so please do not disturb the occupants.)

Map by Larry Van Dyke

The Haight-Ashbury Walking Tour.

Continue up Delmar. Before you get to the first cross street, Piedmont, you will see virtually every house style imaginable— Tudor, Mission Revival, as well as Victorians of different styles. Turn right on Piedmont and then right on Ashbury. One and a half blocks down, on the right side of the street at 710 Ashbury, is a Queen Anne row house where the Grateful Dead lived and where they were once busted for drug possession.

Continue down another block and a half until you reach the famous intersection of Haight and Ashbury. Turn left on Haight. On the south side of the street at 1535 is where The Psychedelic Shop, the first shop devoted solely to "psychedelic" paraphernalia, opened in 1966. Now it's a pizza parlor.

Walk to Clayton Street and cross to the north side of Haight. Just around the corner at 558–560 is the Haight-Ashbury Free Clinic. The idea of a medical clinic open free of charge to indigent and needy people was a radical one when the clinic first opened, in June 1967, but since then many other cities have opened such facilities. The Free Clinic was the idea of Dr. David Smith, who started it in response to increasing drug overdoses and drug-related health problems experienced by the hippies and young people who had descended on the Haight. Still in its original location in an upstairs Victorian flat, the Haight-Ashbury Free Clinic is going strong today, staffed entirely by volunteers, and now treats a wide array of health problems, not just those related to drugs.

Keep walking west on Haight Street to Stanyan, at the edge of Golden Gate Park. You will get a first hand taste of the Haight's street life, since you will surely be beseeched by panhandlers along the way. Turn left on Stanyan and finish your tour at the Stanyan Park Hotel (built in 1904) at the corner of Waller. It is a step back in time to the early days of Haight-Ashbury when the district was a resort area for the wealthy. This proud building, now a registered National Historic Landmark, survived 1906, the hippie invasion, and the 1989 earthquake. With such a record it may well make it through The Big One that someday surely will strike.

The 1989 Earthquake

1989 Earthquake Epicenter – Forest of Nisene Marks, Aptos.

Location: The town of Aptos is seven miles east of Santa Cruz, just off Highway 1. To reach the epicenter trail, from Highway 1 take the Seacliff Beach/Aptos exit to Soquel Avenue. Go right on Soquel for a few blocks. Look for "Forest of Nisene Marks" signs, and turn left onto Aptos Creek Road. Drive all the way to the end of the hard-packed dirt road—about two miles. The epicenter trail starts beyond the gate, near the east end of the parking lot. **Hours:** The park is open from sunrise to sunset. There is no phone and no ranger station at the site. **Admission:** Free. **Website:** www.parks.ca.gov.

A hike to the epicenter of the October 17, 1989 earthquake will not provide a better understanding of the tremor, but for many it seems to serve as a symbolic journey to the heart of darkness.

The trail to the epicenter is in two parts. The first part is a wide, solid fire road. You have to cross a stream on the way, but it is easy enough to hop from rock to rock to avoid getting wet. After half a mile you will come to an official-looking sign that says "epicenter Area/6.8 Earthquake/5:04 p.m. October 17, 1989."

The actual epicenter is half a mile farther into the woods, but the narrower trail leading there is closed. Frankly, there isn't much to see there anyway. Several huge fissures split the earth in the Santa Cruz mountains, as dramatic newspaper photos of the time showed, but those are elsewhere. Still, you will ponder nature's explosive power when you realize that a shifting deep in the earth here caused much destruction and dozens of deaths seventy miles away in San Francisco and Oakland.

San Francisco's Victorian Architecture

The second half of the nineteenth century produced a distinctive style of architecture that is now known as "Victorian." It was named after Queen Victoria of England (1837–1901), the leading figure of an age in which Britain dominated the world and set the trends in social behavior, fashion, and architecture.

Victorian architecture was definitely not a style in which less is more. It was characterized in some instances by a veritable riot of ornamentation, as designers outdid themselves dressing up façades with decorative flourishes such as garlands, egg and dart molding, dentils, fluting, pilasters, collonettes, sunbursts, lattices, spindlework, and false turrets and towers. It seemed that the bigger the house, the more excessive the embellishments. Both the darkly Gothic Mark Hopkins mansion and the Second Empire-style chateau of Charles Crocker on Nob Hill, before they burned in 1906, were noted for their extravagantly detailed exteriors. They even became targets of ridicule. Local architect Willis Polk derided the Crocker house as being the product of "the delirium of the woodcarver."

Victorian architecture took root in many foreign countries as well as in the U.S. In some parts of the country Victorians were built mainly of brick and stone. In San Francisco, wood, particularly California redwood, which was abundant and easily worked by hand or machine, was the building material of choice.

The heyday of the Victorians ended as the nineteenth century came to a close. The twentieth century has not been kind to these noble structures. The 1906 disaster razed San Francisco's downtown, leveled the grand Victorian mansions of Nob Hill and Van Ness Avenue, and destroyed virtually all of the abundant commercial Victorian office buildings that once lined the streets of The City's financial district.

One of the few remaining business buildings from the Victorian era can be seen at the southwest corner of Buchanan and North Point streets in the Marina district. This stately Richardson

Romanesque brick edifice with a Queen Anne tower was built in 1893 as the headquarters of the San Francisco Gas Works. Today it houses a real estate development company.

The Victorian architecture that survived 1906 is located primarily west and south of downtown—residential areas that were untouched by the fire. The remaining Victorians are mainly single-family homes or flats that were mass-produced, affordable (from $750 to $7,000) workingmen's homes, roughly equivalent to the suburban tract houses that went up all over the U.S. after World War II.

Today only about one-half of The City's approximately fifteen thousand remaining Victorians are still unaltered. The rest have been modified, some so severely that it is hard to imagine how they originally looked. Many of the façades were remodeled in the first decades of the twentieth century. Some were redone simply to modernize the ornate nineteenth-century style that had become passé, while others fell prey to the pitches of siding salesmen who told homeowners they could reduce their fire insurance premiums by removing the flammable Victorian gingerbread and covering their houses with asbestos shingles, roll-a-brick, stucco, or other fireproof materials. It was only in the 1960s that this modernizing trend came to an end, and property owners and the public experienced a newfound appreciation for these overdressed "painted ladies." In recent years, some of the previously modernized Victorians have been painstakingly restored to their former appearance.

San Francisco's distinctive residential Victorian architecture might not have come to pass had it not been for the greed of real-estate developers. Back in the 1860s, when the claims of Mexican land grant holders, squatters, and other titleholders to lands outside San Francisco's downtown area were finally settled by the courts, homestead associations and real-estate development companies divided large parcels of raw land into lots just big enough to hold a house—typically twenty-five feet wide by one hundred feet deep. The developers chose the smallest lot size they could get away with, because smaller lots meant more potential buyers and more profit for the developers.

Such a small, narrow lot size forced architects and carpenters to be creative in their designs and ornamentation. One early distinctive feature that emerged was the bay window, which gave a building not only more floor space but also increased the available light and ventilation—important considerations in houses occupying the width of their lots and standing shoulder-to-shoulder. The bay window also provided additional room for exterior decoration. The builders fully utilized this space as well as that on the rest of the façade, adding embellishments as their imaginations dictated. One could also speculate that the profusion of decoration resulted from a desire to compensate for the small lot size.

As early as the 1880s San Francisco was gaining a reputation for its colorful, even eccentric, Victorian architecture. A *New York Times* reporter on a visit to The City in 1883 captured the scene perfectly when he filed the following dispatch:

> Nobody seems to think of building a sober house. . . . Of all the efflorescent, floriated bulbousness, and flamboyant craziness that ever decorated a city, I think San Francisco may carry off the prize. And yet, such is the glittering metallic brightness of the air, when it is not surcharged with fog, that I am not sure but this riotous run of architectural fancy is just what the city needs to redeem its otherwise hard nakedness.

Some of these houses, and sometimes even whole blocks of houses representing "this riotous run of architectural fancy," stand today, having weathered more than a century's worth of the corrosive effects of the elements and several big earthquakes. Some of the best and most characteristic examples can be found in the Western Addition—the roughly triangular area west of Van Ness Avenue to Divisadero Street and from California Street south to Market. The main east-west thoroughfares of Bush and Pine streets contain many beautiful specimens. Haight-Ashbury, the Mission district, and Noe Valley, among other neighborhoods, also contain good selections.

The Victorian homes in San Francisco can basically be placed into one of four periods, each with its own prevailing style, although some houses are difficult to categorize since builders frequently mixed elements of different periods depending on what materials and designs they had available. Houses sporting decorations from more than one style also prevailed during times of transition from one period to the next.

At the risk of oversimplification, the four styles and their approximate periods are:

Cottage Style/Carpenter Gothic	1850s – 1860s
Italianate	1870s
Stick	1880s
Queen Anne	1890s

Cottage/Carpenter Gothic

The cottage style is summed up by the name itself—a modest dwelling with few rooms and simple adornment, usually fronted with a balcony or a porch. Some of the more fancy ones have Gothic windows, sculpted bargeboards, and rooftop finials.

The best examples of this style are to be found on Telegraph Hill, the eastern slope of which was spared by the 1906 fire. The 200 block

Rand Richards

228 Filbert Street.

of Union Street has several of these houses side-by-side. At 287 and 289 are two modest dwellings with Carpenter Gothic flourishes. Both have been modernized somewhat, but the basic structures date from the late 1850s or early 1860s. The much taller building at 291, probably built about the same time, is a good example of the Western false front that could be found in frontier towns all over the West in the mid-nineteenth century. Next door at 293, by way of contrast, is a one-story cottage built in the 1860s.

Just half a block to the north, at 31 Alta Street, is a three-story house with two balconies. Constructed in 1852, it is one of the oldest houses in San Francisco.

Half a block farther north is what is officially a San Francisco street, the Filbert Street steps. Down the wooden steps and to the left, partly hidden by the profusion of green foliage at 228 Filbert, is a nice example of a house in the Carpenter Gothic style; it dates from 1873. Number 224, two doors down the hill, is a fine, small cottage built in 1863.

A few cottages survive in other parts of the city. Two residences that are usually overlooked are at the western edge of the Mission district on Dolores Street, only a block from Mission Dolores. At 220 Dolores is what is known as the Phoenix Cottage. A small sign affixed to its front gives the date of construction as 1852. Its neighbor at 214 is said to have preceded it by a year, which could quite possibly make it the oldest surviving private residence on site in San Francisco. Unlike the houses on cramped Telegraph Hill, these two cottages have front yards.

Italianate

Italianate, a style popular in the 1870s and so named because it incorporated elements of Roman or Italian classical decoration, is characterized by straight roof lines and bracketed cornices. False fronts, which were designed to make these Victorians look more imposing, are also a distinguishing feature. Early Italianates typically had flat fronts, while later ones expanded beyond the traditional flat wall with slanted bay windows.

Probably the finest row of early Italianate flat-front residences can be seen in the

Rand Richards

1818 California Street.

Western Addition from 2115 to 2125 Bush Street, between Webster and Fillmore. These six restored two-story homes were built in 1874.

There is a nice grouping of Italianates with slanted bay windows, three of them dating from 1878, in the Mission district from 120 to 126 Guerrero Street.

On the other side of town, at the edge of Pacific Heights, what is surely the finest free-standing bay-window Italianate left in San Francisco is located at 1818 California Street. Constructed in 1876, this noble survivor, which in recent years was a bed-and-breakfast inn, is once again privately owned.

Stick Style

The Stick style, sometimes called Stick Eastlake (after Charles Eastlake, an English interior designer), is characterized by square bay windows and long ornamental strips or "sticks" affixed to the exterior, giving the façade a strong verticality. Stick-style houses, which typically were capped by false gable roofs, reached the peak of their popularity in the 1880s— the time when the wood-carvers art reached its apogee. Many houses of the period are encrusted with extra ornamental flourishes, such as machine-lathed portico posts, thin, stamped-out wooden strips, and other decorative work.

Rand Richards

1198 Fulton Street.

Virtually a whole block of Stick-style houses can still be seen in the 1801 block of Laguna Street, between Bush and Pine, in the Western Addition. These date from 1889. Most have been refurbished; a couple, however, have been stripped of their gingerbread, reflecting "improvements" made earlier this century. Directly across the street are half a dozen Italianates dating from 1877.

A dozen blocks to the southwest, another grouping of residences representative of the Stick genre can be seen on the south side of McAllister Street between Pierce and Steiner, near Alamo Square. Although not as well maintained as the ones on Laguna Street, these tall units standing shoulder-to-shoulder are fine examples of the Stick style in all its glory. Just a block away, on Alamo Square at the corner of Scott and Fulton streets, is a landmark Stick house crowned with a tower. This gem was built in 1889 for a wealthy baker.

Queen Anne

In the 1890s the Stick style gave way to the final Victorian type, the Queen Anne. Named by a British architect for an earlier queen of England, Queen Anne designs abandoned the false gable roofs of its predecessor in favor of functional gable roofs. The verticality of the Stick houses was also de-emphasized through the use of repetitive horizontal ornamental designs on the cornices, on balconies, and above doorways. Queen Annes were also typically covered with decorative wooden shingles. Most of the homes in this genre were built in row-house fashion, but a few examples have rounded corner towers with "witch's cap" roofs topped by finials. These are rare, however; only some three hundred of the remaining fifteen thousand Victorians are Queen Anne towers.

Steiner Street, on the east side of Alamo Square, has a picturesque line of Queen Anne row houses dating from 1894–95. They are so picturesque that the view as seen from the park, with the downtown high rises in the background, is one of the most photographed in the entire city and has appeared on countless postcards and calendars.

Another fine line-up of Queen Annes can be found in Haight-Ashbury. On the east side of Masonic Avenue between Haight and Waller, a procession of stately homes seems to march up the grade. They were constructed in 1899.

Rand Richards

1701 Franklin Street.

A final Queen Anne worthy of note, this one with a corner tower and complete with beautiful art glass windows, is located on the northwest corner of California and Franklin streets, just down from the previously mentioned Italianate at 1818 California. It was built in 1895.

Sites and Attractions Recap

San Francisco

Alcatraz Island

Alcatraz.
Location: Alcatraz Island is located in San Francisco Bay just south of Angel Island. It can be reached from San Francisco by booking a trip on Alcatraz Cruises (Hornblower) at Pier 33 on the Embarcadero. There is service daily except for major holidays. **Phone:** (415) 981-7625. Ten departures daily starting at 9:30 a.m. Reservations are recommended, especially during the summer. **Admission:** Call for prices or see their **Website:** www.alcatrazcruises.com. **Parking:** Take public transportation if at all possible since parking is hard to find and expensive in the Fisherman's Wharf area. If you drive, there are several garages and surface lots nearby.

The big draw on the island today is the prison that housed Al Capone and other notorious criminals starting in the 1930s. Alcatraz's history, first as a military outpost, and subsequently as a penal colony, goes back to the mid-nineteenth century. The only building on the island surviving from that era is the sally port (1857).

Be sure to wear comfortable shoes, since you will do quite a bit of walking, and wear a jacket or windbreaker, since it is normally breezy on the bay and on the island. (See pages 221–23.)

Cable Car Routes

The Cable Cars.
Location: See the map on page 162 for the cable car routes. **Hours:** Cars start running about 6 a.m. and make their last run between 12:30 a.m. and 1 a.m. Signs at the embarkation point or at most intersections can provide exact times. **Admission:** $3.00 per ride for all ages; $1.00 from 9 p.m. to 7 a.m. for Seniors (65+) and the disabled. All day passes cost $11.00 each and provide unlimited rides on cable cars and the Muni's buses and streetcars as well. **Parking:** If your sole aim is to ride a cable car round trip and see as much of the city in the process, the best bet would be to park at the Fifth and Mission garage and walk one block north to the Powell-Market turnaround and catch the Hyde Street line to Aquatic Park.

The cable cars are likely San Francisco's most popular attraction. There are three lines. The Mason-Taylor and Powell-Hyde lines have terminuses at Powell and Market, at Bay and Taylor, and at Hyde and Beach streets. The California Street line ends at the Hyatt Regency (Market Street) at one extremity and at Van Ness Avenue on the other. (See pages 135–36, 161–63). Cars can be boarded at most intersections, but because they are frequently crowded to capacity within a stop or two of leaving an end station, it is best to wait at one one of the turnarounds to be sure of getting a seat.

Chinatown/Portsmouth Square

A Walking Tour of Historic Chinatown.
Location: The main body of Chinatown, which is sandwiched between Nob Hill and the financial district, is encompassed by California, Stockton, Broadway, Columbus, and Kearny streets. The spine is Grant Avenue, which runs through the middle of Chinatown from Bush to Broadway. This walk will take you from the corner of Jackson and Stockton, three blocks to Sacramento via several alleys, and then will turn back one block to finish at Grant and Clay streets. **Parking:** Metered spaces are available in Chinatown but in this densely populated part of town finding a free one is frequently difficult. Your best bet is to park in the city-owned garage under Portsmouth Square. Drive east on Clay Street and turn left on Kearny to enter it.

This tour takes you through the alleys of Chinatown, which, in the nineteenth century, were havens of vice. Sites where gambling halls, opium dens, and a Chinese slave market stood are noted. (See pages 153–56.)

Chinese Historical Society of America Museum.
Location: 965 Clay Street, (between Stockton and Powell). **Phone:** (415) 391-1188. **Hours:** Tuesday – Friday, Noon to 5 p.m. Saturday, Sunday, Noon to 4 p.m. **Admission:** Adults, $3.00; Students and Seniors, $2.00; Children (6–17), $1.00. Free admission the first Thursday of every month. **Parking:** Same recommendation as for the Chinatown walking tour. **Website:** www.chsa.org.

This small but attractive museum has a wealth of artifacts illustrating the Chinese experience in California. Such items as an opium pipe, and an altar from a Chinese temple are supplemented by descriptive text and historical photographs on the surrounding walls. (See page 124.)

Sub-Treasury Building - Pacific Heritage Museum.
Location: 608 Commercial Street (between Montgomery and Kearny). **Phone:** (415) 399-1124. **Hours:** Tuesday – Saturday, 10 a.m. to 4 p.m., except holidays. **Admission:** Free. Parking: Same recommendation as for the Chinatown walking tour above.

This structure, which until 1906 was a four-story building, opened in 1877 as a federal government sub-treasury. Today it houses the Pacific Heritage Museum and has a permanent display on its role in San Francisco's commercial life during the nineteenth century. (See pages 120–21.)

Portsmouth Square and Yerba Buena Cove.
Location: Portsmouth Square, now the heart of Chinatown, is bounded by Clay, Kearny, and Washington streets, and, at its western edge, by Brenham Alley. The cove, which began just east of Montgomery Street, was filled in as the early city expanded, and now lies beneath San Francisco's financial district. **Parking:** A city-owned parking garage is located beneath Portsmouth Square. The entrance is on Kearny Street between Clay and Washington.

Portsmouth Square was the center of activity of Yerba Buena and early San Francisco and was the scene of many historic incidents, including the raising of the American flag by John B. Montgomery in 1846 and the hanging of wrongdoers by the First Committee of Vigilance. A half a block away on Grant Avenue, a plaque marks the site of William Richardson's first dwelling of 1835. (See pages 54–55.)

The Civic Center

City Hall, the New Main Library, and the Civic Center.
Location: The city government's complex—the Civic Center—is bounded by Van Ness Avenue, McAllister, Hyde, and Grove Streets. City Hall's main entrance faces Polk Street. The New Main Library is on Larkin Street, across the plaza from City Hall. **Hours:** City Hall is open weekdays, 9 a.m. to 5 p.m. The Library's hours vary. Call (415) 557-4400 for information. **Parking:** There are plenty of parking meters surrounding the plaza. If these are all full, try the parking garage underneath. The entrance is on McAllister Street. Rates there are the same for the first two hours as above ground at the parking meters, and slightly more expensive thereafter.

San Francisco's Civic Center is a fine example of Beaux-Arts classicism. All the major buildings surrounding the plaza date from 1915 to 1917 with the exception of the California State Office Building on McAllister Street which was built in 1925. The centerpiece of the complex is the Renaissance style city hall. Be sure and see its interior as well if you are there on a weekday. (See pages 215–17.)

The Financial District

A Walking Tour of Gold Rush San Francisco.

Location: Downtown San Francisco from First and Market streets north to Broadway and Battery, ending at Clay and Sansome streets. **Parking:** The least expensive parking in the area is at the city-owned Stockton-Sutter garage. Entrances are on Stockton Street between Sutter and Bush or on Bush Street between Stockton and Grant. It is only a few blocks walk to First and Market and to the Wells Fargo History Museum and the Bank of California Museum, both of whose descriptions follow this one.

On this walking tour you will trace, as closely as possible, the shoreline as it was at the time the gold rush started. Along the way you will pass the locations of several ships of the era whose remains are entombed below the street level. This tour will also take you by the two museums mentioned below. If you are taking this tour on a weekday be sure and see both of those as well. They are not open weekends. (See pages 71–75.)

The Bank of California Museum.

Location: In the basement of the main branch of Union Bank of California, 400 California Street (between Sansome and Montgomery). There is no phone for the museum. **Hours:** Monday – Friday, 9 a.m. to 4:30 p.m. Closed bank holidays and weekends. **Admission:** Free. **Parking:** As with the walking tour just mentioned above, the Stockton-Sutter garage is the recommended place.

This small museum is packed with artifacts from a number of periods of San Francisco history. There are gold coins from 1849 and the early 1850s, most of them rare private issues, and dueling pistols, perhaps brought by David C. Broderick to his famous duel with David S. Terry. From the Comstock era there are the original 1859 assay pellets that confirmed the richness of the strike. There are also several lithographs of Virginia City in its heyday. Nearby is a quite rare gold ingot stamped with the name of William Sharon, the Bank of California's Virginia City manager. There are also a few coins and medallions from the Panama Pacific International Exposition of 1915. (See pages 71, 91–92, 113, 214.)

> **Wells Fargo History Museum.**
> **Location:** 420 Montgomery Street (between California and Sacramento).
> **Phone:** (415) 396-2619. **Hours:** Monday – Friday, 9 a.m. to 5 p.m. Closed
> bank holidays and weekends. **Admission:** Free, plus free audio tours in
> English, Spanish, and Chinese. **Parking:** Same recommendation as for
> the museum listed above. **Website:** www.wellsfargohistory.com.

This attractive museum is spread over two floors. There are gold samples from every Mother Lode river and a members' medallion from the Second Committee of Vigilance, as well as souvenirs from the PPIE. There are also artifacts from the 1906 fire, including charred silverware and coins. In the very back of the museum across from the elevator is a color panorama of San Francisco in 1863 with major streets and buildings labeled and identified. (See pages 70, 90–91, 187, 213.)

Fort Mason/Aquatic Park

> **Fort Mason.**
> **Location:** Fort Mason is located on Bay Street between Van Ness Avenue
> and Laguna Street. Auto access is via Franklin Street. Fort Mason is part
> of the Golden Gate National Recreation Area (GGNRA). The headquar-
> ters for the park is the old hospital building on MacArthur Avenue at
> Fort Mason. **Phone:** (415) 561-4700. **Hours:** The park headquarters is
> open Monday – Friday, 9:30 a.m. to 4:30 p.m. Fort Mason itself, like the
> rest of the GGNRA parkland, is open from 8 a.m. to sunset. **Admission:**
> Free. **Parking:** There is free parking on MacArthur Avenue in front of the
> park's headquarters and there is a free parking lot at the west end of
> MacArthur. **Website:** www.nps.gov/goga.

Fort Mason is one of the few locations in San Francisco that has buildings dating from the 1850s. The highlights are the three houses north of the Officers Club at the east end of the fort. (See pages 95–96.)

The Hyde Street Pier.

Location: 2905 Hyde Street (on the bay at the foot of Hyde Street).
Phone: (415) 561-7100. **Hours:** Open daily Memorial Day to mid-October, 9:30 a.m. to 5:30 p.m.; mid-October to Memorial Day, 9:30 a.m. to 5 p.m. You can board the *Balclutha,* the *C.A. Thayer,* and the *Eureka* ferryboat for self-guided tours. There are ranger-guided tours of the *Balclutha,* and periodically of the *Eureka* (of the engine room only). **Admission:** The pier it self is free, but it costs $5.00 for Adults (16+) to board the ships. Children 15 and under are Free. **Parking:** Street parking is quite limited in the area. There is a garage underneath the nearby Cannery. The entrance is on Jefferson Street. A better bet is take the Hyde Street cable car, which terminates at Aquatic Park just a few steps from the Hyde Street Pier's entrance. **Website:** www.nps.gov/safr.

The Hyde Street Pier has some of the few remaining sailing ships left in existence. Among them are the three-masted square rigger *Balclutha* and the three-masted lumber schooner *C.A. Thayer.* You can board both vessels. Be sure and see the Victorian captains' cabins on both and contrast them with the Spartan sailors' quarters. Across the dock is the ferryboat *Eureka* which ferried people and autos across San Francisco Bay until 1957. (See pages 157–60.)

The National Maritime Museum

Location: At the foot of Polk Street adjacent to Aquatic Park. **Phone:** (415) 561-7100. **Hours:** Open daily, 10 a.m. to 5 p.m. **Admission:** Free. **Parking:** There are a few free parking spaces (four-hour limit) just to the west of the museum's entrance on Beach Street. Metered street parking is also available, but sometimes difficult to find in this heavily touristed part of town. The closest parking lot is a block away under Ghirardelli Square. Or, take the cable car to Aquatic Park and walk two blocks west. Closed until 2009 for renovation. **Website:** www.nps.gov/safr.

This National Park Service museum has two floors of exhibits. On the ground floor, among other items, is a model of the U.S.S. *Portsmouth,* the ship that brought Captain Montgomery and his sailors to Yerba Buena cove for their flag raising on July 9, 1846. Upstairs are relics taken from the gold rush ship *Apollo,* and other artifacts recovered during excavations in the Financial District. From a later era, there are several photos of the *Balclutha* as well as harpoons and other equipment from San Francisco's whaling days. (See pages 55, 75–76, 160–61.)

Visitor Center, Haslett Warehouse.
Location: 499 Jefferson Street, corner of Hyde. **Phone:** (415) 447-5000. **Hours:** 9:30 a.m. to 5 p.m., with extended summer hours. **Admission:** Free. **Parking:** Same recommendation as for Hyde Street Pier. **Website:** www.nps.gov/safr.

The Visitor Center has historic photographs, ships models, and artifacts depicting seafaring life in the 19th and 20th centuries. There are relics from the gold-rush ship *Niantic* and scale models of the major vessels at Hyde Street Pier. (See pages 75, 160.)

Golden Gate Park

The Conservatory of Flowers.
Location: Off John F. Kennedy Drive at the east end of Golden Gate Park. **Phone:** (415) 666-7001. **Hours:** Tuesday - Sunday, 9 a.m. to 4:30 p.m. Closed Mondays. **Admission:** Adults, $5.00; Youth (12–17), Students with ID and Seniors (65+), $3.00; Children (5–11), $1.50; under 5, Free. **Parking:** Look for parking along John F. Kennedy Drive. **Website:** www.conservatoryofflowers.org.

The oldest structure in Golden Gate Park (1879), it is modeled after one in Kew Gardens, London. It houses a large collection of native and exotic plants. (See pages 164–66.)

The Japanese Tea Garden.
Location: On Tea Garden Drive across from the Spreckels band shell in Golden Gate Park. **Phone:** (415) 752-4227. **Hours:** March to October, Tea Garden open daily, 9 a.m. to 6 p.m.; November to February, 9 a.m. to 4:45 p.m. **Admission:** Adults, $4.00; Seniors, $1.50; Children (6–12), $1.50; under 6, Free. Free admission Monday, Wednesday, and Friday, 9 to 10 a.m.

The Japanese Tea Garden is the only surviving building *in situ* from the 1894 Midwinter Fair. The main gate and the tea house are replacements for the original structures. Legend has it that the tea house is where the fortune cookie was invented. (See pp. 166–67.)

The Music Concourse.

Location: Between the California Academy of Sciences and the de Young Museum in Golden Gate Park. **Parking:** Same as above.

The Music Concourse, the scooped-out area between the two major museums, was created for the 1894 Midwinter Fair. The groundbreaking was held at the spot where the statue, Roman Gladiator, now stands across from the de Young. (See page 166.)

Haight-Ashbury

A Walking Tour of 1960s Haight-Ashbury.

Location: The heart of Haight-Ashbury is the area south of the Panhandle in the blocks bounded by Oak, Masonic, Frederick, and Stanyan streets. This walking tour starts at the intersection of Haight and Masonic and concludes at the corner of Stanyan and Waller. **Parking:** Unmetered street parking can be found on most area streets except Haight Street, which has two-hour parking meters. Oak Street, bordering the Panhandle, is also a good place to look for free parking.

Highlights of this walking tour include houses where two seminal rock bands lived in the 1960s—the house at 130 Delmar where the Jefferson Airplane lived, and the former Grateful Dead Queen Anne row house at 710 Ashbury. At 558–560 is the Haight-Ashbury Free Clinic, still doing business at the same location where it opened it doors in 1967. Also to be seen on this tour, on the east side of Masonic, between Haight and Waller, is a lineup of representative Queen Anne row houses, built in 1899. (See pages 242–44.)

Jackson Square Historic District

Jackson Square and Sherman's Bank.

Location: Downtown San Francisco. The area of prime interest is Montgomery Street between Washington and Jackson, and Jackson Street from Montgomery to Sansome. **Parking:** There are metered parking spaces in the vicinity, and a city parking garage under Portsmouth Square, two blocks to the southwest. The entrance is on Kearny Street via Clay Street.

Jackson Square is home to San Francisco's oldest remaining commercial buildings. The highlight is the Lucas, Turner & Co. bank, sometimes called "Sherman's Bank," at the corner of Jackson and Montgomery streets, opened in 1854 by William Tecumseh Sherman. Other buildings of note in the district are Hotaling's warehouse at 451 Jackson Street, and the Belli Building and Annex at 722 and 728 Montgomery Street, respectively. (See pages 88–90.)

Lake Merced

The Broderick - Terry Duel Site.

Location: 1100 Lake Merced Boulevard, San Francisco, near the San Mateo County line. **Directions:** From Lake Merced Boulevard look for the brown historical signs and turn in at the sign, "Lake Merced Hill, Private Club," at the above address. **Admission:** Free. **Parking:** There are a few free spaces next to the tennis courts. From there, walk to the end of the lot where the state historical marker is. Follow the trail past the small granite plinth until you get to the two opposing stone markers.

This site marks the location of the celebrated Broderick - Terry duel. The two light-colored stone markers show where each man stood at the time the shots were fired.

The Mission District

Mission Dolores.
Location: Sixteenth and Dolores Streets. **Phone:** (415) 621-8203. **Hours:** Open daily during summer, 9 a.m. to 4:30 p.m.; during winter, 9 a.m. to 4 p.m. Restricted visiting hours on religious and major holidays. Closed Thanksgiving and Christmas. **Admission:** Adults, $5.00; Students, Seniors (65+), $3.00. **Parking:** There is no parking lot at the church; check Dolores or nearby streets for parking spaces. **Website:** www.missiondolores.org.

Mission Dolores, completed in 1791, is the oldest building in San Francisco. The chapel is richly evocative of the time when Spain, and later Mexico, ruled California. The cemetery next to it contains the graves of some early and notorious San Franciscans. (See pages 47–48.)

Mission District Victorians.
Location: Cottage/Carpenter Gothic style houses can be seen at 214 and 220 Dolores Street, just one block from Mission Dolores. A few blocks away, from 120 to 126 Guerrero Street, are three fine examples of the bay window Italianate style. **Parking:** These are residential neighborhoods; look for available street parking.

The two cottages on Dolores Street apparently date from 1851 and 1852 respectively, making them among the oldest residences in The City. The Guerrero Street Italianates are lucky survivors of 1906; the fire somehow skirted them before continuing up to Dolores Street where it was finally stopped. (See pages 251–52.)

Nob Hill

A Walking Tour of Nob Hill.

Location: For the purposes of this walk, Nob Hill is the area bounded by the following streets: Powell, Pine, Jones, and Sacramento. Start the walk at the southwest corner of Powell and California streets. **Parking:** Street parking is available but is sometimes hard to find. There are several parking garages on Nob Hill; they are rather expensive on an hourly basis. Your best bet is to park elsewhere and take either the California or Powell-Hyde cable car lines. Both stop at the intersection of Powell and California streets.

This walking tour takes you past the original retaining walls of the Leland Stanford and Mark Hopkins estates, up to the only remaining mansion, that of James Flood, and on to Grace Cathedral, the site of the Charles Crocker residence. Parts of the original sidewalk, laid down in the late 1870s, can still be found on the east and north sides of what was the Crocker estate. (See pages 142–44.)

The Cable Car Barn and Museum.

Location: 1201 Mason Street (at Washington). **Phone:** (415) 474-1887. **Hours:** Open daily, April thru September, 10 a.m. to 6 p.m.; October thru March, 10 a.m. to 5 p.m. Closed Thanksgiving, Christmas, and New Year's Day. **Admission:** Free. Parking: Same recommendation as for the Nob Hill walking tour. **Website:** www.cablecarmuseum.org.

The Cable Car Barn and Museum is located just three blocks to the northeast from the end of the Nob Hill walking tour. A highlight here, beyond the novelty of watching the cable machinery come winding in and out of the building, is Andrew Hallidie's original 1873 car. (See pages 163–64.)

North Beach

The Barbary Coast.

Location: The Barbary Coast initially was centered around lower Pacific Avenue and Broadway, and included the area east to the waterfront. Later it expanded west toward Chinatown and south toward the financial district. **Parking:** Street parking in the area of interest—Broadway and Pacific from Columbus Avenue to Montgomery Street—is difficult. You might look for parking spaces closer to the Embarcadero, or if you don't want to walk more than a few blocks there are two small parking lots on Broadway between Kearny and Montgomery streets.

The few topless clubs near the intersection of Broadway and Columbus are but a pale shadow of the Barbary Coast that was. The long-closed former Hippodrome at 555 Pacific Avenue, with its frieze of naked maidens and carnival-bulb lighting, is the only surviving building that provides a hint of the neighborhood's old character. (See pages 152–53.)

City Lights Bookstore.

Location: 261 Columbus Avenue (near Broadway). **Phone:** (415) 362-8193. **Hours:** Open every day 10 a.m. to Midnight. **Parking:** Same recommendation as for the Barbary Coast. **Website:** www.citylights.com

---

City Lights Bookstore opened in June 1953 and soon became the headquarters for the emerging Beat movement. The store's owner, Lawrence Ferlinghetti, became a First Amendment hero when he was tried and acquitted of obscenity charges in 1957 for selling Allen Ginsburg's poem *Howl*. (See pages 240–41.)

Vesuvio Café.

Location: 255 Columbus Avenue. **Phone:** (415) 362-3370. **Hours:** Open daily, 6 a.m. to 2 a.m. **Parking:** Same recommendation as for the Barbary Coast and City Lights. **Website:** www.vesuvio.com.

This bar, located right across the narrow alley from City Lights, was a favorite hangout for Jack Kerouac and other leading lights of the Beat generation. (See pages 241–42.)

The Presidio

The Old Hospital - Former Presidio Museum
Location: Funston and Lincoln streets in the Presidio. No phone. Interior not open to the public. **Parking:** There are spaces across from the museum's entrance reserved for patrons, or sometimes there are spots available on Funston Avenue in front of the museum.

Located under the porch of this building, the Old Hospital, is one of the remaining cannon from the Castillo de San Joaquin, the Spanish fort where Ft. Point is now.

Behind the building are two "refugee shacks" from the 1906 earthquake.

The new visitor center, when it finally reopens in Building 102 on Montgomery Avenue by the parade ground will likely contain relics formerly on display here from several periods of San Francisco history. (See pages 49–50, 183–84.)

The Palace of Fine Arts.
Location: 3601 Lyon Street (between Bay and Jefferson). The main pavilion is outdoors and is open to the public free of charge. **Parking:** Street parking is usually available on Baker Street, which borders the Palace on the east.

The Palace of Fine Arts is the only remaining structure remaining on site from the PPIE. This replacement copy, which was erected in the 1960s, is not as colorful as the original, which was shaded in reds and greens. (See pages 210–12.)

Fort Point

Location: In the Presidio at the end of Marine Drive underneath the south end of the Golden Gate Bridge. **Phone:** (415) 556-1693. **Hours:** Open Friday - Sunday, 10 a.m. to 5 p.m. Closed Thanksgiving, Christmas, and New Year's Day. Park ranger-led tours are given at regular intervals. **Admission:** Free. **Parking:** There is a free parking lot adjacent to the fort. **Website:** www.nps.gov/fopo.

This brick and masonry fort, constructed between 1853 and 1861, is open for self-guided tours as well as for ones led by park rangers. On the ground floor in the courtyard just to the left of the entrance is one of the cannon from the Castillo de San Joaquin. The second room to the left houses a scale model of that Spanish fort along with a model of a soldier of the period. In the powder magazine, one door down, and on the second and third floors, exhibits and artifacts describe the life of soldiers and officers at Fort Point and the less than ideal conditions under which they operated.

Bring a windbreaker or jacket to Fort Point, since it is invariably breezy and cool. (See pages 52, 93–94.)

The Golden Gate Bridge.

Location: The Golden Gate Bridge spans the entrance to San Francisco Bay, connecting The City to Marin and the other northern counties. The single deck bridge provides for six lanes of vehicular traffic. There are ten-foot-wide walkways on each side of the bridge. Generally, pedestrians are allowed on the east side and bicyclists on the west side. **Parking:** There is a parking lot next to the toll plaza on the San Francisco side and one at Vista Point on the Marin side. Pedestrian access starts from these lots as well. **Website:** www.goldengatebridge.org.

The world famous Golden Gate Bridge, which opened in 1937, is one of San Francisco's most enduring landmarks and symbols. Its timeless design makes it a visual delight. (See pages 219–20.)

South of Market

The Old Mint.

Location: Fifth and Mission streets. The Old Mint currently is **closed**, but will reopen as a museum of San Francisco history after refurbishing, at some unspecified date. **Parking:** There is a city-owned parking garage on the opposite corner of Fifth and Mission. **Website:** www.sfhistory.org

The Old Mint has a wide array of interesting displays. Artifacts from the gold rush period include an original timber from Sutter's Mill at Coloma, and gold mining equipment from Mother Lode mines. Also on view are gold bars and coins. From the Silver Age, there are silver dollars, and from the Comstock region, several chunks of unprocessed silver ore and two bank drafts drawn on Virginia City banks. Photographs on the main floor include several showing the mint as it looked after the city was devastated. (See pages 69–70, 118–20, 186.) The museum closed as of January 1995 for seismic upgrading.

The Palace Hotel.

Location: Market and New Montgomery streets. **Phone:** (415) 512-1111. **Parking:** There are short term parking meters on Mission and nearby streets or, if you don't mind walking three blocks, park at the Fifth and Mission garage. Sundays, when meters are not enforced downtown, are less of a problem; you shouldn't have much trouble finding a space then. **Website:** www.sfpalace.com.

William Ralston's Palace Hotel perished in 1906, but the Garden Court restaurant in the center of the newly remodeled hotel evokes the earlier era. A good place for Sunday brunch. (See pages 115–16.)

South Park.

Location: In the center of the area bounded by Bryant, Brannan, Second, and Third streets. The easiest access by auto or on foot is from either Second or Third streets. **Parking:** Street parking nearby should not be a problem, but it is best to stay out of this area on late weekday afternoons to avoid traffic headed for the Bay Bridge for the commute home.

Rincon Hill and South Park were once the most desirable residential locations in San Francisco. Nineteenth- and twentieth-century development have changed the area completely. Only South Park's oval common remains. (See pages 97–98.)

The San Francisco–Oakland Bay Bridge.

Location: The 8.4-mile-long Bay Bridge extends from the Alameda shore to (and through) Yerba Buena Island, and feeds into San Francisco in the Rincon Hill area south of Market Street. It is a double-deck bridge: the lower deck has five lanes of automobile traffic eastbound, the upper deck five lanes westbound. Like the Golden Gate Bridge, it never closes (an exception was for four weeks after the October 1989 earthquake). Unlike the Golden Gate Bridge, there is no pedestrian access. **Parking:** Because of the lack of pedestrian access, there are no parking lots at either end where you can view the bridge. The bridge is best seen from the top of various hills in San Francisco or from the Embarcadero.

Although not the landmark the Golden Gate Bridge is, the Bay Bridge is even more vital to San Francisco, as residents and commuters found out during the aftermath of the October 1989 earthquake, when it was shut down for a month. You cannot walk across it as you can the Golden Gate Bridge, so the best way to see and appreciate this span is by driving across it. (See pages 220–21.)

Sutro Heights

Sutro Heights, The Cliff House, and Sutro Baths.

Location: All these sights are located on Point Lobos Avenue at Ocean Beach, where San Francisco meets the Pacific Ocean. Sutro Heights is a public park, part of the Golden Gate National Recreation Area, as are the Sutro Baths ruins below the Cliff House. U.S. park rangers periodically give tours of both sites. **Phone:** (415) 561-4323 for tour information. **Parking:** There is parking on Point Lobos Avenue on both sides of the Cliff House, and in a lot adjoining Sutro Heights Park. There is also more parking available on Merrie Way, the dirt promenade overlooking Sutro Baths ruins. **Website:** www.nps.gov/goga.

None of Adolph Sutro's turn of the century buildings—the
Sutro Baths, Cliff House, or his home—has survived, but you can
wander the grounds of his former estate and see the ruins of his
public natatorium (only the foundation remains). His Gothic castle
Cliff House burned in 1907. The present day Cliff House is the sixth
to occupy the site. (See pages 168–70.)

Telegraph Hill

Telegraph Hill Victorians.

Location: Telegraph Hill is in the northeast corner of San Francisco. Coit
Tower rises from its summit. The Cottage/Carpenter Gothic Victorians
are clustered on Union Street, Alta Place, and the Filbert Street steps.
Parking: Parking is very tight here any time of day or night. If a search
produces nothing in the vicinity, you might try parking in North Beach
and taking the Union Street bus up the hill.

Probably the best example of this early Victorian style is the
house at 228 Filbert Street. Others of the genre are located at 287
and 289 Union Street and at 31 Alta. The latter was built in 1852 and
is one of the oldest houses in San Francisco. (See pages 250–51.)

Treasure Island

Treasure Island Museum.

Location: Treasure Island is a man-made appendage on the north side of
Yerba Buena Island in the middle of San Francisco Bay. It can only be
reached via the Bay Bridge. Going either way on the bridge, stay in the
far left lane. Slow to 15 mph as you exit. The museum, containing artifacts from the Golden Gate International Exposition, is located in the
Administration Building to your right as you pass through the gate.
Hours: Open weekdays, 10 a.m. to 3:30 p.m.; until 4:30 p.m. weekends
and holidays (no admission later than one-half hour before closing).
Admission: Free. **Parking:** In front of the building or in the lot to the
north. **Closed indefinitely. Website:** www.treasureislandmuseum.org.

Flanking the front entrance of the Administration Building are six statues from the GGIE. Inside, the museum itself has a wealth of artifacts from the fair, including souvenir programs, towels, drinking glasses, and other items. Numerous photographs round out the exhibit. (See pages 223–24.)

Western Addition/Pacific Heights

San Francisco Fire Department Museum.
Location: 655 Presidio Avenue (between Bush and Pine). **Phone:** (415) 563-4630. **Hours:** Thursday – Sunday, 1 p.m. to 4 p.m. Closed the rest of the week and all holidays. **Admission:** Free. **Parking:** Nearby street parking in this residential neighborhood should not be a problem, but since a Muni lot and yard is only a block away, plenty of buses criss-cross the area. **Website:** www.sffiremuseum.org.

This interesting museum has a wide variety of historic relics related to fire fighting in San Francisco. From the 1850s you can see riveted buffalo-hide water buckets used for fighting fires, as well as fused window glass from an 1851 fire. Artifacts from the 1906 fire include melted glass bottles, charred coins, and a fire station log book open to April 1906. (See pages 87–88, 185–86.)

The Haas-Lilienthal House.
Location: 2007 Franklin Street (near Jackson). **Phone:** (415) 441-3004. **Hours:** Wednesday and Saturday, Noon to 3 p.m.; Sunday, 11 a.m. to 4 p.m. Docent-led tours at regular intervals. **Admission:** Adults $8.00, Children and Seniors, $5.00. **Parking:** Look for street parking on Franklin and nearby cross streets but watch for posted time limits. **Website:** www.sfheritage.org.

Built in 1886, the Haas-Lilienthal House is the only Victorian house containing its original furnishings that is open to the public. Tours of the interior give a taste of what late Victorian domestic life was like. (See pages 151–52.)

Western Addition/Pacific Heights Victorians.

Location: The Western Addition is that part of the city west of Van Ness Avenue. Since this was the main part of San Francisco spared by the 1906 fire, many examples of Italianate, Stick, and Queen Anne Victorian homes are to be found here. **Parking:** Look for street parking in this heavily residential part of town.

A nice row of flat-front Italianates is located from 2115 to 2125 Bush Street (between Webster and Fillmore). Five blocks to the east and two blocks north at 1818 California Street is a fine example of a bay-window Italianate.

Stick Style houses can be seen in the 1801 block of Laguna Street (between Bush and Pine), and a dozen blocks to the southwest on McAllister between Pierce and Steiner. Probably the most classic Stick house in The City sits on the northeast corner of Scott and Fulton streets, one block from the McAllister houses just noted.

A picturesque row of Queen Anne row houses adorns Steiner Street between Hayes and Grove streets; another such line-up is located in Haight-Ashbury on the east side of Masonic between Haight and Waller. A representative Queen Anne Tower can be seen on the northwest corner of Franklin and California streets, just down the street from the bay window Italianate at 1818 California Street. (See pages 251–54.)

Alameda County

Berkeley

The Bancroft Library.

Location: On the campus of the University of California at Berkeley. Anyone who is at least eighteen years old and a high school graduate can use the library and its extensive collection of non-circulating materials related to the history of California and the West. **Phone:** (510) 642-6481. **Hours:** Monday – Friday, 9 a.m. to 5 p.m.; Saturday, 1 p.m. to 5 p.m. (while classes are in session). **Admission:** Free. **Parking:** Street parking anywhere in Berkeley is difficult. If you are only planning a short visit, one- and two-hour meters can be found on Bancroft Way and nearby streets. If you don't mind walking several blocks, there is a parking garage with reasonable rates just west of Telegraph Avenue between Durant and Channing Way (you can enter from either street). The Bancroft Library is **closed** for renovation. **Website:** http://bancroft.berkeley.edu.

On display in the lobby is Francis Drake's "plate of brasse," now proven to be a forgery. In the reading room is the "Wimmer nugget," which is purportedly the first gold nugget discovered in the tailrace at Coloma by James Marshall. (See pages 26–27, 68.)

P. A. Hearst Museum of Anthropology.

Location: Kroeber Hall, across from the corner of Bancroft Way and College Avenue on the University of California campus, Berkeley. **Phone:** (510) 643-7648. **Hours:** Wednesday – Saturday, 10 a.m. to 4:30 p.m.; Sunday, Noon – 4:00 p.m. Thursday until 9 p.m. Closed Mondays and Tuesdays. **Admission:** Free. **Parking:** Same recommendation as for the Bancroft Library above. **Website:** www.hearstmuseum.berkeley.edu.

Some of Ishi's personal possessions, including some bows and arrows he made, are on view here. The other exhibits change periodically, so its possible that other California Indian artifacts may be on display at the time of your visit. (See page 13.)

Fremont

Ohlone Village – Coyote Hills Regional Park.
Location: 8000 Patterson Ranch Road (off Paseo Padre Parkway). **Phone:** (510) 795-9385. Located within this pleasant county park is an Ohlone shellmound and a reconstructed village. Both are fenced off and are accessible only through docent-led tours. **Hours:** Tours of the shell-mound are given Saturdays or Sundays once or twice a month. It is best to call in advance to check dates, times, and to make reservations. There is a visitor center in the park that is open Tuesday – Sunday, 9:30 a.m. to 5 p.m. **Admission:** $5.00 per vehicle. **Parking:** It is best to get there early because the gravel parking lot where the shellmound tour starts can fill up. If that happens there is plenty of additional free parking in the paved lot at the visitor center half a mile away. **Website:** www.ebparks.org.

This informative tour provides a vivid look at how the Ohlone lived and adapted to their surroundings. On top of the shell-mound, which dates to 400 B.C., is a reconstructed village. The visitor center, a short distance away, has a fine display of artifacts, including tools discovered during archeological digs at the site. (See pages 9–10.)

Oakland

The Oakland Museum – History Gallery.
Location: 1000 Oak Street (two blocks from Lake Merritt), Oakland. **Phone:** (510) 238-3842. **Hours:** Wednesday – Saturday, 10 a.m. to 5 p.m.; (First Friday to 9 p.m.); Sunday, Noon to 5 p.m. Closed holidays. **Admission:** Adults, $8.00; Seniors, Students, $5.00; Children (under 5), Free. **Parking:** There is a garage under the museum (entrance on Oak Street), or parking can be relatively easy to find on nearby streets—either posted two-hour time limit or metered spaces. **Website:** www.museumca.org.

The Oakland Museum History Gallery, which covers California history from the time of the Indians to the present day, has a wide array of artifacts that illustrate San Francisco's history. As you progress through the gallery from the Indian baskets and utensils you will see items illustrative of the days when Spain and then Mexico ruled California, such as priest vestments, an olive press, and a leather saddle of the period.

The gold rush was a watershed event—on display are gold mining paraphernalia, nuggets, daguerreotypes of forty-niners, and an assay office taken from a Mother Lode town.

From the Comstock era there are stock certificates from defunct mines and a model of the Virginia & Truckee Railroad.

A highlight of the 1906 earthquake is a fire engine of the time. From the Panama Pacific International Exposition there are life-size statues from the Japanese pavilion and, from more recent times, mementoes from the Beat and Hippie eras. (See pages 11–12, 28, 55–56, 69–70, 123, 186, 212–13, 242.)

Marin County

Angel Island

Angel Island State Park.

Location: Angel Island, the largest island in San Francisco Bay, is located off the Tiburon peninsula. Ayala Cove, on the northwest corner of the island, is the landing point. Camp Reynolds is located on the west side of the island in the West Garrison area. Immigration Station is on the northeast corner in the North Garrison area. There is a visitor center at Ayala Cove that can provide maps and more information. **Phone:** (415) 435-3522. Public access to the island is by ferry only. Primary points of departure are San Francisco and Tiburon. The Blue & Gold Fleet, **Phone:** (415) 705-5555, located at Pier 41, San Francisco, and the McDonough ferry, **Phone:** (415) 435-2131, which departs from 21 Main Street, Tiburon, both serve the island daily during the summer. Call the above numbers or check the web for departure times and the winter schedule. **Admission:** Angel Island itself is free. The ferry tolls on the Blue & Gold Fleet are: Adults, $14.50; Children (6–12), $8.50; under 6, Free. The McDonough ferry: Adults, $10.25; Children (5–11), $8.00; Bicycles, $1.00. **Parking:** In San Francisco, all day parking around Fisherman's Wharf is a tough proposition. Your best bet is the garage across from Pier 39, but leaving your car there all day would be expensive. It would be best to park your car elsewhere and take public transportation or a taxi to the wharf. At Tiburon, there are three all day lots—all are on the east side of Tiburon Boulevard—and they are progressively cheaper the farther away from the dock at Main Street. The nearest lot, which is behind the new shopping center with the pond and fountains, costs $11.00 a day. Farther north on Tiburon Boulevard, behind the Bank of America, is a $5.00 a day lot, and about .4 mile farther still is a gravel lot for $2.00 a day. **Websites:** www.angelisland.org and www.parks.ca.gov.

Three historic sites worth visiting on Angel Island are: Ayala Cove where Juan Manuel de Ayala spent most of his time anchored in 1775 while his officers mapped San Francisco Bay; Camp

Reynolds, a Civil War-era fort with some remaining officer housing; and Immigration Station, one of whose buildings houses a museum documenting the experience of the mainly Chinese immigrants who were processed through there between 1910 and 1940. (See pages 30, 96–97, 217–19.)

Novato

Marin Museum of the American Indian.
Location: Miwok Park, 2200 Novato Boulevard, Novato. **Phone:** (415) 897-4064. **Hours:** Tuesday – Friday, 10 a.m. to 3 p.m., Saturday and Sunday, Noon to 4 p.m. (but call ahead on weekends to be certain that volunteer staff are on site). **General Admission:** $5.00 donation; Seniors, $3.00. Children, Free. **Parking:** Free in the adjoining lot. **Website:** www.marinindian.com.

This museum has replica artifacts such as the Coast Miwoks would have used in their daily lives. The adjacent park has plants native to the time of the Indians. (See page 12.)

Point Reyes

Point Reyes National Seashore.
Location: On the western edge of Marin County. The park's entrance is located just north of the town of Olema, at the junction of Highway 1 and Sir Francis Drake Boulevard. The Bear Valley Visitor Center is a short distance from the park's entrance. To reach the Kule Loklo Miwok Village, follow the trail from the visitor center four-tenths of a mile north. The 1906 epicenter trail starts across the parking lot from the visitor center. To get to Drakes Bay, drive sixteen miles west on Sir Francis Drake Highway to Drakes Beach. Drakes Estero, where the landing site monument is, is a half a mile walk northeast on the beach. **Hours:** The park itself is open from sunrise to sunset. The Bear Valley Visitor Center is open weekdays, 9 a.m. to 5 p.m.; weekends and holidays, 8 a.m. to 5 p.m. **Phone:** (415) 464-5100. The visitor center at Drakes Beach is open only weekends and holidays, 10 a.m. to 5 p.m. **Phone:** (415) 669-1250. Park rangers are on duty at both stations during business hours. **Admission:** Free. **Parking:** Free parking at both visitor centers. **Website:** www.nps.gov/pore.

At the Bear Valley Visitor Center, in addition to maps, are exhibits on the flora, fauna, and history of the area. Among the items illustrating the latter are a few pieces of Ming Dynasty porcelain recovered from the wreck of the *San Agustin* in 1595. The Kule Loklo village nearby is a reconstructed Coast Miwok encampment. The 1906 epicenter trail takes you to the San Andreas fault past a fence that moved sixteen feet on that April 18. The Drake monument at Drakes Estero marks the most likely location of Drake's landing in 1579. (See pages 10–11, 24–26, 182–83.)

San Rafael

China Camp State Park.
Location: From Highway 101 in San Rafael, exit at either North San Pedro Road or at Third Street (which leads into Point San Pedro Road). It is about an eight-mile drive to the park and fishing village from either exit. **Phone:** (415) 456-0766. **Hours:** The park is open daily from 8 a.m. to sunset, and the visitors center and museum from 10 a.m. to 5 p.m. **Admission:** $5.00 per car. **Website:** www.parks.ca.gov.

The visitors center and museum chart the growth and decline of this once active Chinese shrimp-fishing village. (See pages 124–25.)

Sausalito

San Francisco Bay Model Visitor's Center.
Location: 2100 Bridgeway, Sausalito. **Phone:** (415) 332-3871. **Hours:** Tuesday – Saturday, 9 a.m. to 4 p.m., with additional summer hours of Saturday, Sunday, and some holidays, 10 a.m. to 5 p.m. Closed federal holidays. Ranger-led tours are available for groups of ten or more. **Admission:** Free. **Website:** www.spn.usace.army.mil/bmvc.

This huge working-model of San Francisco Bay is the best place to see how ancient geologic changes have shaped the geography of San Francisco and the bay. Off in the corner is an exhibit devoted to Marinship. (See pages 8, 240–41.)

San Mateo County

Belmont

Ralston Hall – Notre Dame de Namur University.
Location: 1500 Ralston Avenue, Belmont. **Phone:** (650) 508-3501. Docent-led tours weekdays by appointment only. Call Monday – Friday, 9 a.m. to 5 p.m. **Admission:** $5.00 per person. **Parking:** Ample free parking on the grounds. **Website:** www.ndnu.edu.

Ralston Hall was once William Ralston's country estate. The ballroom—which resembles the Hall of Mirrors at the Palace of Versailles—gives an idea of the splendor of the age. Upstairs, in the loge, are a few of Ralston's personal effects. (See pages 116–17.)

Pacifica

Portolá Discovery Site.
Location: Sweeney Ridge, San Mateo County between Pacifica and San Bruno. **Phone:** (415) 556-8371. Sweeney Ridge is part of the Golden Gate National Recreation Area. **Hours:** Open daily, 8 a.m. to dusk. **Admission:** Free. There are several trails leading to the discovery site. The easiest and most accessible one starts from behind Sneath Lane in San Bruno. Others start from parking lot #2 behind Skyline College in San Bruno and from behind the Shelldance nursery off Highway 1 in Pacifica. **Parking:** Free parking is readily available at the trailheads. **Website:** www.nps.gov/goga.

A stone plinth atop the ridge marks the approximate site from which Gaspar de Portolá first sighted San Francisco Bay, on November 4, 1769. On a clear day you can see the same landmarks Portolá would have seen—the Farallon Islands, Point Reyes, and Mount Hamilton. (See pages 28–29.)

San Mateo

San Mateo County History Museum.
Location: 2200 Broadway, Redwood City. **Phone:** (650) 299-0104. **Hours:** Tuesday – Sunday, 10 a.m. to 4 p.m. **Admission:** Adults, $4.00; Students, Seniors, and Children, $2.00. **Website:** www.sanmateocountyhistory. com.

This museum has artifacts illustrative of San Francisco's history ranging from the time of the Indians to William Ralston's day. Indian artifacts include arrowheads, shells, and bone tools. The history of the Portolá expedition is marked by a map showing the route to the discovery site. There is a reproduction of a painting believed to be a likeness of Portolá. From the days of the Californios there is an 1850's saddle trimmed in silver, and some candles made of tallow. From William Ralston's peninsula estate are a plate with gold trim and a big "R," a salt cellar, and some silverware. (See pages 13, 29, 56, 118.)

Santa Clara County

Palo Alto

Stanford University and the Cantor Arts Center.
Location: Stanford University is located in Palo Alto. The campus is bounded by El Camino Real on the east, Interstate 280 on the west, Willow Road on the north, and Page Mill Road on the south. It is located at Museum Way and Lomita Drive on the Stanford University campus. **Phone:** (650) 723-4177. **Hours:** Wednesday – Sunday, 11 a.m. to 5 p.m. (Thursday to 8 p.m.). Closed Monday, Tuesday, and holidays. **Admission:** Free. **Parking:** Parking is hard to find anywhere on the Stanford campus when classes are in session. Museum Way, next to the Art Museum, has parking meters. **Website:** www.museum.stanford.edu.

A highlight here is the golden spike used at the transcontinental railroad ceremony held at Promontory Point, Utah on May 10, 1869. The museum has other Stanford family memorabilia including interior and exterior photos of Leland Stanford's various mansions. (See pages 122–23, 149–51.)

While on campus you might want to stroll around the main quad, which was conceived by Frederick Law Olmsted, the designer of New York's Central Park.

Sonoma County

Petaluma

The Petaluma Adobe.
Location: 3325 Adobe Road, Petaluma. **Phone:** (707) 762-4871. **Hours:** Open daily, 10 a.m. to 5 p.m. Closed major holidays. **Admission:** Adults, $2.00; under 17, Free. **Parking:** Free parking in the adjacent lot. **Websites:** www.parks.ca.gov and www.petalumaadobe.com.

Mariano Vallejo's Petaluma Adobe has the only remaining Californio rancho buildings in northern California. None of the original furnishings has survived on site, but the replicas and period pieces prove fine substitutes in re-creating the atmosphere of the 1830s and 1840s. (See pages 52–54.)

Outside the Bay Area

Santa Cruz County, Aptos

1989 Earthquake Epicenter – Forest of Nisene Marks.
Location: The town of Aptos is located seven miles east of Santa Cruz, just off Highway 1. To reach the epicenter trail, from Highway 1 take the Seacliff Beach/Aptos exit to Soquel Avenue. Go right on Soquel for a few blocks. Look for "Forest of Nisene Marks" signs, and turn left onto Aptos Creek Road. Drive all the way to the end of the hard-packed dirt road— about two miles. The epicenter trail starts beyond the gate near the east end of the parking lot. **Hours:** The park is open from sunrise to sunset. There is no phone and no ranger station at the site. **Admission:** Free. **Parking:** There is a free parking lot at the trailhead. **Website:** www.parks.ca.gov.

This slightly less than two-mile hike will take you through the woods and across a stream to the epicenter of the October 17, 1989 earthquake that killed sixty-seven people in northern California. (See pages 245–46.)

El Dorado County, Coloma

Gold Discovery Site.
Location: The Marshall Gold Discovery Site State Historic Park is located northeast of Sacramento on Highway 49 between Auburn and Placerville. **Phone:** (530) 622-3470. **Hours:** The visitor center and the park's other buildings are open daily, 10:00 a.m. to 5:00 p.m., until 4:30 p.m. November - April. The park itself is open from 8 a.m. to sunset. Closed Thanksgiving, Christmas, and New Year's Day. **Admission:** Fees are collected at the visitor center or at the main parking lot across the street: $5.00 per vehicle. **Parking:** There are parking lots both in front of the visitor center and across Highway 49 next to the reconstructed sawmill. **Website:** www.parks.ca.gov.

The town of Coloma, where James Marshall found the nuggets that started the gold rush on January 24, 1848, is now a state historic park. The area still retains its bucolic feel since commercialization has been kept to a minimum. Besides the reconstructed sawmill there is a museum at the visitors center. Marshall's cabin is located in the hills nearby. (See page 76).

Virginia City, Nevada

Virginia City.
Location: On Highway 341 in western Nevada, twenty miles southeast of Reno. **Parking:** Usually available on C Street, which is the main artery, or else try the cross streets.

Virginia City's heyday has long since passed but you can still see mine tailings and ruins of buildings in the nearby canyons. A few cars from the Virginia & Truckee Railroad make a short haul for tourists during the summer months. (See pages 121–22.)

Chronology

1542   **November 15 or 16.** Explorer Juan Rodríguez Cabrillo fails to see the entrance to San Francisco Bay as he sails past, but discovers the Farallon Islands twenty-seven miles offshore.

1579   **June 17.** Francis Drake, in his ship *Golden Hind*, likely lands at what is now known as Drakes Bay, north of the Golden Gate.

1595   **November 5 or 6.** Sebastián Cermeño anchors in Drakes Bay and names it La Bahía de San Francisco. This is the first recorded use of the name San Francisco in the region.

1769   **November 2.** Soldiers from the overland Gaspar de Portolá expedition become the first Europeans to sight San Francisco Bay.

1775   **August 5.** Juan Manuel de Ayala, on the packet boat San Carlos, sails through the Golden Gate and shortly afterward conducts the first nautical survey of San Francisco Bay.

1776   **June 29.** The first mass is held at Mission Dolores. This marks the official founding of San Francisco.

1776   **September 17.** The Presidio is dedicated. San Francisco is officially claimed for Spain.

1791   **April 3.** The current Mission Dolores is dedicated.

1794   The Castillo de San Joaquin, the fort on the bluff overlooking the Golden Gate, is completed.

1821   **September 27.** Mexico declares its independence from Spain. San Francisco, along with the rest of California, becomes a province of Mexico.

1835   William A. Richardson, a former mate on an English whaling ship, builds the first permanent structure at Yerba Buena (as San Francisco was then called).

1835 The Calle de la Fundacion—now part of Grant Avenue—is established as a street.

1839 Jean Vioget officially lays out Yerba Buena's first streets—Kearny, Grant, Sacramento, Clay, Washington, Jackson, and Pacific.

1846 **July 9.** Captain John B. Montgomery of the U.S.S. Portsmouth lands at Yerba Buena and raises the American flag in front of the custom house.

1847 **January 23.** Alcalde Washington A. Bartlett issues a proclamation changing Yerba Buena's name to San Francisco.

1847 Alcalde Bartlett asks Jasper O'Farrell to make the first formal survey of the town. O'Farrell extends and re-aligns the Vioget survey and lays out Market Street.

1847 San Francisco's population: 500 (est.)

1848 **January 24.** Gold is discovered on the American River at Coloma, 130 miles northeast of San Francisco.

1848 **February 2.** The war between Mexico and the United States formally ends when the Treaty of Guadalupe Hidalgo is signed. San Francisco and the rest of California officially become U.S. territory.

1849 **February 28.** The first ship bearing gold-seekers from the East Coast arrives in San Francisco Bay.

1849 **August.** San Francisco's population: 6,000 (est.)

1849 **December 24.** The first of six great fires that devastate San Francisco during the next year and a half.

1850 **September 9.** California is admitted to the Union as the thirty-first state.

1850 San Francisco's population: 25,000 (est.)

1851 The First Committee of Vigilance is formed to combat lawlessness plaguing the city.

1853	Construction of Fort Point begins.

1855 The first anti-Chinese laws are enacted by the California legislature.

1856 The Second Committee of Vigilance is formed in the wake of several notorious killings.

1859 The great Comstock silver rush begins when rich ore deposits are discovered in western Nevada.

1859 **September 13.** Senator David C. Broderick is mortally wounded in a duel near Lake Merced.

1860 San Francisco's population: 56,800

1863 Construction starts in Sacramento on the western end of the transcontinental railroad.

1869 **May 10.** The golden spike is driven at Promontory Point, Utah, completing the transcontinental railroad and providing San Francisco with a direct link to the East Coast.

1870 Construction starts on Golden Gate Park.

1870 San Francisco's population: 149,500

1873 **August 1.** The cable car makes its first run in San Francisco: down Clay Street from Nob Hill to Portsmouth Square.

1874 The U.S. Mint at Fifth and Mission streets opens.

1875 The Stanford residence, the first of the major Nob Hill mansions, is built.

1875 **August 26.** The Bank of California shuts its doors as a Comstock-led financial panic hits the city.

1875 **October 2.** The Palace Hotel opens.

1877   Anti-Chinese riots led by Denis Kearney and other
agitators occur periodically until U.S. Army troops are
called in to help local authorities put an end to
the violence.

1879   The Conservatory of Flowers is erected in Golden
Gate Park.

1880   San Francisco's population: 234,000

1886   The Haas-Lilienthal House is built.

1890   San Francisco's population: 299,000

1894   The California Midwinter Exposition is held in Golden
Gate Park.

1896   The third Cliff House and the Sutro Baths open to
the public.

1900   San Francisco's population: 342,800

1906   **April 18.** San Francisco is hit by a massive earthquake.
Over the next three days the ensuing fire devastates a
large portion of the city.

1910   Immigration Station on Angel Island opens.

1910   San Francisco's population: 416,900

1915   The Panama Pacific Exposition is held on filled-in land
along the city's northern waterfront to celebrate the
opening of the Panama Canal the previous year.

1916   **March 1.** The Beaux-Arts city hall opens for business.

1917   The notorious Barbary Coast dance halls are shut down
after the California State Legislature passes a red-light
abatement law designed to end prostitution.

1920   San Francisco's population: 506,700

1930   San Francisco's population: 634,400

1931   **January 7.** "Sunny Jim" Rolph steps down after nineteen
years as mayor to become governor of California.

1934   Alcatraz changes from a military prison to a maximum security federal penitentiary.

1936   **November 12.** The San Francisco-Oakland Bay Bridge opens.

1937   **May 28.** The Golden Gate Bridge opens.

1939-40 The Golden Gate International Exposition is held on Treasure Island in San Francisco Bay.

1940   San Francisco's population: 634,500

1945   **August 14.** V-J Day. Celebrants jam Market Street and cause a near riot.

1950   San Francisco's population: 775,400.

1953   City Lights Bookstore opens.

1957   Lawrence Ferlinghetti is arrested, tried, and acquitted of obscenity charges for selling Allen Ginsburg's poem *Howl*.

1960   San Francisco's population: 740,900

1967   The "Summer of Love" takes place as hippies converge on Haight-Ashbury.

1970   San Francisco's population: 715,700

1980   San Francisco's population: 679,000

1989   **October 17.** An earthquake measuring 7.1 on the Richter scale strikes northern California. The quake causes billions of dollars in property damage and kills sixty-seven people, thirteen of them in San Francisco.

1990   San Francisco's population: 724,000

2000   San Francisco's population: 777,000

Select Bibliography

Asbury, Herbert. *The Barbary Coast.* Garden City, NY: Garden City Publishing, 1933.

Beebe, Lucius, and Charles Clegg. *San Francisco's Golden Era: A Picture Story of San Francisco Before the Fire.* Berkeley: Howell-North Books, 1960.

Bronson, William. *The Earth Shook, The Sky Burned.* 1959. Reprint. San Francisco: Chronicle Books, 1986.

Caughey, John Walton. *The California Gold Rush.* 1948. Reprint. Berkeley: University of California Press, 1975.

Clary, Raymond H. *The Making of Golden Gate Park: The Early Years: 1865–1906.* San Francisco: California Living Books, 1980.

Cole, Tom. *A Short History of San Francisco.* San Francisco: Don't Call It Frisco Press, 1986.

Delehanty, Randolph. San Francisco: *The Ultimate Guide.* San Francisco: Chronicle Books, 1989.

Dillon, Richard, Thomas Moulin, and Don DeNevi. *High Steel.* Berkeley: Celestial Arts, 1979.

Gilliam, Harold. *San Francisco Bay.* Garden City, NY: Doubleday, 1957.

Hansen, Gladys. *San Francisco Almanac.* 1975. Reprint. San Francisco: Presidio Press, 1980.

Hansen, Gladys, and Emmet Condon. *Denial of Disaster: The Untold Story and Photographs of the San Francisco Earthquake and Fire of 1906.* San Francisco: Cameron and Company, 1989.

Heizer, Robert F., and Theodora Kroeber, eds. *Ishi, the Last Yahi: A Documentary History.* Berkeley: University of California Press, 1979.

Hoover, Mildred Brooke, Hero Eugene Rensch, and Ethel Grace Rensch, 3d ed., rev. and enl., William N. Abeloe. *Historic Spots in California.* Stanford, CA: Stanford University Press, 1966.

Horton, Tom. Superspan: *The Golden Gate Bridge.* San Francisco: Chronicle Books, 1983.

Jackson, Donald Dale. *Gold Dust.* 1980. Reprint. Lincoln, NB: Bison Books, University of Nebraska Press, 1982.

Kennard, Charles. *San Francisco Bay Area Landmarks: Reflections of Four Centuries.* Palo Alto: Tioga Publishing, 1987.

Kennedy, John Castillo. *The Great Earthquake and Fire: San Francisco, 1906.* New York: Morrow, 1963.

Lavender, David. *California: Land of New Beginnings.* 1972. Reprint. Lincoln, NB: Bison Books, University of Nebraska Press, 1982.

————. *Nothing Seemed Impossible: William Ralston and Early San Francisco.* Palo Alto: America West Publishing, 1975.

Lewis, Oscar. *The Big Four.* 1938. Reprint. Sausalito CA: Comstock Editions, 1971.

————. *Mission to Metropolis.* 2d ed. San Diego: Howell-North Books, 1980.

————. *Silver Kings.* New York: Alfred A. Knopf, 1947.

Lewis, Oscar, and Carroll D. Hall. *Bonanza Inn.* 1939. Reprint. New York: Ballantine Books, 1971.

Margolin, Malcolm. *The Ohlone Way.* Berkeley: Heyday Books, 1978.

McGloin, Father John B., S.J. *San Francisco: The Story of a City.* San Rafael, CA: Presidio Press, 1978.

Perry, Charles. *The Haight-Ashbury: A History.* New York: Random House, Vintage Books, 1985.

Reinhardt, Richard. *Treasure Island: San Francisco's Exposition Years.* 1973. Reprint. Mill Valley, CA: Squarebooks, 1978.

Scott, Mel. *The San Francisco Bay Area: A Metropolis in Perspective.* 2d ed. Berkeley: University of California Press, 1985.

Thomas, Gordon, and Max Morgan Witts. *The San Francisco Earthquake.* Reprint. New York: Dell Publishing, 1971.

Watkins, T.H., and R.R. Olmstead. *Here Today: San Francisco's Architectural Heritage.* San Francisco: Chronicle Books, 1968.

————. *Mirror of the Dream: An Illustrated History of San Francisco.* San Francisco: Scrimshaw Press, 1976.

Wollenberg, Charles. *Golden Gate Metropolis: Perspectives on Bay Area History.* Berkeley: Institute of Governmental Studies, University of California, 1985.

Van der Zee, John. *The Gate.* New York: Simon and Schuster, 1986.

Index

(Numbers in *italics*
refer to illustrations.)

About the Author

Rand Richards has been a private investigator, insurance claims adjustor, and advertising executive. He has a B.A. in history and an M.B.A. degree. He has lived in San Francisco since 1972 except for a year spent at Schiller College in Paris, France where he taught international marketing. An avid student of history, he combined that interest with his love for San Francisco to create this book.

© 2007 Gus Figuerola

He is a member of the California Historical Society and several other historical associations. Since writing and publishing *Historic San Francisco*, Rand has come out with two more books—*Historic Walks in San Francisco: 18 Trails Through the City's Past*, and *Haunted San Francisco: Ghost Stories From the City's Past*.